Linguistic Universals

The discovery of "linguistic universals" – the properties that all languages have in common – is a fundamental goal of linguistic research. Linguists face the task of accounting for why languages, which apparently differ so greatly from one another on the surface, display striking similarities in their underlying structure. This volume brings together a team of leading experts to show how different linguistic theories have approached this challenge. Drawing on work from both formal and functional perspectives, it provides a comprehensive overview of the most notable work on linguistic universals – with chapters on syntax, semantics, phonology, morphology, and typology – and explores a range of central issues, such as the relationship between linguistic universals and the language faculty, and what linguistic universals can tell us about our biological make-up and cognitive abilities. Clear, succinct, and fully up-to-date, it will be invaluable to anyone seeking a greater understanding of the phenomenon that is human language.

RICARDO MAIRAL is Professor of English Language and Linguistics in the Departamento de Filologías Extranjeras y sus Lingüísticas, Universidad Nacional de Educación a Distancia (UNED).

JUANA GIL is Senior Lecturer in the Departamento de Lengua Española y Lingüística General, Universidad Nacional de Educación a Distancia (UNED).

Linguistic Universals

edited by
Ricardo Mairal
and
Juana Gil

CAMBRIDGE
UNIVERSITY PRESS

CAMBRIDGE UNIVERSITY PRESS
Cambridge, New York, Melbourne, Madrid, Cape Town, Singapore, São Paulo

Cambridge University Press
The Edinburgh Building, Cambridge CB2 2RU, UK

Published in the United States of America by Cambridge University Press, New York

www.cambridge.org
Information on this title: www.cambridge.org/9780521545525

First published 2006

Printed in the United Kingdom at the University Press, Cambridge

A catalogue record for this publication is available from the British Library

ISBN-13 978-0-521-83709-5 hardback
ISBN-10 0-521-83709-X hardback

ISBN-13 978-0-521-54552-5 paperback
ISBN-10 0-521-54552-8 paperback

Contents

Contributors

RICARDO MAIRAL, Professor of English Language and Linguistics, Departamento de Filologías Extranjeras y sus Lingüísticas, UNED, Madrid

JUANA GIL, Senior Lecturer in Linguistics, Departamento de Lengua Española y Lingüística General, UNED, Madrid

KEES HENGEVELD, Professor of Theoretical Linguistics, University of Amsterdam

CEDRIC BOECKX, Assistant Professor, Department of Linguistics, Harvard University

IAN MADDIESON, Professor, Department of Linguistics, University of California, Los Angeles

ANDREW SPENCER, Professor of Linguistics, University of Essex

BERNARD COMRIE, Professor, Max Planck Institute for Evolutionary Anthropology, Leipzig

ROBERT D. VAN VALIN, JR., Professor, Department of Linguistics, University at Buffalo, The State University of New York

JOAN BYBEE, Professor of Linguistics, University of New Mexico

Preface

Any mention of linguistic universals means the continuation of a journey begun many years ago, and refers to a topic of debate among both linguists and philosophers, which has been a constant in the history of linguistics throughout the ages.

The debate regarding universals is one of the most fundamental chapters – perhaps the most fundamental – in the history of grammar, and its genesis can be traced back to the very dawn of linguistic reflection. Furthermore, it is a subject that transcends boundaries between academic disciplines since it is one of the cornerstones of the philosophical debate between rationalism and empiricism. Consequently, it is of vital interest not only to linguists, but also to philosophers, psychologists, anthropologists, psychobiologists, and ethnologists – in other words, to researchers of all academic disciplines that are involved in what is known today as *Cognitive Science*.

However, linguistic universals are currently in the limelight because any linguistic theory that aspires to explanatory adequacy must offer a satisfactory answer to the question of why languages that are so apparently different on the surface at the same time present undeniable regularities in their underlying structure. It is no longer a question of merely discussing the existence of universals, but rather of making their existence compatible with the epistemological premises of different theoretical approaches. This book is an explanation of how these approaches have dealt with this task.

Thus, the organization of the book is as follows: in chapter 1, we have endeavored to present concisely and selectively the major theoretical positions regarding universals, from the beginning of linguistic reflection up until modern times. Our purpose in providing such a panorama is to offer readers (even those without previous knowledge of linguistics) an overview of the multiple perspectives regarding this issue, which, in our opinion, will help to contextualize the research in this volume. Furthermore, one of the strong points of this chapter is that we maintain that an approximation between formal and functional approaches is not only possible, but crucial for a deeper comprehension of certain aspects of linguistic behavior; the fact that certain grammatical phenomena are motivated by factors derived from cognitive processing limitations in human beings does not necessarily mean that the explanation of *all* linguistic events need be set out in these terms, and, conversely, the fact that certain grammatical principles cannot be externally justified by cognitive or communicative factors should not lead to the rejection of such a possibility for *all* other principles. In essence, although this duality between formalism and functionalism still persists, now, more than ever, there is the necessity for formalist and functionalist theories to work together and offer an integrated explanation of the phenomenon of linguistic universals.

After this introductory chapter which is intended to serve as a backdrop for the rest of the book, chapters 2 and 3 offer very accurate and rigorous accounts of specific aspects that have guided research into linguistic universals from the viewpoint of formal and functional theories. Thus, Hengeveld, as a representative of the functional-typological paradigm, concentrates on the explanatory scope of implicational hierarchies for the analysis of language data. In contrast, Boeckx offers an illuminating account of the notion of universals within the different and successive versions of Generative Grammar from Chomsky's *Aspects* to the Minimalist Program.

As a general rationale, these two chapters clearly illustrate the following two apparently contradictory theses on the origin of universals. Whereas formalist theories link universals to specific characteristics of the human language faculty, functionalists tend to view them as a logical consequence of the fact that languages are ultimately devices for communication. These two rather different conceptions of universals are reflected in a series of differences stemming from the methods used and the more internal or external perspective adopted by each framework, something which the other chapters of this volume, which examine the question of universals from the perspective of a specific linguistic component (i.e., phonetics, morphology, syntax, lexis, and diachrony), are eloquent proof of.

In this regard, Bernard Comrie, in his chapter on relative clauses, shows how typologists attempt to establish a workable hypothesis regarding the geographical distribution of a phenomenon or linguistic structure; how this hypothesis is confirmed by studying a set of languages; and, above all, how this whole process contributes to a deeper understanding of this or that structure or phenomenon, and, subsequently, to a deeper understanding of the mechanisms and strategies that make up the language faculty.

Accordingly, in the chapter on phonetic and phonological universals, Ian Maddieson, after pointing out four basic characteristics shared by all languages (orality, being sound-based, sequential variation, and paradigmatic contrast), argues that although the linguistic analysis of a wide range of languages can clearly provide the key to the specification of a series of universals, the interest of such shared characteristics and other similar factors will only be truly significant if it is used to lay the foundations for more ambitious and far-reaching ideas regarding the biological setting of language, as well as other human cognitive abilities. In other words, the issue of universals inevitably leads us to more ambitious research regarding the language faculty.

The specificity of this faculty is questioned by Joan Bybee in her chapter on the diachronic dimension of universals. In this chapter the author argues that the true universals are not synchronic patterns but rather the mechanisms of change which underlie those patterns and create them. What is even more meaningful from a theoretical perspective is that those mechanisms of change that function in language (e.g. the repetition of linguistic structures and their subsequent automatization) are much the same as those of other cognitive and neuromotor abilities. The author thus maintains a theoretical position that is clearly different from that defended in more orthodox formalism.

In contrast, Andrew Spencer is very skeptical about the existence of morphological universals, or, at least, about the possibility of formulating them with any degree of success at the present time. Spencer argues that, in a way, the specification of morphological universals would necessarily presuppose a prior universal characterization of the word as a unit whose structure has traditionally been the focus of study in morphology. Since there are no clear, generally valid principles that help us to distinguish words from non-words, it is virtually impossible to go beyond the establishment of certain apparently universal tendencies that Spencer analyzes in his chapter.

In the same way as in morphology, but in contrast to phonological and syntactic universals, very little attention has been paid to the study of semantic universals. Accordingly, Van Valin deals with this subject – more specifically, those referring to verb semantics. Based on the work of Vendler, Van Valin's work distinguishes a set of *Aktionsart* distinctions which are common to the verb systems of all languages, and which can be regarded as prime candidates for semantic universals. Furthermore, he develops a system of lexical representation for each of these distinctions and shows their interlinguistic validity by bringing evidence from a wide range of different languages.

All of the aforementioned contributions make this book primarily a monograph on linguistic universals. However, it is also about language as viewed from different perspectives by specialists of recognized prestige, who represent a wide range of theoretical positions, and different ways of understanding linguistics.

We would like to conclude this preface by thanking José María Brucart, Juan Uriagereka, and Robert Van Valin for their ongoing support and encouragement throughout the duration of this project.

RICARDO MAIRAL
JUANA GIL

Abbreviations

ABIL	ability
ABS	absolutive
ACC	accusative
ACT	active
ADJ	Adjective
AOR	aorist
ART	article
ASP	aspect
BENEF	benefactive
CERT	certainty
CMPV	completive
CN, CONN	connective
COLL	collective
CONNEG	connegative
CONT	continuous
COP	copular
DAT	dative
DEM	demonstrative
DM	diminutive
DU	dual
ERG	ergative
F/FEM	feminine
FOC	focus
FUT	future
GEN	genitive
GER	gerund
GG	Generative Grammar
IMM	immediate
IMPFV	imperfect/imperfective
INCH	inchoative
IND	indicative
INFER	inference

INSTR	instrumental
INTR	intransitive
IPA	International Phonetic Alphabet
IPV	imperfective
IRR	irrealis
ITER	iterative
LDP	left detached position
LGB	*Lectures on Government and Binding* (Chomsky, 1981)
LOC	locative
NEG	negative
NFUT	nonfuture
NM	Noun marker
NMZ	nominalizer
NOM	Nominative
NP	Noun Phrase
NSM	Natural Semantic Metalanguage
O	Object
OBL	oblique
OPT	optative
OT	Optimality Theory
P&P	Principles and Parameters
PASS	passive
PF	perfect/perfective
PL	plural
PLD	primary linguistic data
PNCT	punctual
POS	"Poverty-of-Stimulus" argument
POSS	possessive
PP	past participle
PrC	precore slot
PRED	predicate
PREP	Preposition
PRO	Pronoun
PROC	process
PrP	Prepositional Phrase
PRS.PRT	present participle
PST	past
PTCPL	participle
PURP	purposive
RDP	right detached position
RECIP	reciprocal
REDUP	reduplicative

REFL	reflexive
REL	relative
REL.INS	instrumental relative
REL.NS	relative non-subject
REL.OBJ	object relative
REL.OBL	oblique relative
REL.SBJ	subject relative
REM.PAST	remote past
RES	result
RRG	Role and Reference Grammar
S	Subject
SG	singular
TAM	time, aspect, and modality
TOP	topic
TR	transitive
UG	Universal Grammar
V	Verb
VP	Verb Phrase

1   A first look at universals

Ricardo Mairal and Juana Gil

> *Grammatica una et eadem est secundum substantiam in omnibus linguis, licet accidentaliter varietur.*
> Roger Bacon

1   The debate on language universals

1.1   Introduction

For the last several decades we have been living in what has been called, for better or for worse, the *postmodern era*, a cultural movement or climate of social sensitivity, which, in contrast to the traditional values of the rationalistic, globalizing version of Modernism inherited from the Enlightenment, defends ideological positions based on heterogeneity, dispersion, and difference. Over the past years, contingency and individuality have gradually taken precedence over permanence and universality. As Harvey (1989) so accurately states, the views that are presently most highly valued in the postmodern world are generally those that concede greater importance to particularism and fragmentation, focus on the individual nature and interest of the parts rather than the whole, and are ultimately conducive to the disarticulation or deconstruction of all human sociocultural and economic activities. In the same way that moral values and instruction are not thought to be universally applicable, many well-known scholars of this era, even in the realm of science – especially the social sciences (e.g. the work of Lyotard) and, to a lesser extent, physics and mathematics (in line with Spengler) – affirm that there are no general principles that can be objectively evaluated independently of the spatiotemporal context in which they were initially proposed.

Given the present state of affairs, all research on language universals (i.e. properties shared by all languages) may now seem almost paradoxical, to say the least, whereas it is hardly accidental that enthusiasm for the analysis

The authors would like to thank Ignacio Bosque, José María Brucart, Violeta Demonte and Carlos Piera for their useful suggestions regarding the first draft of this chapter, which were invaluable for the final version. Of course, any errors or oversights still remaining in the text are our responsibility. This chapter was translated into English by Pamela Faber of the University of Granada, Spain.

of linguistic variation in all of its manifestations has increased. Yet, the quest to discover what is invariable and what is shared still persists, as do the results of this quest, because, while certain scholars fervently defend individual truth, many others, who are just as prestigious in their respective fields, strive to find proof of universal reason in all areas of knowledge, including language.

As is well known, the dialectical tension between these two positions is not a recent state of affairs. For several centuries, particularly in the area of philosophy, the same questions have repeatedly surfaced in relation to the possible existence of universal entities: which properties, relations, functions, numbers, classes, etc., can be considered universal, and, supposing that universals actually do exist, what is the exact relation between these abstract universal entities and the "particular" entities that embody them.

The answers to these questions have laid the foundation for philosophical schools of thought throughout the ages: *realism*, in the early Middle Ages; *nominalism*, which dominated the latter part of the fifteenth century – with the sudden appearance of empiricism and positivism – and its variant, the *conceptualist* approach; and finally the *rationalist* revolution[1] in the seventeenth century, which provided an especially fertile context for the discussion of universals, which concerns us here.

To a great extent, the Renaissance was an individualistic and plural era, which fomented the meticulous description of events (and languages), rather than an explanation for them based on general underlying principles. However, in the seventeenth and eighteenth centuries, with the Scientific Revolution or the Enlightenment, the concept of universal *reason* first arose, according to which the general takes precedence over the particular, the abstract over the concrete, and the non-temporal over the historical (Pinillos, 1997, 76ff.). This historical period produced philosophers such as Descartes, Leibniz, Locke, Condillac, Diderot, and Rousseau; linguists and pedagogues such as Bauzée, Comenius, and Wilkins; physicists such as Newton; as well as many other great scholars in all realms of knowledge, an exhaustive list of whom would be too numerous to cite in its entirety. To a greater or lesser extent, all of them influenced the linguistic ideas of the time,[2] which were centered on efforts to

---

[1] In the history of philosophy, the term *rationalist* is generally used as an antonym for *empiricist*, but especially from the nineteenth century on. In its widest sense, *rationalist* refers to any school of thought that is based on the use of reason to obtain knowledge. However, if we interpret the term in this way, it would be extremely difficult to differentiate rationalists like Descartes from empiricists like Locke, since the philosophies of both are based on reason. The divergence between the two is best understood if we consider *rationalist* from a different perspective, in other words, in terms of the treatment that each philosophical school gives to the origin of knowledge (see the discussion in Copleston, 1971, 26ff.).

[2] Bartlett (1987, 24ff.) makes a series of generalizations about the period stretching from the beginning of the sixteenth century to the end of the eighteenth, which, for our purposes, can be summarized in the following three ideas: (1) in those centuries, grammatical and linguistic issues

create new artificial and universal languages,[3] and produced pioneering work in the comparison of languages[4] as well as the publication of philosophical grammars that were theoretical rather than descriptive, the most important of which was the *Grammaire générale et raisonnée de Port-Royal* by Claude Lancelot and Antoine Arnaud (Paris 1660). And in this *Grammaire*, which is *générale* in the sense of aiming to be valid for all languages, and based on the philosophy of Descartes,[5] the authors formulate a series of universal principles underlying language in general.

Cartesian philosophy opened the door to the serious discussion of universals. One of its basic premises was the defence of innateness, or the belief that if objects in the real world are knowable, which they evidently are, it is because of the existence of innate ideas or conceptual structures that have not reached us by way of our senses or imagination, and which are not generalizations made by induction, or are even in need of empirical confirmation. Rather they already *exist* in the mind and constitute an eminently human characteristic. If certain ideas are innate, they must then be shared by everyone, and can thus be regarded as universal. This leads to the conclusion that innate ideas are universal, and experiential data, which can be considered contingent, is deduced and interpreted on the basis of innate ideas.

had a decidedly epistemological dimension; (2) philosophers, rather than grammarians, were the ones who determined how grammatical questions should be theoretically and methodologically formulated; (3) the linguistic discussion shifted from the study of word meaning and word classes to the study of propositional meaning.

[3] Universal languages were proposed by the Czech pedagogue and linguist Comenius, the Scottish linguist Dalgarno, the English linguist Wilkins, and Leibniz himself (his *Characteristica universalis*) (see Koerner and Asher, 1995). These early efforts are noteworthy because they were the forerunners of the formal languages of the twentieth century. However, the truth is that the authors hoped not only to achieve a formal logical expression of states of affairs, but also to create "philosophical" languages, capable of accurately transmitting all of the knowledge derived from the real world. An extremely early and illustrious precedent can be found in the second half of the thirteenth century in Ramón Llull's *Ars magna* (see Slaughter, 1982; Eco, 1994, chs. 10–16; Frank, 1979, on Wilkins; Cram and Maat, 2001, on Dalgarno).

[4] Especially worthy of mention is the work of the German philosopher and philologist, Johann Gottfried von Herder, who published *Über den Ursprung der Sprache* [Essay on the Origin of Language] (1772) followed by *Stimmen der Völker* [Folksongs] (1798), a comparative ethnography on the oral cultural manifestations of different countries. Just as significant in this respect were the earlier studies carried out by Leibniz, which will be discussed in greater detail later on.

[5] Whether the *Grammaire générale et raisonnée de Port-Royal* is primarily a philosophical grammar has been a subject of considerable debate. Its initial purpose may have been pedagogical, although with the passing of the years other objectives have been attributed to it. Regarding the debate concerning Descartes' influence on this grammar, see R. Lakoff (1969) and Salmon (1969). For a more recent analysis, see Aarsleff (1982), particularly the chapter "The history of linguistics and Professor Chomsky," in which he harshly criticizes the vision of Cartesian philosophy offered by Chomsky. In his opinion, the rationalist grammar of the seventeenth century is not, as Chomsky would have it, a direct consequence of the philosophy of Descartes, but a continuation of the logical and grammatical tradition dating back to the Middle Ages. Chomsky's answer to this criticism can be read in Huybregts and van Riemsdijk (1982, 37–38); see Bracken (1983, ch. 7).

It is precisely this conception of the origin of knowledge that is the criterion which established an opposition (more conventional than real) between the two most prominent schools of pre-Kantian philosophy (see footnote 1): the dividing line between continental rationalism (e.g. Descartes, Spinoza, Leibniz) and British empiricism (e.g. Locke, Berkeley, Hume). In vivid contrast to rationalists, empiricists affirmed that all knowledge comes from perception, and thus cannot be derived from innate principles, but rather solely from experience. What is interesting for our purposes is that both schools have had an important impact on the contemporary discussion and consideration of the problem of universals.

Let us first focus our attention on the rationalists. It is well known that rationalism greatly influenced not only the general intellectual panorama of its era, but also the more recent generative model of linguistic analysis, which will be discussed in greater detail in the following sections. These conceptions were passed on to new generations of linguists through the writings of Descartes and his followers, and also thanks to the legacy of rationalist thinkers such as Leibniz, whose ideas on language and thought coincide to a great degree with those of Descartes, e.g. Cartesian *innate ideas* essentially correspond to Leibniz's eternal and necessary *truths of reason*, although part of the difference between *innate ideas* and *truths of reason* is evidenced in the fact that they have been used as the basis for different research perspectives on language universals.

In fact, in the strictly Cartesian concept of language, as Acero (1993, 15ff.) very clearly states, innate universal ideas are always accurate and valid, regardless of the data provided by experience and knowledge: "Whatever the real world may be like . . ., it has no effect on the fact that my ideas regarding objective reality are ideas and thus have a typically representational function. The access of understanding to ideas, to the content within them and to its operations with that content – what Descartes euphemistically calls 'self-knowledge' – does not depend on any connection with the real world. According to Descartes, even if such links were severed, representations would not be affected" (Acero, 1993, 16).[6] Strictly speaking, this Cartesian postulate is static in that it presupposes a predetermined, clearly delimited, and non-externally-modelable schema, to which human knowledge and experience must adapt.

On the other hand, according to Leibniz, truths or innate principles (e.g. principle of contradiction) and ideas or innate concepts (e.g. cause, unity, identity, etc.) are only those that can be derived from pure understanding and common sense, and therefore from the mind, never from the senses. This notwithstanding, experience may be necessary to enable us to know these innate ideas or truths: the mind has the power, faculty or *competence* to find within itself those ideas that are virtually innate, and which experience helps it to discover. As a

---

[6] Translated from the Spanish.

result, there is a dynamic, circular conception of the interrelation between mind and objective experience.

Moreover, Leibniz believes that human beings mentally configure what they apprehend through experience, and that this configuration is, to a certain extent, mediated by language and intimately related by it to the cognitive process of which it is a part. Since there is not one language but many, and all of them are the product of an innate human language faculty and of the diversity of human interactions with their surroundings, experiential data from the outside world will be mentally structured according to the dictates of each individual language.[7] This premise, which is at the same time both philosophical and anthropological, explains the interest shown by Leibniz in the study of different languages as a means of discovering features shared by all of them (Wierzbicka, 2001).[8] It is directly linked to the ideas of other great philosophers and linguists, such as Wilhelm von Humboldt,[9] Franz Boas, and Edward Sapir, who, despite accepting the possibility of the "universal unity of language" (above all, in the case of Humboldt), clearly opted for an anthropological approach based on the principle of linguistic relativity with its extreme corollaries regarding the subjectivity of speech and the social nature of languages.[10]

It thus becomes increasingly evident that even among the so-called "rationalists," there are important differences regarding the conception of innate universal ideas. On the one hand, we have a conception that can be described as more *intrinsic*, in the sense that such intellectual truths are considered to

[7] Leibniz considers language as a means of communication, as a cognitive instrument, given that the present state of language, namely the vocabulary that a generation finds, substantially determines one's knowledge (cf. Arens, 1969).

[8] Heinz Holz (1970, 162ff.) underlines this characteristic, which is not unrelated to the philosophy of Leibniz. This philosopher considered concrete, individual manifestations as a representation of what is universal, and for this reason studied specific languages, which he considered to be realizations or reflections of a general universal language (the still-visible trace of the language of Adam and Eve, according to other authors). Heinz affirms that Leibniz, by contrasting the greatest possible number of languages, made an important contribution to the development of comparative linguistics. For more information on this subject, see Aarsleff (1982) or De Mauro and Formigari (1990).

[9] Leibniz, as well as Humboldt, along with other scholars such as Adam Smith or August and Friedrich Schlegel, are often cited as pioneers in the study of typological linguistics, which had become a separate discipline from historical and comparative linguistics, which had acquired great popularity in the nineteenth century: "Humboldt carefully distinguishes typological affinity from any other sort of affinity – but especially from genetic relationships – and thereby lays the foundations for typological linguistics as an autonomous discipline within linguistics" (Di Cesare, 1990, 173).

[10] Lafont (1993, 51) writes: "In the continental interpretation of Humboldt, the universalist perspective underlying Humboldt's general conception of language is an unquestionable truth. The consideration of Humboldt as a representative of linguistic relativism is typical of the American tradition, in which he is considered to be a representative of the 'principle of linguistic relativity' or, what is the same, his writings are regarded as a European contribution to the Sapir–Whorf Hypothesis" (translated from the Spanish). As Lafont goes on to affirm, Humboldt's stance was never as radical as the position later taken by the two American linguists.

be unconscious (although they can reach our consciousness through introspection), unlearned, hardwired into the human brain by Nature, and vitally necessary for the interpretation of experience and for language learning. On the other hand, there is the *extrinsic* conception, exemplified in the philosophy of Leibniz, centered on experiential data derived from the senses, which seeks to discover a shared grammar through the formal comparative study of individual languages, understood as *indicators* of essential characteristics of human language in general. And so, it is the path of strict Cartesian philosophy with its interest in *general grammars* that Chomsky's work follows, whereas the comparative typological analysis of a wide range of languages led to the work of Sapir, Jakobson, and Greenberg. As will be explained in the next section, these two paths also represent two different ways of understanding linguistic universals, which again came into the spotlight of contemporary linguistics in the second half of the twentieth century.

1.2   The debate continues

As previously mentioned in the first section, in the history of linguistics (as in the history of philosophy in general) the debate regarding universal properties has not been centered merely on how to define them or how they should be approached, but on the acceptance of their actual existence. We previously mentioned the dichotomy established between rationalism and empiricism, and we described and concisely outlined rationalist proposals. Empiricism is associated with philosophers such as Locke, and, above all, Condillac[11] in the seventeenth and eighteenth centuries, and Bréal and Taine at the end of the nineteenth century, whose reflections on language heralded the beginning of the anti-universalist movement – subsequent to romanticism and the positivism of the nineteenth-century Neogrammatical Movement[12] – which would last

---

[11] Certain studies reproduced in Aarsleff (1982) analyze the *Essai sur l'origine des connaissances humaines* (1746) by Etienne Condillac. One of the conclusions that Aarsleff arrives at is that neither Locke nor Condillac can be regarded as dyed-in-the-wool empiricists since, for both of them, reason is the principal source of knowledge (see footnote 1). In this sense, Professor Aarsleff harshly criticizes Chomsky's (1966) interpretation of the ideas of Locke and his followers. For our purposes, it is interesting to underline that these philosophers already used concepts ascribed to twentieth-century structuralism and post-structuralism, movements not generally characterized as being especially interested in the study of universals. The lack of interest in universals was particularly prominent in the anti-mentalist American version of structuralism, though somewhat less so in the European version, which produced clearly universalist studies such as Hjelmslev (1971) and Coseriu (1978).

[12] The nineteenth century effectively developed the evolutionary aspects of language. The historical–comparative philology of this century was empirical, descriptive, and classificatory, and consequently gave no explicit priority to philosophical-linguistic notions underlying the elaboration of a universal grammar. It is true, however, that the phonetic rules formulated by neogrammarians, such as Paul, Brugmann, and Leskien, were considered to be inevitable and applicable to any context and language, and thus could implicitly be regarded as universals.

from Saussure onwards into the twentieth century. Ideas traditionally linked to Saussure, such as the arbitrariness of the sign, its conventionality and surface linearity, the communicative nature of language, and the conception of languages as social institutions, had already appeared in the work of the linguists cited above. Obviously, linguistic universals had no place in the ideological framework that emerged, just as they had no place in most of the structuralism derived from the work of Saussure,[13] nor did they arouse the interest of any of the representatives of post-structuralism. Post-structuralist thinkers, such as Foucault, became the most fervent defenders of the idea that each language should be described in its own terms, and of the arbitrariness of the sign, which transformed it into a product of sociocultural contingency.[14]

However, the twentieth century is not only characterized by the structuralist and, above all, the post-structuralist rejection of the idea of language universals. On the contrary, this century also witnessed a renewed impetus in the search for properties common to all languages by linguists within the Humboldtian tradition (some of whom were mentioned in the previous section) as well as by generative linguists, who, as we have also pointed out, took a different approach to this problem.

The research on language typology outlined in Humboldt (and before that in Leibniz), still speculative and eager to pinpoint connections between perception and the organization of grammars – e.g. a "psychological" tendency, like the one represented by Sapir – linked to a more anthropological one like the one represented by Boas, produced a great number of descriptions and classifications of languages documented on the five continents. These studies were for the most part descriptive, and often limited to the elaboration of new taxonomies. It was not until the mid twentieth century that Jakobson breathed new life into typological studies by establishing laws of general (though not universal) validity. His proposals were further developed by Greenberg (1957), who defined his well-known series of empirically based implicative universals. Just as the contribution of Greenberg and his followers laid the foundations for research methodology in language typology by offering empirical results to explain the nature of universals, at approximately the same time Noam Chomsky – who, in response to structuralism, had begun to create his Generative Grammar

[13] According to Hymes (1983, 42), all linguistic schools have at some time shown a certain interest in universal features of language, and this explains why, even in the days in which the idea of structural diversity was at its zenith in linguistics and American anthropology, the Prague School was enthusiastically seeking universal laws and dimensions of language. Even Hockett showed interest in the features that distinguish human language from other systems of animal communication (i.e. Hockett, 1963, as well as the previously mentioned work of Hjelmslev [1971] and Coseriu [1978]).

[14] Moure (2001, 20) gives the following summary of the structuralist position: "On the one hand, each language arbitrarily relates an expression with a meaning, and on the other, each language selects its meanings from the amorphous continuum of reality. Interlanguage comparison thus becomes meaningless" (translated from the Spanish).

(*Syntactic Structures* had been published in 1957 and *Aspects of the Theory of Syntax* [1965] had just come out) – opened up new horizons in linguistic research by conceiving a model based on hypothetical-deductive criteria. This is thus the period that gave birth to the two great paradigms for the study of universals, which would dominate the linguistic panorama throughout the second half of the twentieth century and the beginning of the twenty-first: the Greenberg approach and the Chomskyan[15] approach.

Put concisely, the Greenberg approach is based on the description and analysis of the greatest possible number of language samples, and accordingly endeavors to establish authentically interlinguistic generalizations or *universals of languages*: in other words, intrinsic properties shared by all languages. In contrast, the Chomskyan approach seeks the specification of *linguistic universals* or those internal aspects of linguistic theory that are regarded as universal. In the latter case, it is the basic premises of the model that are universal and that are explained in terms of the well-known *innateness hypothesis*, and are consequently considered to be part of our genetic make-up (e.g. Hawkins, 1988).

1.3   Past and present

As we have endeavored to explain, any mention of linguistic universals consequently signifies the continuing of a journey begun many years ago, and refers to a subject of reflection on the part of both linguists and philosophers throughout the ages, a topic of debate that has been a constant in the history of our discipline. On the one hand, there have always been those who have defended linguistic homogeneity and shared properties of all languages, whether such properties are derived empirically or through introspection. On the other hand, the opposing side has invariably rejected universality, maintaining that the origins of knowledge, values, and ideas are particular, in other words, that they are dependent on and conditioned by their sociocultural context. The predominance of one belief or the other has always depended on the historical period.

In this present day and age, what we have are different understandings of the idea of universals, determined by the divergent epistemological foundations

---

[15] It is worth remembering that the research within these frameworks invariably appears linked to two linguistic conferences: (i) the Conference on Language Universals held in Dobbs Ferry (New York) in 1961, where Greenberg presented his seminal paper, "Some universals of grammar with particular reference to the order of meaningful elements," which was published with the rest of the conference papers in *Universals of Language* (Greenberg, 1963b); (ii) the Symposium on Universals in Linguistic Theory held in 1967 at the University of Texas in Austin, which brought together an important group of linguists who began to work within the innovative and revolutionary framework of Generative Grammar. Their contributions were afterwards published in Bach and Harris (1968). As other studies have also pointed out (Ferguson, 1978; Moure, 2001), the conference titles illustrate the difference between the two frameworks. In Dobbs Ferry, the notion of empirically based universals was the central topic of discussion, whereas in Austin a more abstract theoretical vision of universals was proposed, one which was rooted in the theory itself (see below).

of each of the two theoretical approaches that accept their existence, and that can be classified in two major categories: formal vs. functional theories of language.

The proponents of formal models consider that the similarities found in all languages can be explained in terms of the human capacity for cognition or knowledge of language (*linguistic competence*), which is innate in all human beings, and thus universal. The primary goal of the generative model, which is the most representative of this type of theory, is the characterization of that knowledge or the elaboration of a universal grammar. In contrast, the *functional approach* (a label covering a variety of linguistic paradigms) can be applied to a wide range of models that, according to Hall (1992, 1), share the idea that form is constrained by function – in other words, the idea that regularities in languages are determined by a number of psychological or general functional parameters which are the natural result of the fact that languages are first and foremost a means of communication.[16]

What is extremely significant, in our opinion, and something that we would like to highlight in this chapter, is that, even though these two schools of thought were initially opposed to each other, the years have not widened this separation, but instead have gradually brought them closer to each other. In this sense, the evolution and gradual approximation of positions have produced a new vision of linguistic theory, since all models, without exception and of whatever tendency, acknowledge the necessity of accounting for grammatical phenomena in a great number of languages. It is very revealing to look at the data in language studies carried out within both formal and functional linguistic frameworks, because it eloquently reflects the prevailing awareness that linguistic models should be capable of explaining not just one language, but many.

The distance between formal and functional perspectives on universals is rapidly diminishing, and being replaced by more complex, integrated approaches. In Section 4, we shall try to explain why we believe that such an approximation is not only positive, but vitally necessary for a deeper understanding of certain aspects of linguistic behavior. Nevertheless, despite vanishing differences, it is obvious that each approach still possesses certain differentiating features, which will be examined in the pages that follow.

2 The underlying causes of the debate

2.1 Language or linguistic universals?

Without a doubt, the debate on universals has its roots in the vision of *universal* held by each of the two linguistic schools. According to Ferguson (1978,

---

[16] For a classification of functional linguistic models, see Nichols (1984), Van Valin (2001b), and Butler (2003, chs. 1 and 2), *inter alia*.

12, 16), the universals formulated at the Dobbs Ferry Conference were statistical and implicative (see footnote 15), whereas those at the Austin Conference were not. This is hardly surprising considering the conference titles and the corresponding difference between linguistic universals and language universals, which lay at the foundation of their respective proposals. In consonance with what we explained in the preceding section, our objective is to examine the principal ideas that constitute the backbone for the study of universals within contemporary linguistics, and which, in our opinion, can be summarized in the dialectical tug-of-war between functionalists and generativists over whether to use internal or external criteria for their study and analysis.

The distinction between internal universals (theoretical linguistic universals) and external universals (empirical universals based on languages and their surface structure) arose from the following theoretical and methodological characteristics of each of the two linguistic frameworks.

(a) Generativist and functional models are based on radically different conceptions of the nature of language. Basic features of the generativist model are its innateness, modularity, and psychological adequacy, whereas functional–cognitive models, which focus on function, meaning, and usage, are non-modular and experience-based.

(b) Generative linguists seek a theory of the language faculty known as Universal Grammar (hereafter UG), as well as the establishment of principles that govern this faculty (Chomsky, 2003, 18), an idea that will be discussed in greater detail later on. For this purpose, they use a hypothetical-deductive approach to the contrasting of the elements within a formal model that will ultimately account for human linguistic abilities. For example, if linguists begin with the hypothesis that speakers mentally associate the sentences of a language with the syntactic structures of their constituents and that these constituents are projections of lexical categories (N, ADJ, V) or functional categories (quantification, determination, subordination), then it is necessary to explain not only how this association is produced, or by means of what operations and principles this occurs, but also why languages differ in regard to the number of their projections as well as the extension assigned to grammatical categories.[17] In contrast, among the methodological postulates that characterize functional linguistic models is their more empiricist orientation. Functionalists start from a representative sample of a number of languages and formulate generalizations based on this data. Consequently, their mode of analysis is inductive.[18]

---

[17] For example, certain languages do not distinguish between Adjectives and Nouns.
[18] For a more detailed description of this process and the variables to be considered, see Hengeveld (this volume, chapter 2).

(c) From the above premise it can be deduced that generativists consider language (Spanish, English, or any language) to be a specific state of the language faculty. This state is known as *I-language* (i.e., internal language) and represents the grammatical knowledge of competent speakers, who activate it as an objective and empirical phenomenon in *E-language* (i.e., external language). According to Chomsky (1981, 4, 7), universals can only truly exist within the context of I-language and never in E-language because the parameter settings selected by individual languages, as well as their peripheral, irregular, or idiosyncratic features, are included in I-language along with universals determined by UG (the general architecture of the system). However, in E-language, extralinguistic constraints intervene, such as limitations imposed by human memory or the pauses introduced when an utterance is emitted. I-language thus represents a speaker's linguistic competence or knowledge of language,[19] whereas E-language is the activation of that knowledge.[20]

(d) By contrast, functional models do not distinguish between I-language and E-language, and identify universals of language and linguistic theory with semantic aspects[21] of language.

(e) It is also the case that both generativists and functionalists use different arguments to justify the existence of universals. In this sense, Generative Grammar, as representative of the formal paradigm, invokes criteria of a higher order than the model itself, such as those regarding the theory of competence and of language acquisition, or, in the most recent version of Minimalism, criteria derived from characteristics of language processing. The basic dichotomy established between I-language and E-language, along with the fact that generativists center their attention on I-language, explains

[19] According to Jackendoff (2002), *knowledge* is not the best choice of words in this context: "It must be stressed, though, that whatever term is used, the linguistic system in a speaker's mind/brain is deeply unconscious and largely unavailable to introspection, in the same way that our processing of visual signals is deeply unconscious. Thus, language is a kind of mind/brain property hard to associate with the term 'knowledge,' which commonly implies accessibility to introspection." He prefers the expression *f-knowledge* (functional knowledge).

[20] Botha (1992, 80ff.) points out that Humboldt anticipated the distinction between I-language and E-language since, unlike American and European structuralists, he did not consider language to be a set of pre-established elements, but rather a generative process (see above, footnote 10). However, he did not clearly distinguish between the abstract generative procedure that assigns structural descriptions to all linguistic expressions and the true "Arbeit des Geistes" by means of which thought is expressed in linguistic performance. Another even earlier example of this differentiation appeared in the divergent conceptions of universals held by realists and nominalists (see Section 1.1). A parallel could be drawn between realists and "external" universalists on the one hand, and nominalists and "internal" universalists on the other.

[21] Relevant examples of such functional models are Role and Reference Grammar (Van Valin and LaPolla, 1997; Van Valin, 2005), experience-based cognitive models (G. Lakoff, 1987; Lakoff and Johnson, 1999), perceptive or articulatory phonetic models (Lindblom, 1986; Lindblom and Maddieson, 1988; Maddieson, this volume, chapter 4).

why they do not use pragmatic, textual, or functional aspects of language to justify universals. In contrast, the use of such criteria is precisely what identifies and unifies the wide range of models that are presently classified as within the functional–typological paradigm.[22]

Factors such as the conception of universal, methodological strategies, as well as the value of language data, pervade contemporary linguistic research on language universals, and at the same time differentiate one linguistic framework from the other (cf. Mairal and Gil, 2003). However, as previously mentioned, the heart of the controversy on this topic resides precisely in the opposition between *internal* and *external* perspectives of language, which first appears, as described in Section 1, in the confrontation between nominalists and rationalists, and which later continued in Descartes and Leibniz (both of whom were rationalists). In other words, there is a dialectical tension between a theory, such as UG, whose goal is explanatory adequacy, and which thus requires the definition of foundational theoretical principles, and a descriptively adequate theory demanding an exhaustive analysis of languages. Curiously enough, throughout successive revisions of their respective models, both generativists and functionalists have largely maintained their respective positions on universals, but yet have endeavored to refine and perfect them, always from within the methodological coherence imposed by the conception of language that each defends.

It is extremely interesting to examine this process of "perfection" as applied to universals from both an internal and an external theoretical perspective. We would like to underline that in all of the various versions of the generativist model, based on the idea of UG, a great amount of effort has been devoted to constraining the descriptive power of grammar in order to refine and "perfect" UG. A similar process, with logical methodological differences, also took place in functional models. However, when it came to "perfecting" interlinguistic generalizations, each of these models followed a different path. A case in point within the functionalist framework is the development of a universal alphabet composed of a set of primitives and combinatorial rules (i.e. Wierzbicka's Natural Semantic Metalanguage) which was gradually refined and perfected in successive revisions of the model (see Wierzbicka, 1972; Goddard and Wierzbicka, 2002).

Consequently, in the following sections, we shall analyze this process of perfection and refinement in both the generativist and functionalist frameworks: a process that is intimately related to the concept of explanatory adequacy.

2.1.1   *Looking at linguistic universals from the inside*

One of the priorities in generative linguistics in Chomsky (1957), as well as in later versions of his theory (i.e. Standard Theory, Extended Standard Theory,

---

[22] For example, Bybee (1985, and this volume, chapter 8), Comrie (1989), Croft (1990, 2001), Dik (1997), Givón (1995), Haiman (1985), Keenan (1972), Lindblom (1986, 1990), Boersma (1997), Goddard and Wierzbicka (2002), etc.

Principles and Parameters, and the Minimalist Program), has always been the development of the constituent structures of UG.[23] In this sense, one of Chomsky's principal methodological preoccupations has always been the formulation of well-defined, robust hypotheses that either provide valid information characterizing the language faculty, or can be immediately discarded because they have been refuted by empirical data. Chomsky (1965, 44–45) explains that one of the most serious problems for linguistic theory seems to be how to abstract away assertions and generalizations from descriptively adequate and particular grammars and, whenever possible, try to attribute these to the overall structure of linguistic theory, thus enriching this theory and imposing more structure on the pattern of grammatical description. That is, if possible, one must formulate generalizations about the essential nature of language, from which particular language-specific grammatical features can be derived.

In this respect, one of the reasons for the development of successive versions of Generative Grammar was the desire to formulate increasingly restrictive theories. In our opinion, the mechanisms controlling such restrictions are precisely what characterize this progressive refinement of UG, which, as will be seen, has been an ongoing process from *Aspects of the Theory of Syntax* to minimalism.

In the Standard Theory,[24] the idea of UG had not yet been fully developed, and as no restrictions had been placed on individual languages, they had considerable potential for variation. Chomsky initially outlined UG in the first chapter of *Aspects of the Theory of Syntax* (1965). This was the same period when he formulated the distinction between formal and substantive universals. Examples of substantive universals include distinctive features in phonology and the inventory of syntactic categories which each language can potentially select from, whereas examples of formal universals are rules such as *rewriting, transformations*, and *lexical insertion*, as well as the specification of how they should be applied.[25] It was thus the task of linguists to describe formally these different types of rules and formulate algorithms that encoded how they operated. This

---

[23] The metaphor that Jackendoff (2002) uses to explain this concept is very eloquent: "I prefer to think of it [Universal Grammar] as a toolkit for constructing language, out of which the child (or better, the child's brain) f-selects tools appropriate to the job at hand. If the language in the environment happens to have a case system (like German), UG will help shape the child's acquisition of case; if it has a tone system (like Mandarin), UG will help shape the child's acquisition of tone. But if the language in the environment happens to be English, which lacks case and tone, these parts of UG will simply be silent."

[24] In *Syntactic Structures* the notion of UG is not made explicit. Chomsky only speaks of a "general theory."

[25] The additional distinction between strong and weak universals introduced by McNeill (1970, 73–74) has remained valid. Generativists defend the existence of strong universals in the same way as they defend modularity of mind and language. The mind is modular since it possesses a certain number of systems or modules (e.g. visual perception), each with a specific set of properties. Language is thus a well-differentiated faculty, whose development follows certain steps and which can be defined by specific mental principles.

was a matter of choosing from among the various descriptions of a language permitted by UG, based on maximum simplicity as to the number of symbols and rules:

UG, though infinitely richer than other contemporary linguistic theories, was still relatively undeveloped. Except for the format of its rules, UG placed no other constraint on specific languages, which could thus vary considerably. (Pollock, 1997, 202; translated from the French)

However, this unified vision of Generative Grammar was subsequently disrupted for two reasons. Firstly, an important disagreement arose that divided generativists into two opposing camps. Whereas one side defended an interpretative semantic component, the other was in favor of a generative semantic component. The restriction of the descriptive power of transformations dictated that these should preserve meaning, thus making them semantically irrelevant. This led certain linguists (Ross, 1967; McCawley, 1968) to identify deep structure with logical form or the semantic representation of the sentence. This assertion, when applied to universals, meant that, since all languages presumably shared the same deep structure, all differences lay at the surface level. In this sense, deep structure constituted a theoretical construct based on formal logic and was regarded as a possible linguistic universal.

One of the principal representatives of this school was McCawley (1974) (along with Lakoff, Bach, Ross, etc.) who proposed that VSO word order was a deep structure shared by all languages, and that interlinguistic variations at the surface level could be explained by means of transformational rules. This notwithstanding, as shown by Fodor (1977, 65), it soon became evident even in the initial proposals of generative semantics that the simplification of the model resulting from the elimination of the syntactic component at the base resulted in a transformational component of greater complexity.[26] The proposal of representations at the level of deep structure that were more abstract and further removed from syntactic structure meant that the transformational component became correspondingly more powerful to compensate for the increased distance between deep and surface structures.[27]

Secondly, the vision of language in *Aspects* also changed for reasons that were fundamentally theoretical (Brucart, 2002, 30ff.). As more empirical

---

[26] Jackendoff (2002) offers the following example: "the theory of Generative Semantics . . . increased the 'abstractness' and complexity of Deep Structure, to the point that the example *Floyd broke the glass* was famously posited to have eight underlying clauses, each corresponding to some feature of the semantics."

[27] Chomsky (1972, 117) argued that certain parts of meaning, such as those related to negation and quantification (never to grammatical relations clearly specified in the deep structure), went unnoticed in deep structures. This made it necessary to postulate the new model of the Extended Standard Theory, which admitted the relevance of surface structure in the semantic interpretation of sentences.

language studies were carried out, it became obvious that the rules to be postulated for each language and for each grammatical construction within individual
languages were so numerous that it was going to be difficult to arrive at conclusions regarding possible universals. Consequently, in view of this problem,
a more viable course was to discover the principles underlying these rules, and
thus to avoid having the rules as primitives of the grammatical theory. This
would be the function of general underlying principles that were more viable
candidates for linguistic universals. On the basis of these very simple, abstract
principles, such as the presence of empty categories in syntactic representations
or the cyclicity of syntactic movements, UG was significantly enriched, and
began to regulate and constrain operations of individual languages with greater
precision. As a result, the work of linguists was greatly simplified because the
options for language description were significantly reduced. Many of the studies published in the seventies were extremely influential in this respect,[28] and
gave rise in the eighties to numerous descriptive and comparative studies of
a broad range of languages. One important result of this "wider perspective"
was the paradox formulated by Pollock (1997, 205) in the following series of
questions:

If the link between the UG language faculty and, say, French is so direct, why is it that UG
also allows (internal) language structures that are so different, such as Chinese, Finnish,
and Welsh?

Why is it that, in the very heart of the Indo-European language family, there are so
many differences between syntactic domains that are regarded as similar? For example,
why are Romance languages so different with regard to the order of clitic pronouns . . .?
Moreover, why did English (in contrast to the other Germanic Languages) in Elizabethan
times suddenly begin to use the auxiliary verb *do* for questions, negation, and emphasis,
whereas German, Dutch, and the Scandinavian languages still manage very well without
it? (translated from the French)

In response to such questions, generative grammarians adopted a modular,
parametrized model (Principles and Parameters Model), which was later continued in the Minimalist Program, according to which linguistic variation is
explained as differences in parameter settings.

Generative Grammar thus went from a rule-based model to a principle-based
model, and it was this basic change in perspective in the Principles and Parameters Model that gave linguistic universals empirical content through the concepts of *principle* and *parameter*, which also appear in the title of the model. For
example, X-bar theory, which was one of the subtheories or modules in which
principles were organized, was proposed as a universal model of constituent
structure, and was said to represent to a certain extent the nuclear syntax of
all languages (Jackendoff, 1977, 30ff.; Chomsky, 1981, 127ff.; Radford, 1988,

[28] See Keyser (1978).

167ff.; Haegeman, 1995, 110ff.). Other examples of UG principles are the *principle of endocentricity*, according to which phrases inherit their category properties from the head, and the *structure-dependency principle* that stipulates that grammatical principles and rules are applied hierarchically.

On the other hand, it is evident that languages differ in many important ways. If this were not so, a child would be able to learn any language simply by acquiring its lexical items or vocabulary, something that obviously does not occur. In contrast, we know that linguistic variation is very wide ranging, and, in order to explain it, generativists postulate that the universal principles of UG undergo parametric variation. As previously mentioned, language-specific questions are explained by an inventory of parameters with a maximally restricted set of options, which are also a part of the universalist model, and which help to bridge the gap between language unity and diversity. In this sense, interlinked sets of principles and parameters constitute an authentically universal core grammar in which options for variation – limited and bounded by the universals themselves – are reflected in the model by means of parameters.

For example, the *wh-parameter* accounts for the difference between languages which permit the fronting of a wh-constituent (interrogative pronouns and adverbs) in questions, and those languages, such as Chinese, which do not. There is also the *pro-drop parameter*, which regulates variation in languages which allow the omission of the subject (e.g. Spanish, Italian . . .) and those which do not (e.g. English). The *head parameter* explains the fact that there are languages which place the complement after the verb, and reflects the distinction between SVO and SOV languages (see Radford, 1997; Haegeman, 1995). The fact that all of these parameters are specified in binary terms has had an important influence on the notion of markedness.[29]

[29] In the Principles and Parameters Model, speakers have a markedness theory which guides them in their choice of options represented by parameters. One of the two possible values of each parameter represents the unmarked or neutral option, which is the initial one that is set by default. This setting only changes if language acquirers deduce from contextual input that the language that they are learning has selected the marked option. They will thus adjust their grammar to the corresponding parameter value. In other words, what the generativist model has always maintained is the idea that markedness should be understood in binary rather than scalar terms. Accordingly, categories are defined by the presence or absence of binary features [±N, ±V]. In fact, it is argued on the basis of very clear phonological and syntactic evidence, as well as the implicit or explicit belief that cognitive processing in language is binary, that all ramifications must be so as well. Consequently, the binary tradition of marked and unmarked pairs for each differentiating feature is one of the most salient features of markedness theory within Generative Grammar. This vision contrasts with that proposed by functional models in which the concept of markedness in recent years has been revised by Givón (1984, 1990, 1995) and Croft (1990), among others. More recently, the functional approach to markedness has been linked to cognitive linguistics. For this reason, Croft (1990, 59–60) no longer believes in discrete binary categories, but rather proposes continuous categories that radially cluster around prototypical elements. Consequently, he does not interpret markedness in the traditional way – nor as the generativists do – by postulating that an element has or does not have a certain feature (thus making possible

The result of this process of revision and change which the theory has under-gone is the version proposed in the Minimalist Program, the most recent development in UG (E_0), which is regarded as the genetic expression of the language faculty shared by all human beings and which is composed of a set of linguistic features reflecting linguistic properties, and computational operations that access these features and thus generate linguistic expressions. Any speaker possessing this faculty, who has been exposed to language, is capable of deducing the grammar of that language, in other words, of *his/her* language. The language faculty connects two independent modules, the sensorimotor system and the conceptual system.

To be usable, the expressions of the language faculty (at least some of them), have to be legible by the outside systems. So the sensorimotor system and the conceptual–intentional system have to be able to access, to "read" the expressions; otherwise the systems wouldn't even know it is there . . . So, for example, the sensorimotor systems will require that the expression has a temporal order . . . The conceptual–intentional systems, which we don't know much about, are plainly going to require certain kinds of information about words and phrases and certain kind of relations among them, and so on. (Chomsky, 2000b, 17, 19)

The only potential levels and units in the grammatical model that accounts for the language acquisition process in human beings are those that are justified by the sensorimotor or the conceptual system, or are required by the computational operation itself. This avoids any unnecessary operations and eliminates redundancy. This desire to reduce computational complexity to its minimum expression is the most salient innovation in Chomsky's model, in which simplification is irrevocably linked to the idea of perfection and efficiency. As a result, all efforts in Generative Grammar have gone towards restricting the analytical tools and models of UG and I-language, and at the same time towards preserving the Principles and Parameters Model – above all, its modular and parametric dimension. Chomsky writes:

The "minimalist program" . . . is a program, not a theory, even less so than the P[rinciples] & P[arameters] approach. There are minimalist questions but no minimalist answers, apart from those found in pursuing the program. (In Alexandrova and Arnaudova, 2001, v)

All of this leads us to the conclusion that this obsession with greater theoretical restriction has been a driving force in the successive versions of the

---

the opposition or neutralization of the opposition in certain contexts), but proposes a gradual differentiation of the marked element from the unmarked one. This differentiation is established through a progressive increase in the structural complexity (of marked elements), a lower textual frequency, and a greater cognitive complexity, as pointed out by Croft himself (1990, 59–60). Once more, this differentiation highlights the tension between the use of internal or external criteria in the formulation of interlinguistic generalizations.

generative model, initially based on rules and constructions, and subsequently on principles and representations. Consequently, the explanatory adequacy and particularly the typological adequacy of the model were greatly enhanced as UG became increasingly restricted by more abstract, general principles of inter-linguistic validity, such as those proposed within the Principles and Parameters Model.[30]

2.1.2   *Looking at universals from the outside*

From a functional perspective, Dik (1997, 14, 17) describes two essential fea-tures of a typologically adequate linguistic model: (i) such a theory should not be too concrete because then it would be impossible to elaborate natural lan-guage grammars with descriptive adequacy; (ii) such a theory should possess a minimum level of abstraction, which is defined as the distance between under-lying structures and the linguistic representations that designate them. Again we are faced with the dilemma of choosing between abstract theoretical gener-alizations and more concrete, specific ones. To illustrate the functionalist view on universals, in this section we shall examine some approaches that share an *extrinsic* vision of universals that is radically different from the conception of universals in UG. Evidently, each proposal differs in the mechanisms used to identify what is truly universal.

In our view, the modular interpretation of language is perhaps the point that most clearly separates cognitivists and proponents of certain other functional models from generativists. Put succinctly, functionalists center their interest on function, meaning, and language use (cf. Langacker, 1987; Dik, 1997; Van Valin and LaPolla, 1997; Cuenca and Hilferty, 1999; Bybee, this volume, chap-ter 8). They focus on *function* because they consider that function and meaning are factors that condition form, and not vice versa. They focus on *meaning* because they believe that grammar is structured by semantic and conceptual content, and is thus dependent upon it. They focus on *use* because they do not separate the study of language from its communicative function. As a result, their primary data source is actual speaker output and not introspec-tion. Based on these premises, functional-cognitive models clearly conceive language as a dynamic entity in which boundaries between different language levels (grammar, lexis, semantics, and pragmatics) are fuzzy, and where cer-tain dichotomies, such as that of competence and performance, are not valid. This signifies that any analysis of universals is necessarily interdisciplinary, and although functionalists do not reject the existence of innate ideas, they prefer to explain language acquisition and the essential properties of language by means of experiential data from the real world, the body, and the relationship between

---

[30] Of all the versions of Generative Grammar, the Principles and Parameters Model was the one that produced the most studies on different languages. In our opinion, this is due to the fact that in this model UG achieves its maximum level of restriction.

the two[31] (cf. Cuenca and Hilferty, 1999, for a more in-depth analysis of these proposals).

Metaphor and metonymy are important areas of research in cognitive linguistics, and their study has produced an extremely innovative conception of universals. For example, cognitivists affirm that metaphor is not only a literary figurative device, but a basic aspect of cognitive processing which allows us to understand complex, abstract ideas in terms of simpler, more concrete ones. We conceive life in terms of basic metaphors which underlie our conceptual system and daily experience. In this respect, the publication of *Metaphors We Live By* (Lakoff and Johnson, 1980) gave rise to a veritable host of similar studies aimed at analyzing the internal structure of the metaphor. More recently, Grady (1998), Grady *et al.* (1999) and Lakoff and Johnson (1999) distinguish between *primary* and *complex* metaphors. Examples of complex metaphors can be found in the following Spanish and English expressions:

(1)   ***Va por la*** *vida sin preocuparse de nada.*

(2)   ***Pasó por*** *la adolescencia sin problemas.*

(3)   *Each of us **goes through** life seeking and searching for that one perfect fit, that thing that will fill the void.*

(4)   *As she **went through** her teenage years her sisters played mother to her.*

These expressions are interrelated because each is an instantiation of the same conceptual metaphor, LIFE IS A JOURNEY, which is in turn composed of simpler or primary metaphors, such as ACTIVITIES ARE MOVING OBJECTS, FINISHING AN ACTIVITY IS REACHING A DESTINATION, and OBJECTS ARE DESTINATIONS. In all of these metaphors, time (an abstract notion) is conceptualized in terms of space (a more concrete notion). They are all based on the visual perception of the temporal end of a certain activity (a trip, life) as a final point in space (which Lakoff, 1987, refers to as END-OF-PATH).[32] Other projections or common correspondences are those that relate difficulties with obstacles, affective emotion with cold, heat, etc., as shown in the following examples:

(5)   AFFECTION IS WARMTH
        She is too frigid for my taste.
        They gave me a warm welcome.
        She has a cold heart.

---

[31] It is in this sense that cognitive linguistic models can be considered "experience-based" (cf. Johnson, 1987).

[32] The *localist hypothesis* postulates that the majority of the fundamental notions that human beings possess have a spatial basis. This can be regarded as the authentic primitive from a semantic and syntactic viewpoint.

(6)   MORE IS UP, LESS IS DOWN
        Prices are soaring.
        Costs have plummeted.
        The number of websites all over the world is skyrocketing.

(7)   GOALS ARE DESTINATIONS
        She is not going anywhere.
        We are moving in circles.
        She has made it to the top.

Since primary metaphors arise from basic domains of experience such as sensory perceptions, and, accordingly, are derived from the human body and its interaction with the real world (experience-based), they are based on a set of corporal patterns or schemas, which, in our opinion, are possible candidates for language universals.

Metonymy conceptually associates two contiguous entities from a conceptual viewpoint. Nevertheless, it is necessary to distinguish between metonymic expressions such as *I will have a cup* or *I bought a Picasso* and the conceptual metonymies from which they are derived. Examples of these are CONTENT FOR CONTAINER, PART FOR WHOLE, WHOLE FOR PART, OBJECT FOR ACTION, etc., but, unlike primary metaphors, simple metonymies do not combine to form more complex ones (Kövecses and Radden, 1998; Panther and Radden, 1999; Ruiz de Mendoza and Díez Velasco, 2003). What should be underlined here is that in cognitive linguistics the analysis of both metaphor and metonymy leads to a cognitive and semantic "primitive" whose universality is by no means ruled out.

A strong affiliation with the cognitive linguistics program can be observed in the work done within most variants of the family of Construction Grammar (especially those compatible with Goldberg's version).[33] The issue of linguistic universals was not a major focus of research within this model until the appearance of *Radical Construction Grammar* (Croft, 2001). In fact, as Croft (2004, 276) and Tomasello (2003, 5) affirm:

vanilla construction grammar is neutral as to any hypotheses as to what types of constructions (if any) are universal, or at least found across languages, or what types of component grammatical categories are universal. (Croft, 2004, 276)

---

[33] This theoretical framework contains a cluster of related models, encompassing both: (i) monotonic (unification-based) variants (Kay and Fillmore, 1999; Fillmore *et al.*, to appear), gradually coming closer to a formalist model along the lines of Head Driven Phrase Structure Grammar; and (ii) non-monotonic variants influenced by cognitive linguistics, including, besides the cognitive linguistics program (Langacker, 2000), the Goldbergian version of Construction Grammar (Goldberg, 1995, 1998, 2003) – which, in turn, owes its greatest debts to Lakoff (1987) and Fillmore (1987) – and, more recently, Croft's (2001) Radical Construction Grammar.

Typological research has also established beyond a reasonable doubt that not only are specific grammatical constructions not universal, but basically none of the so-called minor word classes of English that help to constitute particular constructions (e.g., Prepositions, auxiliary verbs, conjunctions, articles, adverbs, complementizers, and the like) are universal across languages either. (Tomasello, 2003, 5)

From the above quotations it seems reasonable to assume that universals should not be identified with specific linguistic items or constructions since these are unequivocally not universal. This, however, does not preclude acceptance of the fact that nouns and verbs (or at least their prototypical instantiations) are universal (see Croft, Goldberg, Langacker, etc.). Thus, universals do not stem from the inner working of the theory, but, as shown below, from outside factors.

In connection with this, an interesting case is that of Goldberg (1995), who – unintentionally, we presume – presents certain assumptions which could be interpreted as hinting at a universalist position. Although she has never explicitly dealt with universals, constructions (simple-clause patterns) may well be taken to be plausible candidates for universals. Thus, for instance, Goldberg (1995, 39) formulates the *Scene Encoding Hypothesis* that draws a parallel between the semantics of constructions and basic patterns of human experience. Languages select these constructions from a set of abstract structures, which are universal to the extent that they are the result of shared experience. However, this is pure conjecture on our part since Goldberg now withdraws that position and a much more "moderate" view is posited.[34]

More particularly, Goldberg (personal communication to Francisco Gonzálvez-García) contends that motivations, such as general cognition, principles of economy, iconicity, processing constraints, expressive demands, learning constraints, etc., are universal, and it naturally follows that this can give rise to *universal tendencies* in languages. Goldberg acknowledges the fact that many unrelated languages do have a ditransitive construction conveying "transfer" as its prototypical meaning or allow for a metaphorical use of the caused-motion construction. Moreover, it is remarkable how often apparently unrelated languages converge on a number of constructions. Nevertheless, according to Goldberg, it is very rare to find something universal, in other words something found in ALL languages. Thus, Goldberg agrees with Croft (2001c) and others (Tomasello, 2003) that the specifics of argument structure are language-specific and are also often construction-specific.

However, this does not mean that universals do not exist for Construction Grammar. As Tomasello (2003, 5) claims, universals must be sought somewhere else, and not in particular linguistic constructions. Two plausible candidates are human cognition (cf. Croft, 2001c ; Talmy, 2003) or even human communication

---

[34] We wish to thank Francisco Gonzálvez-García for his insightful comments regarding the theoretical premises of Construction Grammar.

(cf. Comrie, 2003). This position is compatible with the cognitive credo, which strongly emphasizes an extrinsic view of language in which language universals are seen from the outside without resorting to theory-internal mechanisms or metalanguage.

Similarly, in their desire to reduce theoretical abstraction, certain functional–typological models reject the idea of abstract predicates, and instead use natural language units (e.g. Dik, 1997; Goddard and Wierzbicka, 2002).[35] For example, Wierzbicka proposes a *Natural Semantic Metalanguage* (NSM),[36] which is based on the method of *reductive paraphrase*, in which the meaning of any complex predicate can be explained by a paraphrase made up of terms that are simpler and more understandable than the original. The NSM operates on the following premises: (i) the meaning of a semantic primitive cannot be paraphrased in simpler terms. For example, primitives such as I, YOU, SOMEBODY, GOOD, BIG, THINK, BECAUSE, etc., are used to define a large number of predicates and grammatical constructions like the following:

(8)   *Person X broke Y (e.g. Pete broke the window)* =
       X did something to Y
       because of this, something happened to Y at this time
       because of this, after this Y was not one thing any more. (Goddard, 2002, 8)

(ii) a semantic primitive should have an equivalent or a set of equivalents in all languages. It may happen, however, that a primitive may belong to different grammatical categories in different languages (e.g. INSIDE is an adverb in English, a noun in Longgu – a Polynesian language of the Solomon Islands – and a verb in Cayuga – an Amerindian language spoken in the northeast United States); (iii) the metalanguage of the primitives should be able to explain all the vocabulary and grammar of a language. In other words, the set of primitives is a miniature natural language in itself; (iv) primitives are regarded as lexical universals, which are the symbolic representation of universal conceptual primitives (cf. Goddard, 2002, 16ff.). According to Wierzbicka (1995, 154), primitives are the basis for the *tertium comparationis* which necessarily underlies all successful interlinguistic communication:

Within a particular language, every element belongs to a unique network of elements, and occupies a particular place in a unique network of relationships. When we compare two or more languages, we cannot expect to find identical networks of relationships. We can, none the less, expect to find corresponding sets of indefinables. (Wierzbicka, 1996, 15)

---

[35] Dik (1978b, 1997) develops a lexical representation system called *Stepwise Lexical Decomposition*, which claims that natural language predicates can be defined by means of other predicates in the same language, as occurs in dictionary definitions.

[36] See Wierzbicka (1988, 1992, 1996), Goddard and Wierzbicka (1994, 2002), and Goddard (1998) for an analysis of individual proposals regarding each primitive.

Given that the NSM is a model of universal and innate *lingua mentalis*,[37] a correspondence can be posited between semantic primitives of all languages and some of their combinations, such that anything formulated in the NSM can be easily and accurately translated into any world language.[38]

From a different angle, regarding clause structure, Role and Reference Grammar (RRG) (see Van Valin and LaPolla, 1997; Van Valin, to appear) imposes the following two requirements on its theory of clause structure:

(a) a theory of clause structure should capture all of the universal features without imposing features on languages in which there is no evidence for them.

(b) a theory should represent comparable structures in different languages in comparable ways (Van Valin and LaPolla, 1997, 22).

Van Valin and LaPolla (1997, 18–24) effectively demonstrate the insufficiency of Immediate Constituent Analysis for explaining clause structure in languages such as Dyrbal, where few constraints operate on constituent order, or Lakhota, which is a "head-marking language."[39]

---

[37] Leibniz believed in the existence of a set of universal innate primitives that provided the basis for conceptual analysis. He called these primitives the *alphabet of human thought*. Since they could not be artificial or arbitrarily designated, they necessarily were natural language terms. These terms were undefinable because their meaning could not be broken down into simpler units. His conception differs from Wilkins', who based his *philosophical language* on an artificial set of primitives. Wilkins' approach is directly linked to those of authors such as Hjelmslev and Lakoff, as well as to the *predicate-centered* approaches of Rappaport and Levin (1998), Van Valin (to appear), and Jackendoff (1990). These linguists use a set of abstract primitive elements of the type CAUSE, BECOME, INGR(essive), DO, etc., as part of the lexical representations they formulate. Such elements raise the question of where the chain of the decomposition finally comes to an end (see Van Valin, this volume, chapter 7).

[38] According to Wierzbicka (1988, 13–14), the Humboldtian concept of the *Inhalt* of a language (i.e. the set of its lexically or grammatically coded contents) not only includes all language-independent universal elements, but also those which reflect its individuality and which cannot be translated into other languages without significant loss of meaning. Wierzbicka believes that Humboldt's idea should be further developed so that lexical and grammatical meaning can be formulated in terms of a universal semantic metalanguage: "The use of a standardized semantic metalanguage could open new possibilities in this area of study. The philosophies built into the grammar of different languages become commensurable if all sentences in all languages can be translated into the universal language of semantic primitives. To put it less strongly: different philosophies are comparable to the extent to which the constructions that embody them can be translated into the universal language of semantic primitives."

[39] Nichols (1986) makes an interesting typological distinction between *head-marking* languages and *dependent-marking* languages. Head-marking languages morphologically encode in the head the relation that the head maintains with dependent elements in a given syntactic domain. In contrast, dependent-marking languages encode in dependent elements the relation maintained with the head in a given syntactic domain. These two types of language have the following patterns:

(a) dependent-marking languages:

Noun + Case morph(eme) Noun + Case morph. Noun + case morph. VP H(ead)

(b) head-marking languages:

Noun_1 Noun_2 Noun_3 Verb + $^{\text{Morph}}\text{Affix}_{\text{N1}}$ + $^{\text{Morph}}\text{Affix}_{\text{N2}}$ + $^{\text{Morph}}\text{Affix}_{\text{N3}}$

In the search for a universally valid representational system, RRG differentiates universal aspects of language from language-specific ones. With respect to universal aspects, it establishes two oppositions for clause structure. The first is between predicating elements and non-predicating elements, whereas the second opposition concerns those elements which are arguments of the predicate and those which are not. This dichotomy defines three syntactic units in the structure of the clause: the nucleus (which includes a Verb, an Adjective or a nominal), the core (which contains the predicate and its arguments), and the periphery (which includes constituents that are not predicate arguments). With respect to language-specific aspects, Van Valin and LaPolla (1997, 35–40) expand RRG to incorporate two new positions in the clause and the sentence. The first contains the interrogative elements (*precore slot*, PrCs), and the second, the extra-clausal elements that appear to the right or the left of the utterance, and are separated by a pause from the rest of the clause (*Right and Left Detached Positions*, RDP and LDP). The clause and the extra-clausal constituents make up the sentence.

What is relevant here for our purposes is the fact that universal distinctions are based on semantic criteria and allow syntactic structures in different languages to respond to the same descriptive pattern (e.g. the analyses of Dyrbal, Japanese, and English proposed by Van Valin and LaPolla, 1997, chapter 2).

Other functional explanations of universals are based on the limitations or conditioning that the human capacity for information processing imposes on the form and organization of messages. More specifically, certain models maintain that phonic universals are based on requirements imposed by our speech perception and production systems (cf. Maddieson, this volume, chapter 4). Especially relevant here is the extensive research carried out by Lindblom (1983, 1986, 1990, *inter alia*), who has created an explanatory model of the structure of different phonic systems, based on the idea that the sound elements of all languages are organized and have evolved in such a way as to facilitate optimally both perception and production. This means, from the speaker's perspective, that he/she will invariably opt for the most distinctive elements[40] as well as for an articulation that involves the least effort and is not overly extreme. In contrast, the hearer will always prefer more perceptually distant and salient

Besides these types of languages, Nichols specifies two more that are a combination of the others:

(c) *double-marking languages* in which both the head and the dependent element are marked (e.g. Quechua).

(d) *split marking languages* in which there are certain patterns typical of head-marking languages and other patterns typical of double-marking languages (e.g. English and Spanish).

[40] Indeed, Trubetzkoy (1939) alluded to the *maximum perceptual distance between segments* as a characteristic of optimal phonic systems. This distance may be syntagmatic as well as paradigmatic.

elements. Lindblom *et al.* (1984, 191–192) explain this by means of the following examples.

If we compare [d ð ɖ] with [b d g], it is clear that the first set of sounds is composed of less discriminable elements than the second one. Consequently, there is greater probability that the latter group will be found in the phonic inventory of a language. At the same time, speakers always tend to apply the law of least effort, thus favoring sounds that involve simpler articulatory movements, and which are closer to the neutral position (the point of conventional reference), or which imply co-articulation in the sequence. In [d ɖ ɖ], the first group of sounds of the preceding example, [ɖ] will always be the least favored sound because it involves the greatest tongue height, as well as retraction of the tongue tip. These two opposing factors – the preservation of sensory discriminability and ease of articulation – tend to interact, and languages are obliged to maintain a delicate balance between the two. According to Lindblom's theory, phonetic universals are also conditioned by acoustic distance and perceptual salience. If back vowels are usually rounded, it is because rounding makes these already low-pitched vowels even deeper in tone quality. This distances them even further from high-pitched front vowels. And if the syllables composed of a velar consonant and a palatal vowel are preferred over the ones made up of a velar consonant and a velar vowel, it is because their perceptual salience is greater. This is the philosophy embodied, for example, in the text below:

Consonant inventories tend to evolve so as to achieve maximal perceptual distinctiveness at minimum articulatory cost. (Lindblom and Maddieson, 1988, 72)

From this succinct description it follows that *perfecting universals* has also been a major research goal within the functionalist framework. Functionalists have accomplished this task by developing, broadening, and testing initial hypotheses in order to explain the grammatical structure of language by reducing it to, and analyzing it in terms of, various types of cognitive and behavioral abilities. Table 1.1 summarizes the content of the preceding sections, and shows the points on which functionalists and generativists differ regarding universals.

As will be shown below, we should not oversimplify things and claim that there is only one way of explaining universals. We feel that the choice of one option over the other means relegating the problem either to the realms of UG, or alternatively locating it within the range of cognitive capacities. However, a more viable option would be to rethink the concept of UG so as to create a more unified version, which would account for the interaction of external factors with pre-established linguistic structures. A reasonable first step would be initially to determine the type and amount of linguistic structure which can be ascribed to UG, and then to complement and enrich these principles with

Table 1.1

Linguistic models	Aspects regarded as universal	Methodology and strategies
Typology and/or the empiricist paradigm	Language data	Inductive, initially atheoretical
Aspects of the Theory of Syntax	Substantive universals (categories and features) and formal universals (rules and modes of application)	Hypothetical-deductive
Generative Semantics	Deep structure. Lexical–semantic analysis	Hypothetical-deductive
Principles and Parameters	X-bar theory, Case Theory, etc. General government and binding properties	Hypothetical-deductive
Minimalist Program	Sets of features and computational operations. Constraints imposed by the interfaces between the language faculty, the conceptual system, and sensorimotor system. Narrow syntactic algorithm.	Hypothetical-deductive
Role and Reference Grammar	Nucleus, core, periphery Semantic component and macro-roles	Deductive; functional; semantic
Cognitive Grammar	Basic metaphors (Lakoff). Prototypical categories (noun, verbs), human cognition, communication, etc. (Goldberg, Croft, Tomasello)	Deductive; functional; cognitive

explanations stemming from perception, cognition, etc. Obtaining a delicate balance between linguistic and more general cognitive capacities should be the rationale behind research in universals since a choice between the two trends leads to an unjustified theoretical dispute. As will be seen below, this is the direction taken by recent models like the one described in Jackendoff (2002) and in the work of others, a theoretical move which we are also greatly in favor of.

2.2   Interpreting data

There are presently more than 6,000 documented languages in the world. Data on them has been compiled in an important body of research called "Linguistic Atlases," which offer information on an extensive range of languages and their geographic locations (e.g. Moreno Cabrera, 1990, 1995; Price, 2000; Comrie, 2001; Wurm *et al.*, 2003, etc.). Although such studies constitute a rich legacy of incalculable linguistic value, they are becoming increasingly scarce, without any steps being taken to remedy this loss.

Nevertheless, our objective in this section is not to discuss the viability of language classifications, but rather to highlight how the rich variation in

languages, with regard to the codification of syntactic, phonological, morphological, and semantic phenomena, can illustrate: (i) the application of typology;
(ii) the difficulty of formulating interlinguistic generalizations; and (iii) how the
detailed analysis of such apparently diverse phenomena can be interpreted in
different ways, i.e. as the result of universal language patterns (e.g. generativist principles of parametric variation) or as broader language types (e.g.
functional–typological models).

We shall thus show examples that reflect the plurality of nuances in certain
language phenomena, as well as the different explanations provided for them by
generativists and functionalists. In this way we wish to illustrate the focal point
of this chapter, which is the dialectic tension between theoretical abstraction
and concreteness with the ensuing use of intrinsic or extrinsic criteria in language analysis. It goes without saying that every linguistic theory must possess
a certain degree of abstraction in order to be able to explain the concept of *natural language*, and in the realm of science maximally abstract theories are those
that evidently have universal scope. However, as we shall endeavor to show,
establishing the boundaries that define optimal degrees of abstraction or concreteness for any model is far from easy. For this reason, this issue, which can
be linked in all its possible nuances to the long-standing controversy between
the various trends of rationalism and empiricism, continues to be the subject of
intense debate (see Section 1).

A. Syntax: word order and morpheme order.   One of the areas where
languages most differ is in word order.[41] Ever since Greenberg (1963a) first
published his seminal study, many other linguists have also analyzed this phenomenon. In this respect, languages are divided into *configurational* (languages
whose constituents must to a greater or lesser degree follow a certain order) and
non-configurational (languages whose constituents apparently have no predetermined pattern). Within configurational languages, the typology established
by Greenberg and his followers highlights, among other things, the position
occupied by the Subject, Verb, and Object, and, as shown in the following
examples, expresses interlinguistic variation in this regard (Van Valin, 2001a, 2).

(9)   *The teacher   is   reading a   book* (English)

(10)   *waúspekhiye ki   wówapi wa yawá* (Lakhota)
        teacher   the   book   a   read

(11)   *manjaha   buju   guru   i*   (Toba Batak)
        read   book   teacher the

---

[41] See Comrie (this volume, chapter 6) for an in-depth analysis of the many different ways that
world languages encode relative clauses.

(12)   *učitel'nica*   *čitaet*   *knigu*   (Russian)
       teacher   read   book

       knigu   *čitaet*   *učitel'nica*
       book   read   teacher

       čitaet   *učitel'nica*   *knigu*
       read   teacher   book

As shown in (9), the canonical word-order pattern for English – the same as in Spanish, French, and Italian – is SVO, where the Subject precedes the Verb, and the Verb precedes the Object. In contrast, in Lakhota (10), an Amerindian Sioux language, the Subject and Object precede the Verb, the same as in Japanese, Turkish, and Navajo, all of which thus have an SOV word order. Finally, Toba Batak, a Malayo-Polynesian language (11) has a VOS word order like Welsh, certain Amerindian languages, and Arabic dialects in which the Verb precedes the Object and Subject. In contrast, constituent order in Russian (12) can vary without affecting the grammaticality of the sentence since Subject and Object roles are marked by fusional case morphemes such as *-a* and *-u*. In this language, it is thus word form that indicates the relational structure of the utterance.

Two important conclusions can be derived from these facts. The first conclusion establishes that a typological approach like Greenberg's can use word-order patterns and their distribution to arrive at universal generalizations such as the following:

In declarative sentences with nominal subject and object, the dominant order is almost always one in which the subject precedes the object. (Greenberg, 1963, 77)

A second conclusion that has often been cited underlines the existing relation between the capacity of a language to vary the order of its constituents and the presence of formal elements such as case affixes or a generally rich morphology, which enable speakers to distinguish sentence elements without basing their understanding exclusively on word order.

However, these two language types are more similar than they may seem at first glance. On the one hand, even in those languages that lack a fixed word order, there is invariably one pattern that is more frequent than the others.[42] And on the other, certain languages have elements that are easily identifiable by their case markers (e.g. the English pronoun system), and which, in spite of these features, have very limited or even zero mobility in the sentence. Conversely, in languages such as Russian, even though variation in word order does not affect

---

[42] See Newmeyer (2004) for a discussion of the concept of "basic word order" from a generative and a functional perspective.

grammaticality, it can certainly affect information structure, which inevitably leads to different presuppositions regarding new and given information.

All of this seems to point to an opposition that is even more basic than that between configurational and non-configurational languages, and which is related to the position occupied by the head of the phrase in both language types. For example, in the generativist framework[43] Chomsky (1986) considers – and this is an authentic universal for generativists – that all phrases are composed of a head and a modifier to which a specifier can be added at a second higher level. Difference in word order basically depends on the position occupied by the head. As a result, there are languages in which modifiers always occupy a position to the right of the head. This is the case in Spanish where the Object in a Verb Phrase (hereafter VP) always follows the verb (e.g. *yo quiero a la chica*) and Noun Phrase (hereafter NP) modifiers follow the noun (e.g. *la casa de la chica*). In contrast, there are other languages in which modifiers occupy a position to the left of the head. In classical Latin the Object in the VP always precedes the verb (e.g. *ego puellam amo*) and NP modifiers precede the noun (*puellae domus*). According to generativists, such typological distinctions are caused by different settings of the Head Parameter.[44]

So, now, if we look at the internal structure of the word from a functionalist perspective, some of Greenberg's universals underline the iconic relation between the conceptual distance of affixes, the position they hold in relation to the head, and their degree of cohesion with it. For example, Universal 39 stipulates that in those cases in which there are both number and case morphemes that follow or precede the noun head, the expression of the number is generally situated between the noun head and the expression of the case.

This leads to the conclusion that the distance between the head and the number affix is less than the distance between the head and the case affix, which

---

[43] This is true in all of its versions up to Kayne (1994), who, in his proposal on the asymmetry of syntax, maintains that, despite appearances to the contrary, the only possible order is specifier-head-complement, and not the reverse. Language differences regarding the linear order of constituents are always the result of movement and correspond to a difference in the hierarchical structure of sentence constituents. The hierarchical structure of the clause and word order are interlinked in this proposal. Cinque (2000) shows how Greenberg's universals can be reinterpreted within the framework of Asymmetry Theory.

[44] Within the generative tradition, basic word order has always been related to the order of elements at deep structure, thus overshadowing other factors such as frequency, which has become a hallmark in the functional–typological tradition. It then follows that a deviation from a canonical word order is explained by movement rules that modify basic order. An interesting case in point is Travis (1989), who offers a set of implicational relations encoded in terms of parameters working at deep structure:
(a) headedness (initial or final);
(b) direction of theta-role assignment (to the left or to the right);
(c) direction of case assignment (to the left or to the right).
An unmarked scenario mirrors typological consistency. For example, unmarked Spanish is head-initial, assigns theta-roles to the right, and assigns case to the right.

supposedly can be explained by the fact that the number affix directly affects the meaning of the head, and should thus be nearer, whereas the case affix, which does not affect the semantics of the head, should be farther away, given that it merely codifies the relation between the verbal event and the referent that participates in the event. In other words, linguistic proximity is a faithful reflection of conceptual distance. In consonance with this premise, Haiman (1985) developed the Distance Principle of Iconicity, according to which linguistic distance between expressions (whether syntactic or morphological) reflects the conceptual distance between them.[45] Haiman (p. 108ff.) applies this principle to causatives, coordination and complementation, possessives, etc.[46]

Similarly, Dik (1997, 401) developed principles regarding word order in languages, such as the following:

Principle of Centripetal Orientation
Constituents conform to (GP3) [General Principle 3] when their ordering is determined by their relative distance from the head, which may lead to "mirror-image" ordering around the head.

The above principle refers to the centripetal configuration of grammatical operators of time, aspect, and modality (TAM), and, in many respects, resembles the Mirror Principle mentioned by Spencer (this volume, chapter 5), which claims an identity between the order of syntactic and morphological operations, as reflected in the order of affixation. This principle was first proposed by Baker (1985), who applied it to valency alternations and certain types of agreement. The idea is that the order of morphemes in the word form reflects the syntactic operations underlying that form.

Assertions regarding the iconicity of language at the syntactic and morphological levels have always been very controversial. In a book recently published in Spain, Mendívil Giró (2003) cogently and objectively examines this issue (whilst analyses are expected to be more or less cogent, objectivity is always a pleasant surprise). In the course of his study, he mentions an example in Radden (1992) of the iconicity between grammatical structure and meaning. The case in point is the *famous delicious Italian pepperoni pizza*, an NP in which the order of the modifiers cannot be changed without making the expression ungrammatical. According to Radden, this occurs because the order of the modifiers reflects a progressive increase in the *conceptual proximity* of the modifiers to the entity designated by the noun *pizza*. Mendívil Giró (2003, 16) makes the following criticism of Radden:

---

[45] In the structuring of clausal constituents all linguistic theories mention Behael's First Law according to which those constituents forming a semantic and conceptual unit with a head (Verb, Preposition, Adjective or Noun) should be close to each other in the linguistic expression.

[46] See Bybee (1985) who analyzes the distribution of verb and noun affixes in thirty languages according to Haiman's Distance Principle.

Presumably, conceptual proximity in Spanish would be the same as in English since the symbolic value of the adjectives and noun in this example is more or less equivalent. Nevertheless, no Spanish speaker would say *la famosa deliciosa italiana pepperoni pizza* or judge it grammatical. The reasons for this have nothing to do with conceptual distance, but rather with permissible morphosyntactic structure in Spanish, which is cognitively unpredictable. A possible utterance in Spanish is *la famosa y deliciosa pizza pepperoni*. However, in this example *deliciosa* and *pepperoni* are equally close to *pizza* regardless of their possible iconic value.[47]

After presenting other similar examples in which the iconic value of the structures is highly questionable, Mendívil Giró (p. 61) arrives at the following conclusion:

Since our mental representation system probably preceded our grammatical system, in all likelihood, evolution selected a grammatical system capable of processing such representations. Even though a certain degree of isomorphism between conceptual representation and grammar is to be expected, it would be extremely rash to conclude that surface structures (syntax) are the direct result of conceptual structures (cognitive categories). However, this is a conclusion that Functionalists have no qualms about leaping to in the frantic desire to exorcise the demon of autonomous syntax.[48]

In our opinion, the argument presented here, along with similar ones presented in other studies, is irrefutable: independently of the fact that all languages may present a certain degree of iconicity in their syntactic structures, it is extremely difficult to predict syntax on the basis of this relation.[49]

As we have seen, linguistic diversity in structure / word order can be interpreted either as the result of different parameter settings (as occurs in the Generative Grammar) or alternatively as a useful indicator that reflects interlinguistic tendencies, and which greatly facilitates typological classification (as occurs in functional–typological models). Moreover, research on differences in word or morpheme order is our first example of the contrast between the autonomous internal view of language within the generative framework and the external view of language held by functionalists who seek an explanation for language diversity in extragrammatical sources.

B. Semantics: evidentiality.   The codification of the semantic phenomenon of *evidentiality* (reference to the speaker's information source or how and when he/she obtained the information) occurs in many languages and can be expressed by lexical or grammatical means. In Spanish, for example, evidentiality is encoded both grammatically (*aparentemente, Juan se entrevistó con el ministro* = Juan seems to have had an interview with the Minister) and

---

[47] Translated from the Spanish.   [48] Translated from the Spanish.
[49] For a discussion of the semantic motivation of grammar, see Gonzálvez-García (2003) and the bibliography cited therein.

morphologically (*Juan se habría entrevistado con el ministro* = Juan seems to have had an interview with the Minister). However, Tuyuca, a language with approximately 700 speakers on the Papuri and Tiquié rivers near the Colombian–Brazilian border, has five types of lexical evidentiality markers, which are necessarily present in all predications. These markers are hyphenated and come at the end of the verb. Although they may also vary depending on the verb tense, this distinction is not relevant here since examples (13–17) are all in the past. In Tuyuca, an expression like *he played soccer* has several possible formulations (Barnes, 1984, 257):

(13)   *diiga apé-wi.*
        He played soccer (I saw him).
        (Cf. Spanish: *Lo vi jugar al fútbol.*)

(14)   *diiga apé-ti.*
        He played soccer (I heard the game and him, but I didn't see it or him).
        (Cf. Spanish: *Lo oí jugar al fútbol.*)

(15)   *diiga apé-yi.*
        He played soccer (I have seen evidence that he played: his distinctive shoe print on the playing field; but I did not see him play).
        (Cf. Spanish: *Hay pruebas de que jugó al fútbol.*)

(16)   *diiga apé-yigi.*
        He played soccer (I obtained information from someone else).
        (Cf. Spanish: *Me han dicho que jugó al fútbol.*)

(17)   *diiga apé-hiyi.*
        He played soccer (it is reasonable to assume that he did).
        (Cf. Spanish: *Parece que jugó al fútbol.*)

Barnes (1984, 257ff.) explains that the evidentiality markers in the preceding five examples respectively correspond to the following categories: (i) *visual* evidentiality indicating that the speaker is witness to the propositional content; (ii) *non-visual* evidentiality indicating that the speaker wishes to describe an event or state that he has heard, smelt, touched, or tasted; (iii) *apparent* evidentiality indicating that the speaker derives conclusions on the basis of circumstantial evidence; (iv) *second-hand* evidentiality indicating that the speaker transmits information obtained from another source; (v) *assumed* evidentiality markers indicating that the speaker has not received any type of information about the state or event expressed in the utterance.

Obviously, if we wished to translate this Tuyuca utterance and find correspondences for the subtle nuances encoded in its lexical markers regarding how and when we obtained the information that the Tuyuca speaker is communicating to us, it would be necessary to use syntactic constructions of much greater complexity (such as those suggested in the examples both for English and for Spanish). In other words, we are faced with lexical or grammatical manifestations – which may or may not be obligatory – of the same basic phenomenon, and it is this contrast between lexical and grammatical features that is one of the basic distinctions made by generativists. It is considered particularly important in minimalism, the most recent version of the model, for the typological classification of languages.

C. Morphology: tense morphemes. From among the examples in Comrie and Haspelmath (2001, 7), we have chosen one that has a striking distribution of tense morphemes. In Kayardild, a language spoken by less than a hundred speakers in the Gulf of Carpentaria in Northern Australia, tense morphemes are affixed not only to verbs, but also to nouns. In (18) and (19), the tense markers *-jarra* (past) and *-ju* (future) appear at the end of the verb, but the morphemes *-na* (past) and *-wu* (future), which modify nouns such as *dugong* and *spear*, are also tense markers.

(18)   *Dangka-a   raa-jarra   bijarrba-na   wumburu-nguni-na.*
         man-NOM   spear-PAST   dugong-PAST   spear-INSTR-PAST.
         "The man speared the dugong with a spear."

(19)   *Dangka-a   raa-ju   bijarrba-wu   wumburu-nguni-wu.*
         man-NOM   spear-FUT   dugong-FUT   spear-OMSTR-FUT.
         "The man will spear the dugong with a spear."
         (NOM = nominative; INSTR = instrumental; FUT = future)

Typologically, this is an "anomalous" or curious situation, because in many languages – more specifically, in Indo-European languages – tense is a feature strictly associated with verbs and not with nouns. Its role is to mark time intervals and temporally situate the event described in the main predicate in reference to the time when the utterance was emitted. It is thus instrumental in distinguishing a well-differentiated morphological type. However, Lecarme (1996) writes that, in quite a few languages,[50] the role played by verb tense morphemes can be played by NPs. This rather surprising idea – as Lecarme himself refers to it – that NPs can possess temporal structure is justifiable on the basis of two widely accepted suppositions: (a) all NPs are predicates from a semantic viewpoint and thus sensitive to tense; (b) time reference is a universal property of language. For this reason, tense as a morphosyntactic notion

---

[50] For instance, Nootka and Kwakiult of the Wakashan language family spoken in the state of Washington and British Columbia; St'at'imcets and Halkomelem of the Salishan language family spoken in the northeast United States and southeast Canada; and the Australian languages, Jingulu and Kayardild (see Lecarme, 1996).

can be parameterized or instantiated in different ways, depending on the language. It thus can be restricted to verbs (e.g. Romance languages), to nouns (e.g. Salishan languages), or appear in both (e.g. certain Afro-Asian languages such as Somalian).[51] When different parameter settings are linked to a general principle shared by all languages, certain linguistic phenomena no longer seem anomalous.

Once again, we observe how linguistic diversity at this level of analysis can be interpreted in different ways. Depending on the research framework, differences in the position of tense morphemes can be regarded as a typological parameter that is useful for language classification (functional–typological models) or as a parameter whose setting may vary from language to language, but which can always be associated with a general universal principle (generativist model).

D. Phonetics and phonology: nasalized vowels. Many world languages have nasal consonants and, furthermore, nasalized vowels, either as a result of the co-articulation of oral vowels with an adjacent consonant (e.g. in Spanish), or simply because the phonological system of the language has an opposition between oral and nasal vowels (e.g. French and Portuguese). This last contrast is generally presented by the binary feature (± nasal), which means that languages are classified either as having contrastive nasalized vowels (+), or as not having them (–). So, from a phonological point of view, this is supposed to be a clearly universally valid binary feature. However, in Palantal Chinanteco, a language spoken in Oaxaca, Mexico, there seem to be three degrees of contrastive nasality: non-nasal (oral) vowel / moderately nasal vowel / very nasal vowel, which results in surface oppositions such as the following:

(20)   *ha* "so, such"   *hã* "(he) spreads open"   *hã̃* "foam, froth"
        (Ladefoged, 1971, 35; Ladefoged and Maddieson, 1996, 299–300)

Up until now only one language has been found with this characteristic, but when more language studies are carried out, this situation might change. Certainly the example in (20) points to the fact that nasality may be a great deal more complex than originally believed. From a typological viewpoint, this could have far-reaching consequences. On the one hand this questioned the universal validity of binary features (see footnote 29), and on the other this

---

[51] This refers to the debate on the referential or quantitative interpretation of time in nouns. According to the referential approach (Enç, 1987), time in NPs is interpreted independently from utterance time and is determined primarily by the context (as if it were a deictic). According to the quantitative approach (Musan, 1995), utterance time affects and conditions the temporal value of any element in its immediate context, including NPs.

could give rise to the recognition of a new type of language in virtue of the property specified.

However, recent acoustic analyses show that the moderate nasalization of the Chinanteco vowels only occurs at the end of their duration. In this respect, they might be more accurately defined as partially nasalized vowels since very nasalized vowels are nasalized throughout their entire duration. The essential difference between these nasalized vowels concerning the temporal synchro-nization of the oral articulation and the functioning of the uvula led Ladefoged and Maddieson (1996) to interpret vowels of the second type (*hã*) as diphthongs (*háã*), in which the first element is non-nasal and the second element, nasal: "the second of these three words can thus be seen to consist of a movement from a vowel like that in the first word followed by a vowel that is more like the third" (p. 300). This way the universal binary codification of nasality remains valid, and no further typological consequences can be derived.

Whether or not this interpretation is confirmed, it demonstrates the abso-lute necessity of in-depth analyses of all candidates for typological universals before making any type of sweeping typological conclusion. Even in phonol-ogy, one must be extremely cautious when making sweeping generalizations that are conducive to new linguistic types or classes. What at first seems to be a qualitative and contrastive difference might ultimately be explicable as a purely phonetic detail.

3   Bridging the gap

According to Aristotle, virtue is the happy median between two extremes. It is thus not surprising that in linguistics, as well as in other fields, more extreme positions tend to become less so with the passage of time, gradually drawing closer to each other in a rational process of integration or complementation of different perspectives and viewpoints. In this sense, more and more authors have trouble understanding why the generativist (i.e. formalist) and typological (i.e. functionalist) perspectives should *necessarily* be in opposition to each other, especially when all indications show that language is the product of the complex interaction of principles belonging to both approaches (cf. Newmeyer, 1998, 2004; Darnell *et al.*, 1999).

Logic certainly seems to point to a conception of language structure as the result of the performance of a purely linguistic or grammatical faculty combined with other cognitive abilities that interact with it. "It is evident," writes Mendívil Giró (2003, 197) – who gives a detailed explanation of the advantages that would result from the approximation of formalist and functionalist positions (pp. 73ff.) – "that the constraints imposed by the language faculty as well as those derived from other cognitive, anatomical, and perceptual abilities play an active role in language variation and change. For this reason, in the present panorama of linguistic research, it would be unwise to lose sight of either of these two perspectives."[52]

The fact that certain grammatical phenomena are motivated by factors derived from cognitive processing limitations in human beings does not necessarily mean that the explanation of *all* linguistic events need be set out in these terms, and, conversely, the fact that certain grammatical principles cannot be externally justified by cognitive or communicative factors should not lead us to reject such a possibility for *all* other principles. As a result, in the specification of language universals, it would be sensible to envision the possibility that some of these universals reflect principles of UG while others can be attributed to other factors that are not necessarily associated with an innate and autonomous language faculty, as defended, for example, first in Hyman (1984) and later in more recent publications. The following quotation from Noonan (1999, 29) illustrates this viewpoint:

Many aspects of the model just presented are similar to proposals made recently by linguists working in the formalist tradition, in proposals by adherents of LFG [Lexical Functional Grammar], GPSG [Generalized Phrase Structure Grammar], and HDPSG [Head Driven Phrase Structure Grammar], as well as to proposals made by Levin, Pinker, Jackendoff, and others. I see all of this as a very hopeful sign. After two decades of operating in very different conceptual (and, indeed, social) worlds, there is for me some hope now that the functionalist and formalist schools of linguists may find new ways to communicate with each other and share the insights that each has gleaned from the study of language.

In our opinion, the marked difference between formalist and functionalist approaches does not necessarily entail their incompatibility, but rather the need for a more flexible vision of how to define the resources of the system.

On the basis of these presuppositions, there are now two clearly defined tasks to be carried out. The first task involves the specification of universals belonging to each approach, but without falling into the trap of automatically attributing them to UG or, conversely, giving them a cognitive, functional or external justification without a previous detailed analysis. The second task entails the merging of both types of properties in one theoretical model, which would thus become the basis for a theory that would integrate formalism and functionalism.

In this sense, phonology and syntax can be two areas of study that offer excellent examples of the implementation of the first of the previously mentioned objectives.

As is well known, according to the formalist (basically generativist) approach in phonology, the principles and processes that give rise to superficial phonic structures and constrain the linguistic organization of sounds are caused by purely internal, language-specific factors. In contrast, the functionalist

---

[52] Translated from the Spanish.

approach, which is basically phonetic, has tried to explain the structure of the phonic systems of world languages on the basis of "functional" notions such as facilitation of articulation and the maintenance of the distinctive nature of phonological units (see Maddieson, this volume, chapter 4, as well as the work of Lindblom, cited in previous sections). More generally, it has endeavored to reduce phonological problems to primitives borrowed from disciplines such as physics or physiology (Ohala 1981, 1983, 1990, 1997).

For example, let us now take a look at one aspect of the syllabic organization of languages that is considered a universal. We are referring to the hypothesis described in great detail in generativist phonological studies (see Harris, 1983, for Spanish) which postulates that syllable segments are organized according to their level of intrinsic sonority (the *Sonority Sequencing Principle*) – in other words, the more sonorous segments occupy the peak position of the syllable (nucleus) while the less sonorous ones occur towards the syllable margins (coda and onset). Moreover, in many languages, a *minimum difference* in sonority must exist between adjacent segments for the sequence to be grammatical. The level of sonority of each element is defined by the universal Sonority Hierarchy, according to which, for instance, liquids are more "sonorous" than voiceless plosives.

Actually, the concept of sonority or perceptibility was not coined by generativist phonologists or even structuralists. It first appeared in the writings of Jespersen, Saussure, Grammont, and other well-known authors, but, despite the fact that it has been around for quite some time, it is not an easy notion to define or explain in phonetic terms. Various parameters have been proposed as possible determinants (i.e. degree of opening of phonological segments, intensity of aspiration, volume, pressure, any combination of these variables, etc.), but, as yet, no definitive conclusion has been reached, and many scholars are doubtful that such an objective will ever be attained. Consequently, research on this issue usually mentions the problem of the real phonetic nature of sonority only to end up treating it as a purely linguistic phonological resource, which is derived a posteriori from the analysis of the syllabic schemas of languages. Paraphrasing Clements (1990), sonority is an abstract construct that is justifiable to the extent that it can be coherently integrated into the logical structure of a predictive linguistic model which permits the formulation of a universal principle of syllabic organization.

Although this theoretical position is perfectly valid, it is also possible to explain universal syllable structure alternatively in terms of empirically measurable sound properties, such as amplitude, period, basic frequency or spectrum representation. This is precisely what Ohala and Kawasaki (1984) tried to show when they proposed the substitution of the monodimensional sonority hierarchy for a conglomeration of acoustic–perceptual parameters whose relative degree of difference depends on possible syllabic combinations. For example, the syllable [sa] is well formed in many languages because its segments show a marked contrast between various parameters, thus making it perceptually detectable. The syllable [nla] is systematically excluded in many syllabic inventories because the modulation between its components is not sufficiently robust.

What we have here are two approaches to the same question, both of which offer an explanation for empirically demonstrated tendencies in syllable composition. The explanation of the first approach is theory-internal and is ultimately dependent on the validation of the theory itself. The second approach bases its explanation of the universality of syllabic structure on external factors of a basically physical nature, which are not exclusively linguistic. In this case, as in others, we believe that linguistics should investigate all possibilities before explaining a universal by attributing it an *internal* or *external* cause, and jumping to the conclusion that formalist and functionalist approaches are either totally or partially incompatible with each other so that their respective explanations cancel each other out.

Another relevant example, in the area of syntax, can be found in the complex issue of word order in different languages, already referred to in previous examples (see above, Section 2.2.A). As mentioned, the position of heads before or after complements can be explained by means of a head parameter provided by UG. However, as Newmeyer (2004, 684) rightly points out, there are other factors to be taken into account, such as those related to the requirements of speech processing in real time, which constrain some of the phenomena associated with the order of discourse elements, and which also show in this case that grammars can be partly affected by considerations linked to performance.

Thus, the extensively documented tendency in grammars to place "lighter" elements before "heavier" ones, as shown in the examples in (21) for Spanish (a VO language), can be explained on the basis of the performance-based pressure to shorten the recognition time for phrasal constituents (see Hawkins, 1994, in Newmeyer, 2004).

(21)   (a) *Compré las flores para que mi madre se pusiera contenta en el día de su cumpleaños, que coincide con la fecha del patrón de la ciudad.*
"I bought the flowers so that my mother would feel happy on her birthday, which coincides with the date of the patron saint of the city."

*Compré para que mi madre se pusiera contenta en el día de su cumpleaños que coincide con la fecha del patrón de la ciudad las flores.
"*I bought so that my mother would feel happy on her birthday which coincides with the date of the patron saint of the city the flowers."

(b) *La blanca nieve.* / **La más blanca que la leche nieve.*
"The white snow." / * "The whiter than milk snow."

(c) *El alarmante sonido.* / **El alarmante por el peligro que entraña sonido.*
"The alarming sound." / * "The alarming for the danger that it implies sound."

In other words, it is not sufficient to know that in this particular language heads precede complements. Irrespective of whether canonical order may vary (e.g. [b] and [c]) or not (e.g. [a]), in both cases it is also necessary to take into account the length of the phrase, since this is a decisive factor in the position of the head. "There is no question in my mind," Newmeyer (2004, 684) concludes, "that grammars have been shaped by processing considerations – that is, by language in use."

The second task, which implies a more hybrid or integrated approach to linguistic problems in general and to linguistic universals in particular, is the design of a theoretical model that makes such an approach possible. In this respect, we wish to highlight, primarily because of its accuracy and eclecticism, the new orientation in Jackendoff's (2002) architectural grammar, which is, in our opinion, a viable framework for such a model.

Jackendoff bases his grammar on a conception of UG that is very different from the traditional generativist model in UG (Principles and Parameters Theory) or the model proposed in Optimality Theory (see below). At the same time he incorporates external factors typical of the functional–typological tradition in order to achieve a compromise between syntax-centered and semantics-centered positions. Jackendoff (2002, 148–149) writes:

Argument structure provides a rich illustration of this decomposition [*of the grammar into independent generative components that interact through interface rules*]: it can be accounted for only in a system that discriminates syntactic formation rules, conceptual formation rules, and rich syntax–semantics interface principles. Thus, on one hand, it constitutes an argument against Chomsky's syntacticocentric architectures. On the other hand, it also constitutes an argument against purely semantically based theories that deny an independent role to syntax, of the sort often advocated by opponents of the generative approach.

Effectively, according to Jackendoff's model, UG is not the sole element upon which language acquisition and the ensuing parametrization of languages are based and developed, as occurs in the orthodox generativist model. Rather it is a module that *influences*, *delineates*, and *shapes* language acquisition with the help, when necessary, of external factors.

I agree that learning which makes more effective use of the input certainly helps the
child, and it certainly takes some of the load off Universal Grammar. But I do not think
it takes *all* the load off. It may allow Universal Grammar to be less rich, but it does not
allow UG to be dispensed with altogether. (Jackendoff 2002, 82–83, emphasis in the
original)

UG is thus conceived as a "toolkit" that a child brings to his/her learning of any
of the languages of the world (2002, 75). As we have pointed out, this theoretical
stance is far removed from the oversimplified vision that the defenders of the
nativist position (e.g. Principles and Parameters Theory) propose. The same is
true of connectionist positions in which UG is similar to a cartoonish "grammar
box," isolated physically and computationally from the rest of the mind (e.g.
Bates and MacWhinney, 1982, *inter alia*).

According to Jackendoff, UG is now made up of a set of skeletal fragments of
rules (also known as *grammatical archetypes* [53]), lexicalized and encoded in the
speaker's memory, as well as of another set of rules that emerge with greater
or lesser difficulty during language acquisition, depending on the degree to
which they conform to the already encoded rules in the mind. Jackendoff calls
these grammatical archetypes *attractors* because he wishes to make clear that
they are not absolute, categorical standards for grammatical patterns, but rather
relatively stable unmarked reference points from which languages can deviate
to a greater or lesser degree in marked cases (i.e. those that differ from the
supposedly universal[54] general tendency).

Consequently, in Jackendoff's model, the relation between syntax and semantics is flexible and far from rigid.[55] The idea of conceptual structure and its basic
architecture is the only innate and universal construct, to which languages give
expression through different syntactic strategies (a position closer to cognitivists
than to formalists). However, since certain aspects of his model are also based
on autonomous syntax[56] which has no semantic motivation, he has evidently

[53] For a description of the type of grammatical fragments that are a part of UG, see Jackendoff
(2002, 192–193).
[54] With regard to these grammatical archetypes, Jackendoff adopts a clinal model similar to the
prototype network and its metaphorical extensions described in Cognitive Grammar and Construction Grammar. Jackendoff (2002, 192) writes: "UG renders certain parts of the design space
for words and I-rules more stable and/or accessible, with gradients of relative 'markedness' as
one moves away from the 'core' cases. This leaves plenty of room for linguistic idiosyncrasy at
all levels of generality."
[55] "If a word's syntactic behaviour (including its syntactic argument structure) were always linked to
its meaning (including semantic argument structure), there would be far less lexical idiosyncrasy
for the child to learn, always a desideratum . . . A lot of syntactic behaviour is predictable from
meaning, but far from all; the syntax–semantics interface is highly constrained but not entirely
rigid" (Jackendoff, 2002, 138).
[56] In reality the model has not only remnants of autonomous syntax, but also three types of defective
items (Jackendoff, 2002, 131–132): (i) "defective" lexical items that have phonology and semantics but no syntax (e.g. *yes, no, hello, thanks*); (ii) words that have phonology and syntax but not

managed to formulate a theoretical compromise between semanticocentric[57] and syntacticocentric approaches, as previously stated. His model is sensitive to parameters derived from the theory of competence as well as those derived from the theory of performance, and in this sense it represents an important, far-reaching step towards the elaboration of an integrated model:

> If this is letting the theory of performance intrude on the theory of competence, so be it. For my own taste, such interaction between the two theories is the proper way for linguistic research to proceed in the future. (Jackendoff, 2002, 194)

Another model reflecting the possible integration of functionalism and formalism is Optimality Theory (Prince and Smolensky, 1993), which originated in phonology but quickly spread to other grammatical areas. There are now many phonologists who believe that no incompatibility exists *a priori*, and who have welcomed the new model explicit in that theory as the ideal solution to give formal expression to this wider, integrated perspective. The conceptual starting point in this model is that the grammar of a language is a specific organization of certain well-formedness constraints, which are *universal* and whose most important characteristic is that on certain occasions they are violated. This means that the only reason that grammars of different languages – and thus phonology as part of those grammars – differ is that they have different constraint hierarchies. The task of the linguist who analyzes the language, the same as that of the child in the process of acquiring it, is thus to discover the hierarchy that governs that particular language. This can be discovered by studying the behavior that the elements of the language show regarding each of the constraints. This is a generativist model and as such it presupposes a series of abstract, underlying lexical entries, which are the patterns that the analysis is based on – i.e., inputs – as well as a series of outputs that are physically perceptible forms. From the various possible surface realizations for each input, the language selects the most *optimal* one. In other words, it chooses the realization that best conforms to its own constraint hierarchy, and that violates the fewest constraints or those that are ranked at the lowest level. As a result, if we know the initial form, the final result, and the families of universal constraints, we can deduce their organization for a specific language.

The set of all universal constraints is a component that is known as CON (from CONSTRAINTS) and is integrated in UG along with another component, GEN,

---

semantics (cf. the so-called *do* of *do*-support); and (iii) some words that are just stored pieces of phonology lacking both syntax and meanings (e.g. nonsense refrains used to fill up metrical structure in songs and nursery rhymes: *hickory-dickory-dock, eenie-meenie-minie-moe* . . .).

[57] Although it is invariably affirmed that all functionalist, and in particular cognitivist, models (e.g. Croft, Langacker, Goldberg, etc.) defend semantically motivated syntax, not all of them defend it with the same fervor. Whereas authors such as Langacker assert that "every valid grammatical construct, including expletives and pro-*it*, have meaning," Goldberg and Croft maintain that *the greater part* of syntax is semantically motivated.

whose task is to generate possible surface forms from a given input. When we say that the task of the GEN component is *to generate all possible surface forms*, we mean its job is to offer a sufficiently wide range of candidates so that any language can choose the one that is most in consonance with its own constraint hierarchy. The third basic element in the theory is E VA L, which is the function that uses the constraint hierarchy to evaluate a set of output candidates provided by GEN and select the most optimal – in other words, the candidate that in each language violates the fewest and lowest-ranked constraints, and, furthermore, violates them to the least degree.

As Hayes (1999, 245) explains, this relatively new theory has the advantage of allowing us to incorporate the general principles of markedness, explicitly formulated as hierarchically organized well-formedness constraints, into specific analyses of individual languages.[58] Just as important, it allows us to justify many of these constraints on *functional grounds*:

> In the case of phonetic functionalism, a well-motivated phonological constraint would be one that either renders speech easier to articulate or renders contrasting forms easier to distinguish perceptually. From the functionalist point of view, such constraints are *a priori* plausible, under the reasonable hypothesis that language is a biological system that is designed to perform its job well and efficiently. (p. 244)

Optimality Theory thus represents another valid means for phonologists, and linguists in general, to integrate formally and functionally based principles into one model.[59] Hayes' conclusion is that such a theory can help to "close the long-standing and regrettable gap between phonetics and phonology," and we could take this further and suggest that such an approach might serve as a bridge in general terms between functionalism and formalism.

4   Conclusions

In this chapter we have endeavored to present, concisely and selectively, the various theoretical positions regarding universals, from the dawn of linguistic

---

[58] McCarthy (2002, 1) affirms: "OT . . . is inherently typological: the grammar of one language inevitably incorporates claims about the grammars of all languages. This joining of the individual and the universal, which OT accomplishes through ranking permutation, is probably the most important insight of the theory."

[59] Obviously, what we have presented so far is just a slight approximation to the major guidelines of Optimality Theory, an approach characterized by a high degree of complexity. In connection with this, we believe that this theory tackles a number of unresolved conflictive issues, an account of which we briefly point out: is the order of restrictions completely arbitrary and language-dependent or is there a set of hierarchies which are already pre-established by UG?; to what extent can UG contain all the restrictions, often very specific, though necessary to account for particular language-specific phenomena?; are there substantive criteria which constrain the restrictions so that one can hinder the easy option of formulating a new restriction for every new phenomenon that appears in the analysis?

reflection up until modern times. The objective of this revision is to offer readers (even those without previous knowledge of linguistics since the debate on
universals is also important for related disciplines) an overview of the multiple
perspectives regarding this issue, which we believe will help to contextualize
the research in this volume.

The conclusions reached in the course of this chapter are various. Firstly, in
contrast to the initially philosophical debate on the existence of universals – a
debate that without a doubt is phylogenetically linked to the discussion of the
role of universals in linguistics – there is now little argument in our discipline
about the existence of such elements. The problem is rather how to account
for them within each theoretical framework. Consequently, what has slowly
and progressively developed is an explicit or implicit acceptance of universal
features of language, which has only been sporadically disrupted by occasional,
but more or less expected, disagreements (see Section 1).

This means that, for the last several years, what linguists have been trying to
do is to make the epistemological premises of each theory compatible with the
undeniable fact that languages share certain features. In this sense, linguistic
models can be classified into two groups: formalist models and functional models (see Sections 1 and 3). These theoretical frameworks are based on divergent
premises, and, for this reason, their basic principles and methodologies also differ, but perhaps their key difference resides in their respective approaches to
the *origin* of universals.

According to formalist theories, whose most extreme exponent is genera-
tivism, language universals exist precisely because of the existence of a universal ability or innate language faculty, which enables all human beings to
acquire language during a specific period of their lives on the basis of a limited
amount of data. This "language faculty," conceived as a genetically transmitted UG whose characteristics have been gradually refined, thanks to successive
revisions of the initial model, is now a basic component of the architecture of
the theory. It is this faculty that ultimately "justifies" the model and gives it
explanatory adequacy. Since languages are regarded as specific states of the
language faculty, they logically have shared properties and only differ in their
surface realizations. Some of these properties are invariably present in all languages (e.g. the fact that all languages combine words according to principles
of hierarchical organization). Other properties, however, show a certain degree
of variation (e.g. some languages accept elliptical subjects, whereas others do
not).

In contrast, functional models are based on the premise that the origin of
universals lies in the fact that human beings use languages for communication. Since communication is a property common to all languages, this is also
conducive to the sharing of certain linguistic features. Languages are used to
convey meaning, and, from the functional perspective, meaning is derived from

physical, cultural, and social experience instead of from aprioristic notions external to this experience. To the extent (and only to the extent) that such experience underlies all languages, language properties will also be shared.

Consequently, our discussion of universals leads us to two different linguistic approaches: (i) one that is more oriented towards the immanent study of language as an autonomous cognitive system, and which regards the influence of experience on language as too limited and fragmentary to be considered; (ii) a second approach that is more inclined to adopt an external perspective, based on language use and its function as a means of transmitting information. This could be a second recurring topic that is present throughout the history of linguistic reflection: the opposition in the philosophy of language between rationalism and empiricism, and the opposition in modern linguistics between generativists, on the one hand, and typologists and cognitivists, on the other.

These divergent ways of understanding universals, and thus linguistics in general, entail a series of differences that are easily comprehended if we are first aware of the contrasts between the basic premises of each of these frameworks. While the adherents of the immanent type of approach use a hypothetical-deductive method to specify the characteristics of the universal structure underlying all languages, the defenders of an external perspective use inductive methods for language study. Whereas formalists propose universals on the basis of abstract theoretical constructs, functionalists do the same on the basis of empirically observable features. And, definitively, while the formalist approach justifies universals by means of theory-internal criteria, the functionalist approach does so by using external criteria.

Finally, a third topic that has appeared with increasing frequency in recent years in relation to the history of universals is the gradual approximation of theoretical positions. The debate on this issue has often been acrimonious and far from objective, but, lately, there appears to be a growing consensus that the study of this complex issue demands the combined efforts of linguists belonging to both perspectives. There have been many manifestations of this new tendency to join forces. For example, from a methodological viewpoint, both approaches are making an increased effort to validate their assertions with the largest possible sample of different languages. In our opinion, the marked difference between formalist and functionalist models does not necessarily entail their incompatibility. On the contrary, the progressive approximation of these two approaches signifies the achievement of a wider, more integrated perspective, as well as the development of a new sensitivity that will allow us to value and benefit from all advances in the understanding of universals, from whatever theoretical framework. As Jackendoff (2002, xiii) writes:

We cannot afford the strategy that regrettably seems endemic in the cognitive sciences: one discovers a new tool, decides it is the only tool needed, and, in an act of academic (and funding) territoriality, loudly proclaims the superiority of this new tool over all others. My own attitude is that we are in this together. It is going to take us lots of tools to understand language. We should try to appreciate exactly what each of the tools we have is good for, [and to recognize when new and as yet undiscovered tools are necessary.]

This is not to advocate a warm fuzzy embrace of every new approach that appears on the scene. Rather, what is called for is an open-mindedness to insights from whatever quarter, a willingness to recognize tensions among apparently competing insights, and a joint commitment to fight fair in the interests of deeper understanding. To my mind, that's what the game of science is about.

2   Linguistic typology

Kees Hengeveld

1   Introduction

This chapter discusses the contribution of linguistic typology to the study of language universals. Language universals research and linguistic typology are closely related fields, and are often not distinguished very clearly. Yet the difference between them can be characterized in the following way (Comrie, 1989): language universals define the restrictions on cross-linguistic variation; linguistic typology studies the restrictions on cross-linguistic variation; so typological research can be seen as the primary method used in uncovering language universals.

After a brief description of the way in which language samples are selected in cross-linguistic research in Section 2, the basic concepts and the methodology used in linguistic typology are introduced in Section 3, in which the notion of *implicational hierarchy* is taken as the point of departure. The implicational hierarchies uncovered through typological research are generally assumed to reflect true language universals, which means that they may be expected to show up in other linguistic domains as well, such as the historical development of languages, the process of language acquisition, language contact phenomena, and the distribution of linguistic phenomena within a single language. Section 4 of this chapter is dedicated to this issue. Conclusions are presented in Section 5. Wherever possible, the examples I present are taken from my own work, since this allows me direct access to the primary data.

2   Language sampling

Typological investigations make use of representative samples of the approximately 6,000 languages of the world. In order to guarantee the representativeness of the sample, three factors have to be taken into account: a sample should be representative from a genetic, an areal, and a typological perspective.

The author is indebted to Lachlan Mackenzie for comments on an earlier version of this chapter.

Languages may share properties because they belong to the same language family. For this reason the languages of the sample have to be selected in such a way that the genetic distance between them is maximal. The classification of languages through genetic reconstruction is complicated, particularly in the case of languages with an exclusively oral tradition. The existing classifications are therefore always tentative and reveal important differences of opinion between specialists.

Languages may also share properties because they are spoken in contiguous or (partially) coextensive areas. For this reason, the languages of the sample have to be selected in such a way that the geographical distance between them is maximal.

Finally, languages may share properties because they are of the same linguistic type. This factor is very difficult to control, since it is still unclear which typological properties should be decisive in assigning a language to a certain type. For the moment, the typological features most often used in controlling typological bias are the morphological type and the basic word order of a language.

One method of drawing representative language samples of various sizes in terms of genetic distribution is that proposed in Rijkhoff *et al.* (1993) and Rijkhoff and Bakker (1998). This method assigns a numerical value to a language family on the basis of the structure and complexity of its genetic tree. This value is then used to calculate the number of languages by which that family should be represented within a sample of a given size. The method is applied recursively to determine the number of languages by which a sub-family should be represented within the sample, etc. An advantage of this method is that it can be applied to any genetic classification. An example of a language sample[1] created using this method, applied to Ruhlen's (1987) genetic classification of languages of the world, is given in Table 2.1.

3   Implicational hierarchies

3.1   Introduction

The main tool that is applied in the study of language universals in linguistic typology is the *implicational hierarchy*. The general properties of implicational hierarchies are presented in Section 3.2, their application to various components of the language system in Section 3.3, and the level of abstraction of these hierarchies in Section 3.4. Sections 3.5 and 3.6 then deal with the interaction between hierarchies and the nature of the explanations given for them, respectively.

---

[1] This is the sample that is used in Hengeveld *et al.* (2004).

Table 2.1 *Example of a language sample*

Afro-Asiatic (2)	Chadic (1)				*Gude*
	Cushitic (1)				*Oromo, Boraana*
Altaic (1)					*Turkish*
Amerind (7)	Northern (2)	Almosan-Keresiouan (1)			*Tuscarora*
		Penutian (1)			*Koasati*
	Andean (1)				*Quechua, Imbabura*
	Equatorial-Tucanoan (1)				*Guaraní*
	Ge-Pano-Carib (1)				*Hixkaryana*
	Central Amerind (1)				*Pipil*
	Chibchan-Paezan (1)				*Warao*
Australian (3)	Gunwinyguan (1)				*Ngalakan*
	Pama-Nyungan (1)				*Kayardild*
	Nunggubuyu (1)				*Nunggubuyu*
Austric (6)	Austro-Tai (4)	Daic (1)			*Nung*
		Austronesian (3)	Malayo-Polynesian (2)	Western (1)	*Tagalog*
				Central Eastern (1)	*Samoan*
			Paiwaric (1)		*Paiwan*
	Austroasiatic (1)				*Mundari*
	Miao-Yao (1)				*Miao*
Basque (1)					*Basque*
Burushaski (1)					*Burushaski, Hunza*
Caucasian (1)					*Abkhaz*
Chukchi-Kamchatkan (1)					*Itelmen*
Elamo-Dravidian (1)					*Tamil*
Eskimo-Aleut (1)					*West Greenlandic*
Etruscan (1)					*(Etruscan)*[2]
Hurrian (1)					*Hurrian*
Indo-Hittite (2)	Indo-European (1)				*Polish*
	Anatolian (1)				*Hittite*

Family				Language
Indo-Pacific (5)	Trans New Guinea (1)			*Wambon*
	Sepik-Ramu (1)			*Alamblak*
	East Papuan (1)			*Nasioi*
	West Papuan (1)			*Tidore*
	Torricelli (1)			*Arapesh, Mountain*
Kartvelian (1)				*Georgian*
Ket (1)				*Ket*
Khoisan (1)				*Nama Hottentot*
Korean-Japanese-Ainu (1)				*Japanese*
Meroitic (1)				*(Meroitic)*
Na-Dene (1)				*Navajo*
Nahali (1)				*(Nahali)*
Niger-Kordofanian (4)	Niger-Congo (3)	Nigen-Congo Proper (2)	Central Nigen-Congo (1)	*Babungo*
			West Atlantic (1)	*Kisi*
		Mande (1)		*Bambara*
	Kordofanian (1)			*Krongo*
Nilo-Saharan (2)	East Sudanic (1)			*Lango*
	Central Sudanic (1)			*Ngiti*
Nivkh (1)				*Nivkh*
Pidgins and Creoles (1)				*Berbice Dutch*
Sino-Tibetan (2)	Sinitic (1)			*Chinese, Mandarin*
	Tibeto-Karen (1)			*Garo*
Sumerian (1)				*Sumerian*
Uralic-Yukaghir (1)				*Hungarian*

2 Parentheses around language name indicate that insufficient data are available for a language that should be in the sample according to the sampling method.

3.2   Universal implications and implicational hierarchies

Language universals are generally expressed in the form of universal implications, which are most often unidirectional. An abstract example of a unidirectional universal implication is given in (1):

(1)   A > B

This universal implication defines the possible combinations of properties A and B listed in (2):

(2)   A   B
                    +   +
                    +   −
                    −   −
          *   −   +

Since the presence of property B in a language implies the presence of property A in that same language, but the absence of B does not imply the absence of A, the only combination of features that is excluded by the implication is the absence of A in the presence of B. Thus, of the logically possible combinations ($2^2 = 4$), one (i.e. 25%) is excluded.

Some concrete examples of universal implications are the following, taken from Keenan and Comrie (1977) and Comrie (1989) (see also Bakker and Hengeveld, 1999):

(3)   (a) Subject   > Direct object
        (b) Direct object   > Oblique object
        (c) Oblique object   > Possessor

These implications were proposed to account for, among other things, the variation in the degree to which languages permit the relativization of constituents that fulfil the relevant syntactic and semantic functions within the relative clause. For instance, languages that permit the relativization of direct objects will also allow the relativization of subjects (3a); those that do not permit the relativization of direct objects will not allow the relativization of oblique objects either (3b); and those that permit the relativization of possessors will allow the relativization of oblique objects (3c).

The implied category in (3c) is the implying category in (3b), and the implied category in (3b) is the implying category in (3a), so that the universal implications in (3) can be combined into the chain in (4):

(4)		S	>	DO	>	OO	>	Poss
		+		+		+		+
		+		+		+		−
		+		+		−		−
		+		−		−		−
		−		−		−		−
*		+		−		+		−
*		etc.						

A chain of universal implications such as the one in (4) is called an "implicational hierarchy." In this case, 11 (67.5%) out of all logically possible combinations are excluded. This shows that the higher the number of categories that can be combined within a single hierarchy, the more constrained the typological description of cross-linguistic variation will be.

In general, two types of implicational hierarchy are distinguished: absolute and statistical ones. Absolute implicational hierarchies are valid for all languages, statistical ones for a significant proportion of all languages. It is important to note that absolute implicational hierarchies are absolute only in relation to our current knowledge of linguistic variation, since, on the one hand, as mentioned in Section 2, typological research is based on samples of the world's languages, and, on the other hand, many of the languages of the world lack documentation. Another limitation that has to be taken into account is that implicational hierarchies are normally based on a sample of oral languages: the study of the typology of sign languages is still in its infancy.

3.3   Implicational hierarchies and the components of the language system

3.3.1   Introduction
Implicational hierarchies are a useful tool in capturing linguistic generalizations pertaining to the different components of the language system. This will be illustrated in this section through the analysis of examples from the areas of phonology (3.3.2), morphology (3.3.3), syntax (3.3.4), semantics (3.3.5), and the lexicon (3.3.6).

3.3.2   Phonology
In Section 3.4 a detailed example of a possible phonological universal will be given. I therefore limit myself here to an example of an implicational hierarchy concerning the distribution of nasal phonemes across languages, presented in (5), which concerns dental/alveolar, bilabial, and palatal voiced nasals, respectively:

(5)   /n/   >   /m/   >   /ɲ/

This hierarchy defines the following possible combinations of nasal consonants in the phoneme inventory of a language:

(6)   /n/   /m/   /ɲ/
        /n/   /m/   –
        /n/   –   –
        –   –   –

Note that this hierarchy, like most typological hierarchies, is not exhaustive.
It does not predict, for instance, under what conditions a language might have
the voiced velar nasal /ŋ/, which does not form part of the hierarchy in (5).

3.3.3   *Morphology*

Important implicational hierarchies in the area of morphology concern the order
of inflectional morphemes expressing tense, aspect, and modality. Bybee (1985)
proposes the generalization in (7):

(7)

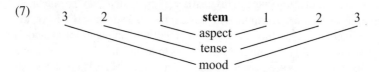

This generalization predicts that aspect will be expressed closer to the (verb)
stem than tense, which in turn will be expressed closer to the stem than mood.
   Elaborating on Bybee's work, Hengeveld (1989) proposes a more detailed
classification, partly inspired by Foley and Van Valin (1984). This classification
is shown in (8):

(8)   5 4 3 2 1 **stem** 1 2 3 4 5
        1. qualitative aspect / agentive modality
        2. tense / realis–irrealis / quantitative aspect / negation
        3. evidentiality
        4. illocution
        5. mitigation–reinforcement

The classification in (8) situates the categories of aspect and mood in various
positions, depending on the subcategories involved. The position of these subcategories within the hierarchy reflects their scope within the sentence. Thus,
qualitative aspect occupies the position closest to the predicate because it affects
just the predicate, while quantitative aspect occupies the second position, since
it modifies the event described within the sentence.

The morpheme order in example (9) obeys the hierarchy in (8):[3]

(9)   Turkish (Altaic)
        Anli-y-abil-ecek-miş-im.
        understand-*y*-A B I L -I R R -I N F E R -1.SG
        "I gather I will be able to understand."

In this example the suffix *-abil* expresses ability (A B I L), an agentive modality;
the suffix *-ecek* expresses irrealis (I R R), which in this case is translated as a future
tense; and the suffix *-miş* expresses inference (I N F E R), an evidential modality.
Applying the classification given in (8) to these categories, example (9) reflects
the hierarchy in (8) in the following way:

(10)   **stem** -1   -2   -3
        Anli-y-abil-ecek-miş-im.
        1. agentive modality
        2. realis–irrealis
        3. evidentiality

Example (11) shows that the hierarchy in (8) can be applied to a language
that is structurally very different:

(11)   Hidatsa (Siouan; Matthews, 1963)
        Wíra   i   apaari   ki   stao   ski.
        tree   it   grow   I N C H   REM PAST   CERT
        "The tree must have begun to grow a long time ago."

In Hidatsa the categories of tense, mood, and aspect are expressed through
grammatical particles, rather than through affixes as in Turkish. In example (11),
the particle *ki* expresses inchoative aspect (I N C H), which is a qualitative aspect;
the particle *stao* expresses remote past (R E M . P A S T); and the particle *ski*
expresses certainty (C E R T) on the part of the speaker, an evidential modality. This example thus reflects the hierarchy in (8) in the following way:

(12)   **stem**   1   2   3
        Wíra i apaari ki stao ski.
        1. qualitative aspect
        2. tense
        3. evidentiality

The translation of example (11) into English shows that even in a language
in which these categories are expressed through auxiliary verbs the hierarchy
in (8) is respected, albeit in the opposite order:

---

[3] The -*y*- is meaningless. It is inserted for phonological reasons.

(13)   The tree must have begun to grow.
                   3   2   1   **stem**

The predictive force of the hierarchy is further corroborated by the fact that the order of the auxiliaries cannot be altered, as can be observed in the following examples:

(14)   (a) *The tree must begin to have grown.
        (b) *The tree has must begin to grow.
        (c) *The tree has begun to must grow.
        (d) *The tree begins to must have grown.
        (e) *The tree begins to have must grow.

The examples from Hidatsa and English serve to illustrate that universals such as the one in (8), which was originally proposed in the area of morphology (affix order), can be applied in the area of syntax (particle and auxiliary order) too, since this universal is semantically conditioned.

3.3.4   Syntax

Many of the studies that have appeared in the field of syntactic typology are dedicated to establishing generalizations with respect to word order. As an example of a universal in this area consider the order of verb and object in relation to the order of standard and quality in comparative constructions. As shown by Greenberg (1966), the relation between these two parameters is as in (15):

(15)   (a) Object–Verb $\diamondsuit$ Standard–Quality
        (b) Verb–Object $\diamondsuit$ Quality–Standard

In this case the implication is bi-directional, i.e. the properties specified within the implication always occur together. It is furthermore important to note that although all languages have ways of expressing comparison, not all languages have a comparative construction. The generalizations in (15) are only valid for languages with such a construction.[4]

The examples in (16) and (17) illustrate the two combinations of properties given in (15). Turkish (16) has the combination of properties of type (15a), English (17) of type (15b):

(16)   *Turkish*
        (a) Object–Verb
            Ressam bize resimlerini$_{Object}$ *gösterdi*$_{Verb}$.
            artist   us   his.paintings   showed
            "The artist showed us his paintings."

---

[4] This statement may be generalized to all implicational hierarchies: they are only valid to the extent that the categories contained within them are relevant to the languages under consideration.

(b) Standard–Quality
    *kurşun-dan*_{Standard} *ağır*_{Quality}

$$kurşun\text{-}dan_{Standard} \quad ağır_{Quality}$$
$$\text{lead-ABL} \qquad\qquad \text{heavy}$$

"heavier than lead"

(17)   *English*
       (a) Verb–Object
           The artist showed$_{Verb}$ us his paintings$_{Object}$.
       (b) Quality–Standard
           heavier$_{Quality}$ than lead$_{Standard}$

   The correlation between the features illustrated in these examples appears to
be absolute or nearly absolute, and is one of the main indicators of the basic
word order of a language.

3.3.5   Semantics

One of the best known hierarchies in the area of semantics is the color term
hierarchy proposed in Berlin and Kay (1969), which is given in (18). This
hierarchy says that if a language has just two basic color terms, these will be
the equivalents of "white" and "black" (or rather "light" and "dark"); if it has
three, the third one will be the equivalent of "red"; etc. For each of the different
systems defined by the hierarchy, an example of a language manifesting the
relevant combination of basic color terms is given.

(18)   *The color term hierarchy*

white and black	> red	> yellow or green	> yellow and green	> blue	> brown

Dani >					
	Koromfe >				
		Babungo >			
		Kobon >			
			Wari >		
				Nkore-Kiga >	
					Punjabi

   In more recent studies in semantic typology, a new method has been introduced that is based on the concept of "semantic map." A semantic map organizes
sets of related meanings in such a way that the different means that languages
use to express those meanings consistently occupy contiguous areas on that
map. By way of illustration, consider the following series of constructions and
the verbs that are used within them:

Table 2.2 *Example of a semantic map*

Locative/+pres.			Possessive/+pres.
Locative/–pres.	Property	Status	Possessive/–pres.

Table 2.3 *Turkish*

Locative/+pres.			Possessive/+pres.
Locative/–pres.	Property	Status	Possessive/–pres.

Table 2.4 *Babungo*

Locative/+pres.			Possessive/+pres.
Locative/–pres.	Property	Status	Possessive/–pres.

(19)   Locative/+presentative
        "There *is* a woman in the garden."

(20)   Locative/–presentative
        "The woman *is* in the garden."

(21)   Possessive/+presentative
        "I *have* a book."

(22)   Possessive/–presentative
        "The book *is* mine."

(23)   Property
        "The woman *is* beautiful."

(24)   Status
        "Charles *is* president."

Hengeveld (1992) shows that these constructions can be organized in the semantic map given in Table 2.2.

Languages subdivide this semantic space in different ways. In Turkish (Table 2.3), the two presentative constructions are expressed in one way, and all the non-presentative ones in another.

In Babungo (Table 2.4) locative constructions use one strategy and all other constructions another.

Table 2.5 *Nasioi*

Locative/+pres.			Possessive/+pres.
Locative/–pres.	Property	Status	Locative/–pres.

Table 2.6 *Spanish*

Locative/+pres. *Haber*				Possessive/+pres. *Tener*
Locative/–pres. *Estar*	Property *Estar*	Property *Ser*	Status *Ser*	Possessive/–pres. *Ser*

Nasioi (Table 2.5) draws the line between adjectival and nominal constructions on the one hand, and locative and possessive ones on the other.

Spanish uses a large number of verbs in expressing the various construction
types. All of these occupy contiguous spaces, as shown in Table 2.6.

More detailed examples of the application of the semantic map methodology
may be found in Haspelmath (1997), van der Auwera and Plungian (1998), and
Croft (2002).

3.3.6   Lexicon

Not only lexical semantics (3.3.5), but the organization of the lexicon in terms
of categories and subcategories has been the object of typological study too. In
particular, the presence and absence of certain parts of speech have drawn the
attention of typologists. Within this field, Hengeveld *et al.* (2004), following
up on Hengeveld (1992), propose the hierarchy in (25):

(25)   Parts-of-speech hierarchy
        Head of   > Head of   > Modifier of > Modifier of
        predicate   referential   referential   predicate
        phrase   phrase   phrase   phrase

This hierarchy should be interpreted in the following way. The part of speech
that languages are most likely to have is a class of verbs, i.e. a set of lexemes
that are exclusively used in predicative function. Languages are least likely to
have a class of manner adverbs, i.e. a set of lexemes that are exclusively used to
modify the head of a predicate phrase. Since languages may furthermore either
have lexemes that can be used within various syntactic slots (flexible systems)
or simply lack lexemes for certain syntactic slots (rigid systems), the hierarchy
in (25) defines seven different parts-of-speech systems, which are presented in
Table 2.7.

Table 2.7 *Parts-of-speech systems*

Parts-of-speech system		Head of predicate phrase	Head of referential phrase	Modifier of referential phrase	Modifier of predicate phrase
Flexible	*1*	lexeme			
	2	verb	non-verb		
	3	verb	noun	modifier	
Differentiated	*4*	verb	noun	adjective	manner adverb
Rigid	*5*	verb	noun	adjective	–
	6	verb	noun	–	–
	7	verb	–	–	–

By way of illustration, consider the following examples:

Warao (Chibchan-Paezan; Romero-Figueroa, 1997, 50, 119)
(26) *yakera*
      beauty
      "beauty"

(27) *Hiaka yakera auka   saba tai nisa-n-a-e.*
      dress beauty daughter for her buy-SG-PF-PAST
      "She bought a beautiful dress for her daughter."

(28) *Oko yakera nahoro-te.*
      we beauty eat-NONPAST
      "We eat well."

In Warao, there is a class of verbs – e.g. *nisa-* in (27) – and a class of non-verbs. One and the same lexeme, *yakera*, is used in (26) as the head of a referential phrase, in (27) as a modifier within a referential phrase, and in (28) as a modifier within a predicate phrase. For this reason, Warao may be classified as a type 2 language in terms of the classification in Table 2.7.

3.4   Level of abstraction

Implicational hierarchies can only be successful predictors of linguistic variation to the extent that the categories, functions, or constructions that they try to capture can be identified cross-linguistically. As a result, the categories, functions, and constructions under investigation should be defined at a sufficiently abstract level. On the other hand, implicational hierarchies have to be sufficiently concrete in order to be applicable to actual linguistic data. The ideal

Table 2.8 *Three consonants*

	labial	coronal	dorsal	glottal
plosive	**X** (p)	**X** (t)	**X** (k)	
fricative				
nasal				
liquid				

Table 2.9 *Six consonants*

	labial	coronal	dorsal	glottal
plosive	X (p)	X (t)	X (k)	
fricative		**X** (s)		
nasal	**X** (m)	**X** (n)		
liquid				

implicational hierarchy therefore reflects both a sufficient degree of abstractness and a sufficient degree of descriptive potential. An example from the area of phonology may help to illustrate this point.

The consonant inventories at the disposition of languages are notoriously variable. A typologist who tries to define implicational hierarchies based on specific phonemes will encounter few generalizations: it is difficult to decide which consonants are less marked than others. A famous exception is the hierarchy of nasal consonants presented in Section 3.3.2. At a higher level of abstraction, however, generalizations may be formulated in terms of combinations of distinctive features of consonant phonemes available in the languages under investigation. On the basis of a small sample, at this higher level of abstraction the following generalizations seem to hold. If a language has just three consonants, it is very likely that these will be characterized by the features represented in Table 2.8. Note that in each case an example of a consonant is given that exemplifies the combination of features under consideration. This specific consonant is, however, not necessarily a phoneme of the language under investigation. For instance, both /b/ and /p/ are instances of the combination of the features /labial/ and /plosive/.

If a language has three more consonants, it is probable that these will display the combinations of features printed in bold in Table 2.9.

The next two consonants would be likely to display the combinations of features that are given in Table 2.10.

And the next two might very well display the features in Table 2.11.

Table 2.10 *Eight consonants*

	labial	coronal	dorsal	glottal
plosive	X (p)	X (t)	X (k)	
fricative		X (s)		**X** (h)
nasal	X (m)	X (n)		
liquid		**X** (l)		

Table 2.11 *Ten consonants*

	labial	coronal	dorsal	glottal
plosive	X (p)	X (t)	X (k)	
fricative		X (s)	**X** (χ)	X (h)
nasal	X (m)	X (n)	**X** (ŋ)	
liquid		X (l)		

This tentative example shows that a phenomenon that at first sight seems to defy generalization does show systematicity at a higher level of abstraction.

3.5   Interaction between implicational hierarchies

In many cases, various implicational hierarchies are simultaneously operative within the same domain of grammar, and give rise to conflicting results. Depending on the weight languages assign to each of these counteracting hierarchies, the final outcome of their application may differ from language to language. This interaction between hierarchies unavoidably leads to counterexamples at the level of the individual hierarchy, which is the main reason for the existence of statistical hierarchies.

As an example of the interaction between hierarchies, consider the following two generalizations in the area of word order, as formulated in Dik (1997, 403–404):

(29)   The Principle of Functional Stability: constituents with the same functional specification are preferably placed in the same position.

(30)   The Principle of Increasing Complexity: there is a preference for ordering constituents in an order of increasing complexity.

As an illustration of the interaction between these hierarchies, consider the following examples:

Table 2.12 *Two-dimensional representation of parameters*

		Time dependency	
		+	−
Presupposedness	+	Dependent verb forms most likely	
	−		Independent verb forms most likely

(31)   *That he left was a pity.*

(32)   **Was a pity that he left.*

(33)   *It was a pity that he left.*

According to principle (29), a construction with a clausal subject in English should be expressed as in (31), in which the subject appears in preverbal position. This sentence is grammatical, although it does not display the preferred constituent order. According to principle (30), the same construction should be expressed as in (32), in which the clausal subject appears in final position. The preferred construction type in (33) can be seen as a compromise between the two counteracting principles: the expletive pronoun *it* occupies the subject position, following principle (29), and announces the subject clause that appears in final position, following principle (30).

In order to account for the interaction between implicational hierarchies one needs a multidimensional model, which is difficult to represent graphically in those cases in which more than two parameters are involved. For a simple example involving two parameters, consider Table 2.12, adapted from Hengeveld (1998, 379).

In Table 2.12 two parameters that exert influence on the expression of the verb forms used in subordinate clauses are represented. Verb forms are classified as dependent or independent. A dependent verb form is one that cannot be used in a main clause, while an independent verb form is one that could also be used in a main clause. The parameter represented horizontally states that subordinate clauses with dependent time reference, i.e. which depend for their temporal interpretation on the main clause, are more likely to be expressed by means of dependent verb forms than those with independent time reference. The parameter represented vertically states that subordinate clauses with a presupposed content are more likely to be expressed by means of dependent verb forms than those with a non-presupposed content. The combination of these

Table 2.13

		Time dependency	
		+	−
Presupposedness	+	Dependent verb forms	Independent verb forms
	−		

Table 2.14

		Time dependency	
		+	−
Presupposedness	+	Dependent verb forms	
	−		Independent verb forms

Table 2.15

		Time dependency	
		+	−
Presupposedness	+	Dependent verb forms	Independent verb forms
	−		

two parameters predicts that presupposed time-dependent subordinate clauses are most likely to be expressed by means of dependent verb forms, while subordinate clauses with the opposite values are most likely to be expressed by means of independent verb forms.

Depending on the weight languages assign to the different parameters, the resulting systems could, for example, be of any of the types represented in Tables 2.13–2.16.

3.6   *The interpretation of implicational hierarchies*

An important general property of implicational hierarchies is that, all other things being equal, features more to the right on the hierarchy are less likely to occur in language systems. A question that arises immediately when an

Table 2.16

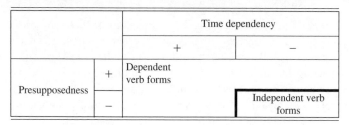

implicational universal is discovered is therefore how this increasing marked-ness of features can be explained in terms of the constraints that are imposed on possible human languages. Explanations given to language universals generally make reference either to (i) cognitive constraints (e.g. ease of processing, innate faculties, iconicity, saliency in perception), or to (ii) communicative needs (e.g. saliency of information, disambiguation, economy).

Another important aspect of the interpretation of typological generalizations concerns the extent to which these are used in the elaboration of a comprehensive theoretical model of language. Often linguistic typology is seen as a goal in itself: the research has a purely descriptive aim. In other cases linguistic typology is seen as a method that can be applied in developing (part of) a linguistic theory, which incorporates typological results to give rise to new predictions. In the first case, the primary goal of the research is an exhaustive characterization of languages; in the second case, an exhaustive characterization of language.

4   Linguistic typology and other branches of linguistics

4.1   Introduction

Typological hierarchies reflect universal properties of language and may therefore be assumed to define restrictions on cross-linguistic variation. But if these hierarchies really have a universal value, they should not only manifest themselves in cross-linguistic variation, but also restrict intralinguistic variation, such as, for instance, diachronic variation, the different phases in language acquisition, the effects of language contact, and the quantitative distribution of phenomena within a single language. In this section, I present a number of examples of intralinguistic phenomena that may be interpreted as the result of the influence of some of the same implicational hierarchies that were introduced earlier in this chapter in relation to cross-linguistic facts.[5]

---

[5] For a more detailed study of the relation between cross-linguistic and intralinguistic variation, see van Lier (2005).

4.2   *Linguistic typology and historical linguistics*

In (8) in Section 3.3.3 I presented an implicational hierarchy in the area of
morphology that defines restrictions on the order in which various grammatical categories may be expressed with respect to the predicate. The categories
are defined in semantic terms. From a diachronic perspective this hierarchy is
relevant too, in the sense that it defines the possible changes in meaning that a
grammatical element may undergo in the course of time. A concrete example
of this is the diachronic development of the auxiliary verb *will* in English, as
described in Bybee *et al.* (1991). In a first stage, this verb only expressed the
agentive modalities Intention and Obligation, which pertain to the first category
of the hierarchy. In the second stage, the verb acquired the temporal meaning
Future, which belongs to the second category of the hierarchy. In the third phase
the verb expressed the evidential modality Prediction as well. This modality falls
in the third category of the hierarchy. Thus, the changes in meaning that this
verb underwent concern contiguous categories of the hierarchy, and follow the
order predicted by the hierarchy.

4.3   *Linguistic typology and language acquisition*

The same hierarchy is relevant in the area of first language acquisition too.
Various studies concerning the acquisition of Turkish (Ekmekci, 1979; Aksu-
Koç and Slobin, 1985) show that the first category in the area of tense, mood, and
aspect that Turkish children acquire is the durative aspect, which pertains to the
first category of the hierarchy in (8). The past tense, which belongs to the second
category of the hierarchy is acquired later, but before the inferential mood, which
falls into the third category of the hierarchy. Thus, in this case the process of
first language acquisition respects the order and the contiguity of categories in
a morphological hierarchy that was developed to capture constraints on cross-
linguistic variation.

4.4   *Linguistic typology and language contact*

Hierarchy (25) in Section 3.3.6 predicts the possible combinations of parts of
speech in a language. These combinations vary from one to four of the parts
of speech that the hierarchy takes into consideration. An interesting question
resulting from this typological observation is what happens when languages
with less than these four parts of speech enter into contact with a language with
all these four parts of speech and start incorporating loans from this language.
If the hierarchy is correct, it is to be expected that in such a situation languages
will tend to incorporate items pertaining to the first category of the hierarchy
that is lacking in their native lexicon in a significantly high degree.

This hypothesis may be verified, for instance, by studying the effects that contact with Spanish has had on various typologically different indigenous languages of Central and South America. A few isolated examples seem to indicate that the typological difference between Spanish and the indigenous language determines which part of speech is borrowed more frequently.

In Quechua there is no clear-cut distinction between Nouns and Adjectives, so that one can say that only the first two categories on the hierarchy are covered. Hekking and Muysken (1995) show that the number of borrowed Spanish Adjectives in this language is surprisingly high, which indicates that the lexicon is being extended with elements from the third category of the hierarchy.

In Pipil there is no clear-cut distinction between Adjectives and manner adverbs in the indigenous vocabulary, so in this language the first three categories of the hierarchy are covered. Campbell's (1985) dictionary shows clearly that the number of manner adverbs borrowed from Spanish is surprisingly high, which indicates that the lexicon is being extended with elements from the fourth category of the hierarchy.

4.5   Linguistic typology and descriptive linguistics

Table 2.12 in Section 3.5 presented two hierarchies that influence the choice of dependent or independent verb forms in subordinate clauses. Many languages of Western Europe allow the use of both dependent and independent verb forms in the same type of construction. The following examples show that one and the same type of adverbial construction may be expressed with a dependent verb form (34a) or an independent verb form (34b):

(34)   a. *Apart from doing the cooking, I look after the garden.*
          b. *Apart from the fact that I do the cooking, I look after the garden.*

Under the hypothesis that typological hierarchies are reflected in intralinguistic variation, it is to be expected that the selection of one of the two alternatives available for expressing a subordinate clause will correspond quantitatively to what is predicted in Table 2.12.

On the basis of a large-scale corpus investigation of Modern English, Pérez Quintero (2002, 132) presents the results given in Table 2.17 for the choice of dependent and independent verb forms in adverbial clauses of the types under consideration. The percentages refer to the proportion of dependent verb forms used.

The percentages in boldface clearly show that dependent verb forms are used much more frequently in constructions that, from a cross-linguistic perspective, are most likely to be expressed by dependent verb forms, and the opposite is true for independent verb forms.

Table 2.17

		Time dependency	
		+	−
Presupposedness	+	**54.39%**	14.58%
	−	40.43%	**6.98%**

5   Conclusion

Linguistic typology studies the restrictions on cross-linguistic variation. These restrictions are formalized as implicational hierarchies, which do not only manifest themselves in the differences between languages, but also in the restrictions that they impose on intra-linguistic variation, since implicational hierarchies represent language universals that manifest themselves in all language systems.

3   Universals in a generative setting

Cedric Boeckx

Scientific endeavors tend, by their very nature, to focus on universal statements like (1), as opposed to existential statements like (2).

(1) $\forall x \ldots [\ldots x \ldots]$

(2) $\exists x \ldots [\ldots x \ldots]$

Statements like (1) give rise to universal formulations or "laws." In the context of the scientific study of language, universal statements (henceforth, "universals") have been formulated along the axes that Gould (2002, 259) identifies as influences underlying the genesis of natural objects: historical, functional, and formal.

In this chapter, I will focus exclusively on the formal axis. This is not to suggest that other axes are unimportant. It is simply that universals have a much more precise meaning in the context of formal approaches to language, by which I mean "Generative Grammar" (GG), hence they allow for clearer exposition.[1]

Let me start by pointing out that GG is a topic, a perspective on language, one that, following a long tradition ("Cartesian linguistics," see Chomsky, 1966), takes language to be a species-specific property, an object of the natural world to be studied like any other ("methodological naturalism," see Chomsky, 2000a). This makes linguistics a part of cognitive science, and ultimately biology.

This biolinguistic approach, as Jenkins (2000) has aptly called it, emerged more and more clearly as research in GG advanced.

The first chapter of *Aspects of a Theory of Syntax* (Chomsky, 1965; hereafter, *Aspects*) firmly places the study of language in a cognitive, and ultimately biological, setting, and arguably remains to this day the clearest statement of the generative enterprise as a whole. Here Chomsky argues that the central problem of linguistics is to account for how children are able to acquire their native languages.

---

[1] I also think that the formal approach, inspired by the goals of Generative Grammar, takes epistemological priority over other aspects of language. But this is not a theme that I will be able to develop here. For some discussion, see Chomsky (1986).

That is, how does the child go from primary linguistic data (P L D), i.e. well-formed, short sentences of the target language, to a grammar for that language, i.e. a procedure for generating an infinite number of linguistic objects? The problem facing the child looks quite formidable when considered from this perspective, as it quickly becomes evident that the linguistic evidence available to the child in the period of language acquisition is simply too impoverished to account for how he generalizes from this small sample of cases to a grammar that generates the infinite set of the well-formed sentences of the language. In light of this gap, the broadest aim of linguistic theory is to discover the "innate linguistic theory that provides the basis for language learning" (Chomsky, 1965, 25). In other words, the aim of a theory of grammar is to outline the biologically given cognitive structures that enable human children to project grammars so reliably and effortlessly from PLD.

Because language acquisition is universal and uniform across the species, the central question of GG is approached by looking for invariances across natural language grammars that can be taken as *innately* constraining the class of possible grammars. This is what generative grammarians mean by *universals*. These are taken to be principles of Universal Grammar that restrict the candidates for possible language-particular grammars. There are several ways of hunting for such invariances. One is to consider many languages and see what commonalities, if any, emerge. Call this the typological approach.[2] However, the way *Aspects* frames the problem suggests an alternative, more abstract method of investigating the invariant properties of the language faculty. The logic behind this approach is known as the Poverty-of-Stimulus argument (P O S). Because the argument is central to the enterprise, and because it has been repeatedly misunderstood, I briefly summarize it in the following paragraphs.

Consider how English forms "Yes/No" questions (questions whose answer is "Yes" or "No").

(3)   (a) *Is Mary at home? (Answer: Yes, Mary is at home.)*
        (b) *Can Bill sing? (Answer: Yes, Bill can sing.)*
        (c) *Will Mary be at the party tomorrow?*
             (Yes, Mary will be at the party tomorrow.)

---

[2] The core text here would be Greenberg (1963). Chomsky (1965, 118) casts doubt on the typological approach thus: "Insofar as attention is restricted to surface structures, the most that can be expected is the discovery of statistical tendencies, such as those presented by Greenberg (1963)." More recently, in light of the work that extended Kayne's (1994) Antisymmetry hypothesis (see, especially, Cinque, 1999), Chomsky has qualified his position, as expressed by the following quote (Chomsky, 1998, 33): "There has also been very productive study of generalizations that are more directly observable: generalizations about the word orders we actually see, for example. The work of Joseph Greenberg has been particularly instructive and influential in this regard. These universals are probably descriptive generalizations that should be derived from principles of U[niversal] G[rammar]." For some remarks on Greenbergian universals and how they may be captured in a minimalist setting, see Kayne (2003).

The questions seems to be related to their (affirmative) answer as follows.

(4)   To form a Y[es]/N[o] question concerning some state of affairs
         described by a structure S, transform S as follows: find the auxiliary
         of S and put it at the front.

So, in (3a), the proposition of interest is described by the sentence "Mary is
at home." The auxiliary in this sentence is *is*. The rule says that one moves this
to the front to derive the Y/N question: *Is Mary at home?*

The procedure in (4) works fine for these simple cases, but it fails for more
complex sentences like (5).

(5)   *Will Mary believe that Frank is here?*
         (Yes, Mary will believe that Frank is here.)

Example (5) is problematic because there is more than one auxiliary, so the
injunction to move *the* auxiliary is inapposite. We must specify which of the
two (*/n*) auxiliaries gets moved. To accommodate (5), we can modify (4) in
several ways. Here are several options:

(6)   (a) Move the main clause auxiliary to the front.
         (b) Move the leftmost auxiliary to the front.
         (c) Move any auxiliary to the front.

Each of these revisions of (4) suffices to generate (5). However, with the
exception of (6a), they all lead to unacceptable sentences as well. Consider
how (6c) applies to the affirmative answer of (5). It can form the Y/N question
depicted. However, it also can form the Y/N question in (7) if the rule chooses
to move *is*. In other words, (6c) overgenerates.

(7)   **Is Mary will believe that Frank here?*

Example (7) is English word salad and will be judged highly unacceptable
by virtually any native speaker. So, we know that native speakers of English
do not use a rule like (6c). We are also confident that they do not use rules like
(6b), based on sentences like (8):

(8)   *The man who is tall will leave now.*

The Y/N question that corresponds to (8) is (9a), not (9b). The latter is terrible.

(9)   (a) *Will the man who is tall leave now?*
         (b) **Is the man who tall will leave now?*

Rule (6b) predicts just the opposite pattern. Thus, (6b) both over- and under-
generates.

Rule (6a) runs into no similar difficulty. The main clause auxiliary is *will*.
The auxiliary *is* resides in an embedded clause and so will not be moved

by (6a). So, it appears that we have evidence that the rule that native speakers of English have acquired is roughly that in (4) as modified in (6a).

Now the typical *Aspects*-question is: how did adults come to internalize (6a)? There are two possible answers. First, the adults were once children and, as children, they surveyed the linguistic evidence and concluded that the right rule for forming Y/N questions is (6a). The other option is that humans are built so as to consider only rules like (6a) viable. The reason they converge on (6a) is not that they are led there by the linguistic data but that they never really consider any other option.

The second answer is generally considered the more exotic. Some resist it until the present day. However, the logic that supports it is, we believe, impossible to resist. It also well illustrates the POS strategy, as I now show.

Let us assume, for the sake of argument, that the correct rule, (6a), is learned. This means that children are driven to this rule on the basis of the available data, the PLD. A relevant question is, what does the PLD look like? In other words, what does the linguistic input that children use look like? What is the general character of the PLD? Here are some reasonable properties of the PLD: first, the data are finite. Children can only use what they are exposed to and this will, of necessity, be finite. Second, the data that the children use will be well-formed bits of the target language, e.g. well-formed phrases, sentences. Note that this *excludes* ill-formed cases and the information that it is ill formed (e.g., [7] and [9b] above will *not* be part of the data that the child has access to in divining the Y/N rule, not part of his/her PLD for this rule). Third, the child uses relatively simple sentences. These will be short simple things like the sentences in (3), by and large. *If* this is the correct characterization of the PLD available to the child, then we can conclude that some version of the more exotic conclusion above is correct. In other words, it is not that the child learned the rule in the sense of using data to exclude *all* relevant alternatives. Rather, most of the "wrong" alternatives were never really considered as admissible options in the first place.

How does one argue for this second conclusion? By arguing that the PLD are insufficient to guide the observed acquisition. Consider the case at hand. First, native speakers of English have in fact internalized a rule like (6a) as this rule correctly describes which Y/N questions they find acceptable and which they reject. Second, one presumably learns the rule for Y/N questions by being exposed to instances of Y/N questions, rather than, for example, seeing objects fall off tables or being hugged by one's mother. Say that the PLD relevant for this are simple well-formed instances of Y/N questions, sentences analogous to the examples in (3). On the basis of such examples, the child must fix on the correct rule, roughly something like (6a). The question now is: does the data in (3) suffice to drive the child to that rule? We already know that the answer is "No!" as we have seen that the data in (3) are compatible with *any* of the rules in (6). Given that there is only a single auxiliary in these cases, the issue of which of several to move never arises. What of data like (5)? These cases involve several auxiliaries but once again all three options in (6) are compatible with both the data in (5) and the data in (3).

Are there any data that could decisively lead the child to (6a) (at least among the three alternatives)? There are. We noted that examples like (9a) argue against (6b) and that (9b) and (7) provide evidence against (6c). However, the child could not use these sorts of cases to converge on rule (6a) *if he/she only uses simple well-formed bits of the language as data*. In other words, if the PLD are roughly as described above, then sentences like (9b) and (7) are not part of the data available to the child. Examples (7) and (9b) are excluded from the PLD because they are unacceptable. If such "bad" sentences are rarely uttered, or, if uttered, are rarely corrected, or, if corrected, are not attended to by children, then they will not form part of the PLD that the child uses in acquiring the Y/N question rule. Similarly, it is quite possible that examples like (9a), though well-formed, are too complex to be part of the PLD. If so, they too will not be of any help to the child. In short, though there *is* decisive linguistic evidence concerning what the correct rule is (i.e., it is [6a], not [6b] or [6c]), there need not be such evidence in the PLD, the evidence available to the child. And this would then imply that the child does not arrive at the right rule *solely* on the basis of the linguistic input of the target language. But *if* he/she does not use the linguistic input (and what other sort would be relevant to the issue of what the specific rule of Y/N questions looks like in English?) and all native speakers of English come to acquire the rule in (6a), it must be the case that this process is guided by some process internal to the language learners. In other words, this implies that the acquisition is guided by some biological feature of children rather than some property of the linguistic input. The conclusion, then, is that children have some biological endowment that allows them to converge on (6a) and not even consider (6b) or (6c) as viable options.

This is a brief example of the POS argument. The logic is tight. Granted the premises, the conclusion is ineluctable. What then of the premises? For example, is it the case that children only have access to acceptable forms of the language (i.e., not cases like [7] or [9b])? Is it true that children do not use complex examples? Before considering these questions, let me reiterate that, if the premises are granted, then the conclusion seems airtight: if the acquisition does not track the contours of the linguistic environment, then the convergence to the correct rule requires a more endogenous, biological explanation. So, how good are the premises?

For the PLD to be the main causal factor in choosing between the options in (6), we would, at the very least, expect the relevant data to be robust in the sense that *any* child might be expected to encounter sufficient examples of the decisive data. Recall that virtually all native speakers of English act as if (6a) is the correct rule. So, the possibility that *some* children might be exposed to the decisive sentences is irrelevant, given that *all* speakers converge on the same rule. Moreover, the data must be robust in another sense. Not only must all speakers encounter the relevant data, they must do so a sufficient number of times. Any learning system will have to be supple enough to ignore noise in the data. So, learning cannot be a single example affair. There must be a sufficient number of sentences like (8) and (9a) in the PLD if such sentences are to be of any relevance.

It is regularly observed that the PLD *do* contain examples like (9a).[3] However, this is not, to repeat, the relevant point. What is required is that there be enough of it. To determine this, we need to determine how much is enough. Legate and Yang (2002) and C. Yang (2002) address exactly this problem. Based on empirical findings in C. Yang (2002), they propose to "quantify" the POS argument. To do that, they situate the issue at hand in a comparative setting and propose "an independent yardstick to quantitatively relate the amount of relevant linguistic experience to the outcome of language acquisition" (C. Yang, 2002, 111). The independent benchmark they propose is the well-studied use of null subjects in child language. They note that subject use reaches adult levels at around the age of 3. This is comparable to the age of children Crain and Nakayama (1987) tested for Yes/No questions (youngest group: 3 years, 2 months). The core examples that inform children that all English (finite) sentences require phonologically overt subjects are sentences involving expletive subjects (e.g. *there is a man here*). Such sentences amount to 1.2% of the potential PLD (all sentences). Legate and Yang suggest, quite reasonably, that the PLD relevant to fixing the Y/N question rule should be of roughly comparable proportion. To be generous, let's say that even 0.5–1% would suffice.

Pullum (1996) and Pullum and Scholz (2002) find in a sentence search of the *Wall Street Journal* that about 1% of the sentences have the shape of (9a), putting it within our accepted range. However, as Legate and Yang note, the *Wall Street Journal* is not a good surrogate for what children are exposed to. A better search would be in something like the CHILDES database, a compendium of child–caretaker linguistic interactions. In a search of this database, it appears that sentences like (9a) amount to between 0.045 and 0.068% of the sentences, well over an order of magnitude *less* than is required. In fact, as Legate and Yang observe, this number is so low that it is likely to be negligible, in the sense of not being reliably available to every child! Just as interesting, of roughly 67,000 adult sentences surveyed in CHILDES (the kind of data that would be ideal for the child to use), there is not a single example of a Y/N question like (9a). If this survey of CHILDES is representative of the PLD available to the child (and there is no reason to think that it is not), then the fact that the *Wall*

---

[3] See, most recently, Pullum and Scholz (2002), Cowie (1998), and Sampson (1999).

Street Journal contains sentences like (9a) is irrelevant. Recall, however, that it is these sorts of sentences that would provide evidence for choosing (6a) over (6b). And if they are missing from the PLD, as seems to be the case, then it seems that the PLD is too poor to explain the facts concerning acquisition of the Y/N question rule in English. In short, the conclusion of the POS argument outlined above follows.

I have spent all this time on this issue as it has recently been advanced (once again) as a refutation of the nativist conclusions of the POS argument. However, to be fair, I should observe that our discussion above is too generous to the opponents of the POS. The discussion has concentrated on whether examples like (9a) occur in the PLD. Even if they did, it would not undermine the argument presented above. The presence of sentences like (9a) would simply tell us that the PLD *can* distinguish (6a) from (6b). It does not yet address how to avoid generalizing to (6c). This option must also be removed or the nativist conclusions are once again required. However, (9a) does not bear on (6c) at all. It is (7) and (9b) that are relevant here. Such data, often called "negative evidence," is what counts. Is negative evidence present in the PLD? If it is, how would it be manifest?

One way would be if adults made the relevant errors and corrected themselves somehow. However, nobody makes mistakes like (7) and (9b). Such sentences are even hard for native speakers to articulate! A second possibility would be that children make errors of the relevant sort and are corrected somehow. However, this too is virtually unattested. Children never make errors like those in (7) and (9b) even when strongly set up to do so (see Crain and Nakayama, 1987, for detailed discussion). If they do not make the errors, however, they cannot be corrected. Moreover, there is plenty of evidence that children are very resistant to correction (see McNeill, 1966; Jackendoff, 1994, 22ff.). Thus, even when mistakes occur, children seem to ignore the best-intentioned efforts to help them along grammatically. A third option is to build the negative evidence option into the learning process itself. For example, we might say that children are very conservative learners and will not consider structures as possible unless they have observed instances of them. (This is often referred to as "indirect negative evidence.") The problem with this, however, is that it is difficult to state the restriction in a way that won't be obviously wrong. Recall that children are exposed to, at most, a finite number of sentences and, therefore, to, at most, a finite number of sentence patterns. Recall that it even seems that a negligible number of sentences like (9a) occur in the PLD so, if children were too conservative they would never form such questions. Moreover, mature native speakers can use and understand an unbounded number of sentences and sentence patterns. If children were conservative in the way hinted at above, they could never fully acquire language at all as they would never be exposed to most of the patterns of the language. So, at least any simple-minded idea of conservativity won't do, and we are left with the conclusion that the assumption that children do not have access to negative data in the PLD is a reasonable one.

To get back to the main point, if what I have said above is correct, then why children don't opt for rules like (6c) is unaccounted for. Recall that only negative data tell against (6c) as the correct option; (6a) is simply a proper sub-case of (6c). It would seem then that both the logic and the premises of the POS argument are sufficient to lead us to conclude that language acquisition is not explicable *solely* on the basis of the linguistic input. More is needed. In particular, I follow Chomsky in asserting the need for some biological, human-specific mechanism for language development.[4]

Considerable progress on Universal Grammar was made possible with the introduction of the Principles and Parameters model in the early 1980s. For the first time, a workable proposal regarding universals emerged in *Lectures on Government and Binding* (*LGB*; Chomsky, 1981), in the guise of a "Principles and Parameters" architecture, to which I now turn.

In a deep sense, the central problem in linguistics is identical to the one in the branch of biology known as "Theoretical Morphology" (see McGhee, 1998). Those that Kauffman (1993) dubbed the "Rationalist morphologists" such as Goethe, Cuvier, St. Hilaire, had already recognized that extant organismal forms are only a subset of the range of theoretically possible morphologies. The primary question of Theoretical Morphology parallels the one within Generative Grammar:

The goal is to explore the possible range of morphologic variability that nature could produce by constructing n-dimensional geometric hyperspaces (termed "theoretical mor-phospaces"), which can be produced by systematically varying the parameter values of a geometric model of form. . . . Once constructed, the range of existent variability in form may be examined in this hypothetical morphospace, both to quantify the range of existent form and to reveal non-existent organic form. That is, to reveal morpholo-gies that theoretically could exist . . . but that never have been produced in the process of organic evolution on the planet Earth. The ultimate goal of this area of research is to understand why existent form actually exists and why non-existent form does not. (McGhee, 1998, 2)

Aspects essentially identified this "ultimate" goal, but no workable mech-anism for generating the "theoretical morphospaces" was available until the 1980s.

In *LGB* the issue was conceived as follows.[5] Children come equipped with a set of principles of grammar construction (i.e. Universal Grammar [UG]). The

---

[4] Exactly which brain property corresponds to the mental property under discussion is far from clear. Hopefully, informed research in neurolinguistics will help us bridge this gap and unify the mind/brain.

[5] For an introduction to the Principles and Parameters approach to language variation and language acquisition that develops this theme in detail, see Baker (2001).

principles of UG have open parameters. Specific grammars arise once values for these open parameters are specified. Parameter values are determined on the basis of PLD. A language-specific grammar, then, is simply a specification of the values that the principles of UG leave open. This conceives of the acquisition process as sensitive to the details of the environmental input (as well as the level of development of other cognitive capacities) as it is the PLD that provides the parameter values. However, the shape of the knowledge attained (the structure of the acquired grammar) is not limited to information that can be gleaned from the PLD since the latter exercises its influence against the rich principles that UG makes available. Much of the work since the mid 1970s, especially the countless studies inspired by Kayne (1975), can be seen, in retrospect, as demonstrating the viability of this conception. And viable it was judged to be! There was an explosion of comparative grammatical research that exploited this combination of fixed principles and varying parametric values that showed that languages, despite apparent surface diversity, could be seen as patterns with a common fixed core. An example, based on Pollock (1989), should provide a flavor of this research.

Consider the placement of adverbs in English and French. In English, an adverb may not intervene between the Verb and the direct object, in contrast with French.

(10)   a. *John eats quickly an apple.
        b. Jean mange rapidement une pomme.
        c. John quickly eats an apple.
        d. *Jean rapidement mange une pomme.

The paradigm in (10) appears to be the result of a parametric variation between the grammar of English and that of French. In both languages, the clause has a structure roughly as in (11).

(11)   [$_S$ Subject [Inflection [Adverb[$_{VP}$ Verb Object]]]]

What makes a sentence finite are features in the Inflection position. These must be added to the Verb in both languages (call this the "Inflection-Attachment" Principle). The languages differ, however, in how this happens (call this the "Inflection-Attachment" Parameter). In English, Inflection lowers onto the Verb, whereas in French the Verb raises to Inflection. The difference is illustrated in (12):

(12)   a. [$_S$ Subj [<del>Infl</del> [Adverb[$_{VP}$ V+Infl Obj]]]]
        b. [$_S$ Subj [Infl+V [Adverb[$_{VP}$ <del>V</del> Obj]]]]

Note that this one difference explains the data in (10). In English, since the Verb doesn't raise, and the adverb is assumed to stay put, the adverb will be to the left, but not the right of the finite verb (12a), whereas in French the opposite holds, due to v-movement across the adverb (12b). So, allowing for one parametric difference accommodates the facts in (10). Note, by the way, that we keep the basic clausal structure the *same* in the two languages. Likewise, the demand that Inflection be attached to the verb remains constant. What changes is how this attachment takes place.

As should be clear, this sort of account can be multiplied to accommodate all sorts of differences between languages (see Baker, 2001). And a good part of research in the 1980s involved exactly these sorts of analyses. It proved to be very insightful, and grammarians came to the conclusion that something like a Principles and Parameters account of the language faculty was essentially correct. Note that this does *not* say which of the many possible principles and parameters theories is the right one. It only says that the right theory should have this general architecture. This consensus opened the door to the most current shift in grammatical theory, the Minimalist Program, to which I now turn.

The Principles and Parameters proposal has three great virtues: (a) it accommodates the fact that what language a person ends up speaking is closely related to the one that s/he is exposed to; (b) it accommodates the fact that acquisition takes place despite a significant poverty of the linguistic stimulus, by having the PLD act against a fixed backdrop of invariant principles; and (c) it is immediately applicable in day-to-day grammatical research. In particular, in contrast to the vagaries of the evaluation metric, the parameter-setting model has been widely used to account for grammatical variation. These three facts have led to a general consensus among linguists that the language faculty has a Principles and Parameters (P&P) architecture.

This consensus invites a new question: granted that the language faculty has a P&P character, which of the many possible P&P models is the right one? In other words, what other conditions on grammatical adequacy are there, and how can they be used to move the generative enterprise forward? Minimalism is an attempt to answer this question. However, because the legitimacy of a Minimalist Program for linguistic theory has been disputed (see Boeckx and Piattelli-Palmarini, 2005, and Boeckx and Uriagereka, in press, for review), I want to stress that the minimalist turn is fully in line with the research agenda initiated in *Aspects* (see Freidin and Vergnaud, 2001, on this point), and pursues questions quite common in the well-developed sciences.[6]

Succinctly put, the Minimalist Program conjectures that the computational system ("syntax") central to human language is an "optimal" solution to the central task of language: relating sound and meaning. This thesis will be vindicated once the complexities apparent in earlier approaches (such as *LGB*)

---

[6] The only note of caution worth bearing in mind is that the Minimalist Program may be premature (Chomsky, 2001, 1).

are eliminated, or else shown to be only apparent, following from deeper, and simpler, properties.

Stated thus, the Minimalist Conjecture is no different from the emphasis in Theoretical Morphology to "model existent form with a minimum of parameters and mathematical complexity" (McGhee, 1998, 2). In fact, minimalism responds to a deep-seated urge characteristic of the sciences. As Feynman (1963, 26) puts it:

Now in the further advancement of science, we want more than just a formula. First we have an observation, then we have numbers that we measure, then we have a law which summarizes all the numbers. But the real glory of science is that we can find a way of thinking such that the law is evident.

Seen in this context, minimalism emerges from the success of the *LGB* program. Because the Principles and Parameters approach "solves" Plato's problem, more methodological criteria of theory evaluation, revolving around simplicity, elegance, and other notions that are hard to quantify but are omnipresent in science, can become more prominent. Until *LGB*, solving the acquisition problem was the paramount measure of theoretical success. Once, however, this problem is taken as essentially understood, then the question is *not* how to solve it but how *best* to do so. By its nature, this question abstracts away from the POS problem and points towards other criteria of adequacy – that is, "beyond explanatory adequacy."

As Chomsky has clearly stated in his most recent technical writings (Chomsky, 2004, 2005), the ambition – perhaps premature, although recent results are, I find, encouraging[7] – of the Minimalist Program is to clearly delineate the three factors influencing language design: (i) genetic endowment, (ii) experience, and (iii) general properties of systems. These match, point by point, the loci of explanation that make up what Lewontin (2000), reviewing the program of biological sciences, called "the triple helix": genes, environment, and organism.

Minimalism thus addresses a fundamental question of the biolinguistic approach, i.e., to what extent are the properties of grammar so far discovered specific to language, or shared by other domains, cognitive or even more general? As is the case with all scientific quests, answers to general questions must proceed through a first stage of what one might call extreme modularization or specificity. At first, it appears that the effect of the moon on the tides is distinct from the reason behind apples falling off trees, electricity is nothing like magnetism, space and time are two irreducible dimensions, and so on. Likewise, at first, focalization in Gbe looks radically different from wh-movement in Bulgarian and topicalization in English, to say nothing of relative clause formation

---

[7] For review, see Boeckx and Uriagereka (in press).

in French. Gradually, commonalities are extracted, and disparate phenomena are unified, with surface differences relegated to extraneous factors. That is, gradually, principles emerge, and arbitrary aspects (parameters) can be clearly localized.

Arguably, the clearest example of this development revolves around analyses of sentences like (13) and (14).

(13)   *What did John say that Peter bought t?*

(14)   **What did John wonder whether Peter bought t?*

All native speakers of English consider (13) acceptable, and most consider (14) unacceptable (whence the asterisk that precedes it). Every native speaker perceives it as sharply less well formed than (13). The general line of thinking (see Chomsky, 1986) to explain a variety of such phenomena was that traces of movement are subject to two kinds of licensing (technically known as "proper government"): licensing by neighboring element such as a verb ("head-government") or licensing by the moving element itself ("antecedent government"). Rizzi (1990) argued that the definition of the two kinds of licensing can be made symmetric by relativizing the so-called Minimality condition on government to the type of licenser. The technical details here don't matter. What is important is that Rizzi's effort was driven towards a simplification of a technical definition. The definition itself has now fallen into disrepute, but, crucially, Chomsky and Lasnik (1993, 89f.) were able to see beyond the technicalia and extracted a condition on movement that is now taken to reflect a fundamental "minimalist" feature of language. As Chomsky and Lasnik note, "the basic and appealing intuition that lies behind the principle of Relativized Minimality [Rizzi (1990)] is not really captured by the mechanisms proposed, which list three arbitrary cases and add unexplained complexity" (p. 89). They note further, "[t]he basic intuition is that the operation [of movement] should always try to construct 'the shortest link'" (p. 89). This is schematized in (15):

(15) $x_a \ldots y_a \ldots z_a$

That is, in (14), movement of *what* crosses an element of the same type (*whether*) that occupies a position that could be occupied by *what* (cf. *John wondered what Peter bought*).

Chomsky and Lasnik go on to elevate Relativized Minimality to a "general principle of economy of derivation" (p. 90). Since then, considerations of economy have been the major focus of research in syntactic theory. Chomsky and Lasnik's perspective on Relativized Minimality has allowed numerous cases that originally did not fall within the definition of trace licensing to be incorporated into the general guideline of economy, thereby strengthening the central minimalist thesis that syntactic computation is optimal.

Research in the Minimalist Program is driven towards finding other instances of efficient computation, symmetric representations, and other features of optimal systems, and establishing them as principles of UG, that is, as universals in a minimalist setting.

4   In search of universals

Ian Maddieson

1   What are universals?

In everyday life we are struck by the *differences* between languages. When we overhear a conversation between people speaking a language we have no knowledge of, we find it completely impenetrable. There is something disturbing, even sinister, about a language you do not understand at all. The fear this engenders is part of what tempts authoritarians everywhere to ban the use of unfamiliar languages, and enforce the use of the familiar. Unfamiliar languages are also frequently looked down on as unstructured and incapable of serving to convey more than simple messages. Linguists confront this fear and contempt, and it is part of the value of the mainstream traditions of linguistics as a humanistic discipline that they insist on the equal worth of every language. Every language is considered equal, in the sense of meriting equally serious consideration, akin to the way that all people are declared to be "equal in dignity and rights" in the Universal Declaration of Human Rights (United Nations, 1948). In contrast to lay emphasis on linguistic differences, for linguists the demonstration of *similarities* between languages functions at the same time as one of the ways in which the proposition of equality is supported and as one of the reasons why linguists hold this view. We feel justified in constructing general theories within which the peculiarities of individual languages can be described, rather than taking it as our task to build quite separate theories for different languages. The nature of some of these similarities, some methodological considerations involved, and some of the factors which may account for similarities will be the topics of this chapter. Naturally enough, the focus will be on examples from the domain of phonetics and phonology, but methods and types of explanations may be parallel in other subfields of linguistics.

There are three very different takes on the nature of linguistic similarities that I am familiar with. In one, the perspective is that the problem of describing all languages can be attacked using similar methodologies, yet the linguist makes no commitment that the similarities are ones of substance rather than of method. Those familiar with work in the tradition of "prosodic phonology" associated with the name of J. R. Firth may recognize this trait in that work. Its practitioners would surely assert that the phonology of any language can be described using the concepts of phonematic units and prosodies, and phonetic exponents of these categories. However, the nature and content of the categories is so dependent on language-particular interpretations by individual linguists that it makes no sense to compare descriptions of different languages in this model. One of Firth's main concerns was to find a way round what he saw as the excessive inflexibility of competing linguistic models, which threatened to mask differences not only between languages but equally between different subsystems within the same language. By providing flexible descriptive tools he permitted an escape from this rigidity, and accepted the fact that comparability of descriptions only existed at the level of the tools used. Despite it being one of Firth's targets, some linguists of the heyday of American structuralism maintained a somewhat similar view that language descriptions were only similar at the level of their methodology, a view jocularly dubbed "hocus-pocus" at the time.

An opposite extreme of thinking about language similarities is the postulation of an innate Universal Grammar (hereafter UG) which underlies the grammars of all individual languages and structures the process by which they are acquired in childhood and how they are represented in the adult brain. The existence of such a UG is a fundamental assumption within the generative tradition of linguistics, and the discovery of its properties is taken to be one of the main objectives of the science. UG in this sense is sometimes discussed as if it was a rather mystical immanent entity – a "language organ" which appeared somewhat mysteriously at some point in human ancestry, with no precursors – but Pinker (1994), Deacon (1997), and other scholars have shown how the idea can be set comfortably in the mainstream of thinking in evolutionary biology. From this perspective, all languages are similar in certain important ways and cannot be otherwise because humans come "pre-set" with principles of language design. It is, of course, not necessary to assume that all similarities observed between languages should be attributed to innate adaptation for language. Some shared characteristics could, for example, be due to properties of the human organism that are not specific to language, or to properties of the external environment in which language is used. This point seems sometimes to be missed, by both adherents and opponents of the UG hypothesis.

A third perspective is found in the tradition of work that actually bears the title of linguistic universals, or is discussed in terms of universals and typology. An underlying assumption here is certainly the hypothesis that all languages are constructed on similar principles, or at least that the range of their variation is circumscribed within quite definite limits. However, the explanation of any shared properties or limits on language variability is the subject of further specific hypotheses which may be based on a variety of different factors. Although special innate adaptations for language are not excluded, it is clear that many of the linguists working in this tradition would prefer to find their explanations elsewhere. Work in this tradition tends to have a strongly empiricist orientation: universals can (and should) be inferred directly from comparing descriptions of different languages (Greenberg, 1966; Croft, 1990). In order to do this, it has to be assumed that the descriptive terms and constructs used to describe properties of different languages can be sufficiently well equated for generalizations to be meaningfully made, a quite problematic issue which will not be discussed here.

The meaning of the term "universal" when used in this context needs to be clarified, since in only relatively few cases is this work focused on properties that are literally shared by all languages. Rather, the interest is in trying to define the limits within which variation among languages is confined, and to study the relative frequency of various traits – a reasonable hypothesis being that a more frequent pattern may represent in some sense a "better" design feature for a language than one which is significantly less frequent. "Universals" are thus essentially distributions of individual properties and of patterns of related properties. What justifies the term "universal" is that these distributions are being studied over the universe of known languages. Studying the universe of known languages offers one way to approach the goal of understanding what the essential nature of human language is – that is, what is to be found in the universe of possible languages.

An interesting convergence between the generativist UG tradition and empiricist work on language universals has been apparent in recent years in work on language origins (see introduction to Hurford *et al.*, 1998). A combination of several factors, including new lines of thinking about emergent organization, new techniques for studying human brain activity, and greater sophistication in handling experiments with young children and animals, has reinvigorated an area of research which not long ago was largely neglected as sterile, if not downright unrespectable. Any innate endowments of modern humans that make language possible and the attributes manifested in language itself cannot be other than different reflections of the evolution of our species. There are many aspects to consider – biomechanical and cognitive development, environmental and social setting, purposive action vs. emergent self-organizing patterns, and so on. UG theorists may be more likely to emphasize cognitive elements and empirical universalists more likely to emphasize biomechanical, environmental, and social factors, but there is a good deal of overlap. Some of the comments below reflect an attempt to place universals research in an evolutionary context: it will be apparent that I am on the side of those (e.g. Ulbaek, 1998) who consider that it was indeed communication of information (including "social" information about group solidarity) which was *the* evolutionary advantage of the development of language.

2 How do we find universals?

It follows from what was said above that knowledge of universals comes from surveying what is found in known languages. But, as has often been pointed out before, actually conducting such surveys is laden with both practical and theoretical difficulties. In the first place, there is the sheer impracticality of literally surveying the entire universe of known languages, in whatever way that task is conceived. This practical reason is the first thing that drives the universalist to turn to using a *sample* of languages. The laziest way to construct a sample is just to think of the languages you know about, or can find descriptions of in the books and journals in your office. Let us charitably call this an informal sample. It is a part of human nature to generalize from the familiar, and linguists are as prone to do this as anyone. Implicitly or explicitly they may extract "universals" from such informal samples. Thus, for many linguists, Standard Mandarin, being the most familiar example of a tone language, comes to serve as the tacit prototype of one, even though wider surveys show that a tone system with only one level tone is typologically very unusual.

Clearly, an explicit sample is preferable to an informal one, since the basis for any conclusions drawn from it can be seen and verified by another linguist. Explicitness alone, however, is not enough, as the sample also needs to be carefully constructed to avoid bias if the results are to be meaningful. Language samples are hard to construct, however. This is not least because of the difficulties of determining and consistently applying appropriate criteria for deciding whether two related speech varieties should be considered two different languages or two dialects of the same language. For example, the 1992 edition of *Ethnologue* (Grimes, 1992) distinguishes seven modern Romance languages spoken primarily within the borders of mainland France, whereas Posner (1996) is reluctant to recognize more than two, each encompassing more dialectal variation. If you want to compile a sample of fifty languages, how many eligible targets for inclusion are there in France? This makes language sampling very different from conducting a public opinion poll asking 2,000 people whether they prefer Pepsi or Coke. Human beings, unlike languages, have rather well-defined boundaries, so they can be enumerated and a random subset easily picked.

The appropriate structure of a sample will naturally vary according to the purpose for which it is designed. A sample to examine the global frequency of some property or pattern of properties must be structured to sample the whole universe of known languages, whereas one designed to examine the strength of association of property x and property y may be limited to languages in which at least one of these properties occurs. The UPSID sample, originally described in Maddieson (1984), subsequently expanded, and now consultable on the web in several implementations, is designed to study global patterns in the structure of phoneme inventories and the frequency of occurrence of particular segment types or classes in those inventories. It was constructed using a sampling grid based on a genetic classification of the world's languages, and this for a very good reason.

All linguists working on universals, whether their approach is to assume a UG or to look for universals empirically, intend to be describing characteristics that are general attributes of being a language. But we know that similarities between languages can have a historical origin, whether due to descent from a common ancestor or from contact; in fact, it is precisely the presence of similarities which makes it possible to reconstruct the historical connections among languages. The fact that the word for the warmest season of the year is "summer" in English and that synonyms with similar shapes are found in the other German languages is the result of some arbitrary association of sound and meaning dating back to Proto-Germanic, and carried down to the modern languages with relatively little change. Highly specific similarities, such as here in the shape of particular words, are clearly not candidates for universal status. What we would consider typological patterns, however, can also be continued down through language families, and some proportion of these patterns may be the result of factors just as arbitrary as the choice of making "summer" mean what it does. For English words like "star," "stone" and "still" we can also find cognates in other Germanic languages. Here we may be tempted not just to note the lexical similarities but to conclude that the initial clusters in these words provide evidence for a generalization that sibilant fricatives have a special freedom to occur before stops in onset position. Yet the apparently privileged occurrence of sibilants in two-obstruent clusters may be just another inherited peculiarity of Germanic, and more generally of Indo-European, languages: other languages give wider freedom to lateral or velar fricatives.

Moreover, it should always be remembered that the selection of languages available for examination today is the cumulative result of all the accidents of the past, which have led to the extinction of Sumerian, Etruscan, Tocharian, Beothuk, Ningi, Island Carib, Tasmanian, and many other languages, including many thousands of which we know nothing at all; the reduction of some language groups to a handful of survivors or isolates, such as Basque, Burushaski, Ket, Hadza, Albanian, Greek, and Armenian; and the explosion of numbers of languages in other groups such as Austronesian or Benue-Congo. Some arbitrary features will thus have had the opportunity to propagate in a large number of daughter languages, while other patterns which existed in the past will be found nowhere today. The raw pattern of relative frequencies is thus not simply a function of how "natural" (for want of a better word) a particular pattern is, but the outcome of the interaction of naturalness, arbitrariness, and accidents of history. Exactly parallel problems arise in relation to contact. Some of the features spread by contact may be arbitrary ones, and languages have quite unequal chances of participating in contact situations that result in typological-looking change. There is no way to avoid completely the risk of error that these facts create, the principal one being that of interpreting common patterns as being "natural" when they may just have been lucky, and of thinking that a typology based on existing languages is exhaustive when other possible patterns just happen not to be around at the moment. However, constructing a sample using *genetic distance* between the languages as a major criterion for inclusion reduces the risk of over-valuing shared inherited features. The majority of carefully drawn-up explicit samples follow this criterion in one way or another. Nonetheless, it is still prudent to examine explicitly any putative universal in the light of its distribution across genetic groupings, and to check that the patterns are not plausibly explained by contact.

Sampling is also required for another reason. Many of the observed patterns in universals research consist of relationships between properties. In such a case it is necessary to show that the properties that appear to be related are not just associated by chance. This can best be done by examining the statistical patterns of an explicit sample. I will illustrate this with an intentionally silly example. In the expanded UPSID sample of 451 languages, all the languages with clicks in their consonant inventories also have bilabial nasals. Should we conclude that having clicks specifically entails the presence of a bilabial nasal? About 95% of the languages have bilabial nasals; there are only 5 languages with clicks. Given this frequency of bilabial nasals, we can calculate that for any random subset of 5 languages from the sample there is about a 77% chance that all 5 will include a bilabial nasal. The association of clicks and bilabial nasals in inventories is therefore overwhelmingly likely to be due to chance, as any set of five languages – regardless of whether any clicks occur – is far more likely to all have bilabial nasals than not. It is easy to be misled by the co-occurrence of properties in one or more familiar languages into thinking that their co-occurrence is "natural" but we can only be confident of such an interpretation when the data have been assembled in a way that allows chance association to be ruled out.

We would in any case have been unlikely to consider that the co-occurrence of clicks and bilabial nasals taken as an isolated fact in this way was likely to be of importance. We need a reason to think that any facts we observe have importance. Confidence that a particular phenomenon is reasonably viewed as a universal comes finally from the ability to formulate a theory drawing on factors that are appropriately universal in their scope and which provide a reason for its existence. The particular shape of the English word "summer" may be arbitrary, but the fact that all its component sounds are produced in the mouth – rather than, say, by stamping the feet – is open to a universally general explanation if we can show that oral sounds possess advantages for the construction of a human communication system that foot-stomping and other alternatives do not have.

It is perhaps also worth re-emphasizing here that success in acquiring speakers has nothing to do with "fitness" as a system of communication. The most widely spoken languages did not achieve their dominance because they are better equipped than others, but because of the political and demographic success of the communities using these languages. English has no greater claim to be representative of "language" than Tewa, Ogoni, or Manam. Forcing the inclusion of all the major languages in a sample, or, worst of all, constructing a sample that consists of only the most widely spoken languages, risks introducing some serious distortions, particularly if one wishes to count the relative frequency of properties. For example, many of the most widely spoken languages, e.g. English, Arabic, French, and Russian, are very deviant from the most common pattern of segment sequencing, and many of these widely spoken languages also have particular kinds of comparatively rare sounds in their phonological inventories, such as the [ʁ] (and its variants) of standard French, and the [ɹ] of standard American English in words like "bird."

Conducting surveys for universals involves other practical considerations besides sample design. Many of the languages in the world today have only been described in quite sketchy fashion. The investigator has the options of considering collecting information with first-hand field-work (usually impractical), or working with information collected by others (which may not include the facts being sought). In practice, therefore, it is what one might call the "lowest denominator" theoretical elements that are most readily amenable to broad cross-linguistic study. This is one reason why, in the domain of phonological universals, a great deal of attention has been devoted to analyzing the structure of phoneme inventories and patterns of syllabification, since even the relatively modest publications which are all that are available for most languages usually include a phonemic level of analysis and some information on syllable structure. Even here, though, there are significant gaps; for example, we cannot say how common contrast of tongue root position is in phonemic vowel systems since many descriptions do not consider this possibility, while others use the feature +/− Advanced Tongue Root to make up for deficiencies in the features available to distinguish vowel height or other properties. For many other aspects of phonological structure, for example intonation and phrasal structure or patterns of segmental alternation, it can be hard to assemble a sufficiently large database or to find descriptions that are commensurable. For more detailed phonetic aspects of language, such as acoustic variation in different contexts, there is only a small amount of data of any sort on most languages, and the risk of drawing misleading conclusions from inadequate data is correspondingly great.

3   Where do universals come from?

There are certainly two easily distinguishable kinds of constraints which produce observable universal phonetic and phonological patterns, and perhaps it
would be useful to distinguish more. The two I have in mind were labelled
"mechanical" and "ecological" in an earlier publication (Maddieson, 1997).
The names are chosen to be suggestive rather than to be strictly construed in
narrow senses of these terms, and it is not claimed that there is any strikingly
novel insight behind their choice. Rather, this is an attempt to present in a relatively clear and transparent fashion a distinction which it seems important to
draw. "Mechanical" constraints are those which are necessarily so, for example
because of physical laws or limits on what human beings are capable of doing
(which may be ultimately explicable in terms of physical laws too, although it is
often convenient to bypass this explication). "Ecological" constraints are those
which direct selection within the range of what is possible in certain directions
rather than others.

   If we think about vowels, for instance, it is clear that there are "mechanical"
limits on the range of articulatory and spectral diversity that it is possible to
produce. There is a limit to how wide we can make the vocal tract at any point
(although the particular distances will vary according to individuals), and if we
narrow it beyond a certain degree it becomes no longer possible to produce a
vowel. These and other restrictions on the geometry of the vocal tract mean that
it is possible to delimit a "vowel space" with articulatory, acoustic, or perceptual
coordinates. Vowels will necessarily fall within this space. For example, if we
consider a very simplified acoustic representation of vowel space in terms of the
two lowest formant frequencies, a given speaker will be able to produce a certain
highest first formant frequency and a certain highest second formant frequency.
Although it can provide many hours of harmless entertainment for a phonetician
in search of distraction to see how close one can get to the impossible, there
is no way that these two values can be produced at the same time. Hence,
within the rectangle defined by the minimum and maximum values of F1 and
F2 shown schematically in Figure 4.1 there is a smaller space that contains all
the possible combinations of F1 and F2 values. This space is represented as
bounded by the curved line inside the rectangle. The excluded area in the lower
left of the figure (lightly stippled) represents all those combinations of values of
high F1 and high F2 that cannot be attained. (There is also an excluded area in
the lower right of the figure, but for a quite different reason. By definition, the
frequency of F2 cannot be lower than the frequency of F1. This area represents
those combinations of values where this definition would be violated.)

   The configuration of the standard IPA vowel quadrilateral, shown in
Figure 4.2 with cardinal vowel symbols conventionally placed, represents a

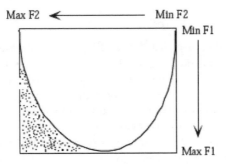

Figure 4.1   Rectangular space defined by range of first two formants, and interior limits.

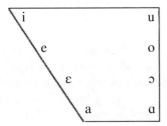

Figure 4.2   The standard IPA vowel quadrilateral.

similar kind of understanding that there are limits to the vowel space, and that these limits have some interesting asymmetries. The shape of the figure implies such constraints as "a vowel with the quality [a] cannot be assimilated to a fronter vowel without also being raised." This example, of courses, begs many questions about the nature of the parameters which define vowel space, but the details are not crucial to illustrating that there are some "mechanical" limits to respect.

But there are other factors that are clearly not of this necessary sort. An illustration can be provided by considering the arrangement of vowels in sets of vowel phonemes. Considered cross-linguistically, vowel systems display a number of quite clear trends which have been widely studied (Lindblom, 1986; Schwartz *et al.*, 1997). More languages have a system of five distinctive vowels than of any other number. Having five vowels, however, is clearly not a necessary pattern as so many other possibilities are also found. The common arrangements of five vowels place them so well dispersed in phonetic vowel space that it is evidently not a case of running up against limits on human ability to resolve differences. Such "preferred" arrangements in contrastive sets must therefore be due to a different kind of factor or factors. These are viewed as "ecological" partly by analogy with, say, a predator's choice of foods within its ecological setting – when times are good and the animal is strong, it will go after its favorite foods, but less desirable foods will serve the purpose of keeping it alive just as well. What the animal actually eats is thus a result of the interaction of variables affecting food supply and the animal's strength. There are some single scales to consider (e.g. food preference), but crucially any outcome requires considering how several factors interrelate. And it is this aspect of considering factors in context that is the essence of an "ecological" perspective. But the term is not just chosen for the analogy; it seems likely that many of the choices made in language design do result directly from the ecological setting in which language developed or in which it is now used.

The distinction of "mechanical" vs. "ecological" factors is not as sharp as the foregoing discussion of a couple of prototypes related to vowels suggests, and it may perhaps be better to think of a scale from "more mechanical" to "more ecological." It is certain that we do not always know where to place effects between these poles. There are many things we still do not know about the mechanisms of speech production, and about the auditory system, and we know less about perception and the representation of linguistic knowledge in the brain. There are surely limits imposed by the "hard-wiring" of elements in the auditory and perceptual systems, which put bounds on the system's capacity to resolve difference between, say, two vowel tokens. We cannot always experimentally see, however, where such physical limits lie, and how they are distinguishable from more functional limitations, shaped by, for example, the learning of some particular language.

4   What are some universals we know about?

In the remainder of the chapter I will talk briefly about a few selected universals or classes of universals, starting with some which touch on very basic aspects of language. One popular pseudo-universal will also be mentioned, to illustrate that it is also very easy to construct explanations for pseudo-facts.

4.1   Language uses sound

The most basic phonetically related universal is that all human ethnic groups make use of a language which is based on sound (see Locke, 1998). Another type of language exists which uses our sense of sight, that is, the transmission of a message involves an encoding of the signal in terms of patterns of light (created by movements in space). These languages, like good small children in the English saying, are seen and not heard. I will call them light-based languages to contrast them with sound-based languages, but, of course, they are more ordinarily called signed languages. The light-based languages known from around the world seem invariably to be the preserve of particular subcultures, most often composed of individuals with impaired hearing and their close associates, who form a group within a larger society using a language based on sound.

Why is it the case that sound-based languages are universal across societies in this way? We know that the spatial–visual medium is fully capable of supporting languages adequate to all the demands people make on them, and that such languages are as complex in their structures as sound-based languages. Yet nowhere in the world do we find a family of languages used by hearing people and employing a light-based system for its primary organization, nor do we have evidence to suggest that such a family ever existed. This is perhaps surprising in view of the fact that, for humans, sight is considered the most sensitive of the various senses through which we acquire information about the world around us, and our sight is certainly more acute than our sense of hearing. In view of the well-established fact that visual cues significantly aid in comprehension of languages transmitted by sound (e.g. MacDonald and McGurk, 1978), we might also have expected to find language families in which there is primarily light-based encoding but with some secondary support from sound.

It seems appropriate to consider the relative balance of advantage between sound and sight in very ecological terms, since it is clear that what is involved is a strong *preference* for sound-based systems, not complete uniformity. Light-based systems have an advantage over sound-based ones in that they can function well in situations where there are other sources of sound present which would interfere with a sound-based system. The world was undoubtedly a much quieter place before the invention of internal combustion engines and amplified music, but there are many natural sources of sound which might have impeded our ancestors' efforts to communicate. With a light-based communication system you can have a conversation in a howling gale, or standing next to Niagara Falls, or while on an egg-stealing expedition to a colony of thousands of screeching seagulls. A slightly similar advantage is that the medium does not interfere with itself. Within a group of people assembled together, several different conversations can be going on at the same time with relatively little interference. A light-based system also does not exclude that fraction of the population with impaired hearing (although of course it does exclude that fraction with impaired vision). Despite these advantages, it is not hard to see where a sound-based system scores over a light-based one. This is precisely because the light-based system requires the presence of light and that the sender of the message be in the line of sight of the receiver. Using sound, messages can be sent and received in the dark, and between people who are out of line of sight or who just happen not to be looking at each other. Using sound, one can communicate in an unlit hut or cave, or outdoors on a night when the moon is new or veiled by clouds. People walking in single file along a path can communicate with each other without the need to turn around. You can call back a child who has wandered away from home, or warn someone that a scorpion is about to sting their foot, regardless of where their eyes are turned. The advantages of a sound-based system over a light-based one seem decisive.

Just for completeness, we might briefly consider whether the other senses, apart from hearing and sight, could serve as a basis for a language. We can probably eliminate smell and taste at once, since humans cannot generate a range of tastes and smells on demand, out of which to create a complex sig- nalling system. Our sense of touch appears sensitive enough to use variation in localization, strength of contact, and movement as well as sequencing to form a language system, but one drawback is the necessity for message-sender and receiver to be within touching range. While this is not always unwelcome, it does limit the distance of possible transmission rather narrowly. Another dis- advantage is the inability to use this method to communicate with a number of people at the same time. Touch-based communication systems have found a role in communication for individuals with complex disabilities, but outside this special situation they could not compete with sound-based ones.

4.2   *Language is oral*

Not only do all human societies have a sound-based language, but all these sound-based languages use only what I will call rather loosely "oral sound" – ones made in and around the mouth and using what we generally call the vocal tract for their production (see Kohler, 1998). It's easy enough to generate sound at will in a variety of other areas. We can click our fingers, clap our hands, slap our thighs, stamp our feet, squeeze the air out from under the armpits, and so on. Why is it that our sound-based languages use only oral sound and not other possibilities, either alone or in combination with oral sound? We may speculate that, compared to using the various other possibilities, when the mouth is used it is easier to produce a suitable range of variation in sound with appropriate continuity. It is, however, hard to conceive how we could persuasively demon- strate these points to be so, since our available experimental population has such extensive prior practice in oral skills, and so much less in, say, distinctive thigh-slapping. A more readily demonstrable advantage of oral sounds is that considerable amplitude can be generated with comparatively little expenditure of energy. This is, as our military brethren might say, thanks to the use of air power. Passing the air we breathe through constrictions which require only very small muscle movements for their creation produces much louder acoustic output than can be produced by movements of similar magnitude elsewhere. Another definite advantage for oral sound is that when communication occurs in close proximity, that is, when the visual channel is used in support of the auditory one, attention can be directed to a limited area, i.e. the face. This is an area which gives a great deal of information about such things as emotional state and direction of visual attention, which can guide and influence the linguistic interaction. Another advantage of using only oral sounds is that this leaves the hands – the most obvious alternative means of producing sound – free to do something else at the same time, for example to carry a child or tools, or to work or demonstrate a craft. This advantage also counts in comparison with a light-based system using the hands, as those we know all do.

Of course, the oral channel is employed for more limited sound-based communication systems across a very large range of terrestrial vertebrate life forms besides humans. Some general capacity to make use of such signals is evidently very ancient but there is not one single evolutionary continuum involved, and the oral channel can be dispensed with when no longer appropriate, as in marine mammals. This raises some very interesting questions concerning precisely what aspects are directly biologically specified, what aspects are best understood as due to the self-organization which emerges in complex systems without being specified (Kauffman, 1993; de Boer, 2000), and what aspects remain free. It is obvious that humans inherited some use of vocal signals from pre-human ancestors, even if in humans this limited inheritance has developed into a very different kind of tool. The average human is born equipped with some clever circuitry to help figure out the connection between speech noises heard and the actions in the vocal tract required to produce a near-equivalent. Does this machinery also include something which determines which oral sounds are possible linguistic sounds and which are not? It is my intuition that some kinds of sounds, such as pure whistles or the Donald Duck kind of noises you can make by squeezing air into the cheek cavity through a lateral constriction, are inadmissible as linguistic sounds, while other sounds that are equally unknown to occur in any actual language – for example, linguo-labial trills – are possible, if unlikely, linguistic sounds. Is this intuition founded on anything more than the ability to describe the second class but not the first in the technical terminology of phonetics? We'll revisit this question again briefly later.

4.3   Language shows sequential variation

To construct a useful signalling system out of sound, there must be some differentiation between different parts of the signal in time. It appears that a basic organization of this differentiation of sound in all (spoken) languages consists of an alternation between louder and quieter levels of sound, with a period not too far from 150–200 ms (by informal survey!). This is what creates the notion of organization into syllables. Although any modulated sound stream will inevitably contain peaks and valleys of amplitude, there are ways in which one can be organized without this particular periodic pattern, for example, with long plateaus or with sequences of steps upwards or downwards. In fact, among the most discussed phonological universals are those which relate to sequence of consonants in syllable- or word-initial and final positions, and the broadest generalizations drawn are exactly those which organize complex onsets and codas into crescendo and decrescendo patterns respectively (Greenberg, 1966). The effort devoted to explaining these sequences perhaps distracts attention from the fact that such clusters are strikingly rare. In a survey of the lexical frequency of syllable types in a sample of 30 languages drawn from around the world, I found that 21 of them (70%) had no consonant clusters or a negligible number of them (frequency of less than 1%). In every one of these languages, at least 85% of the syllables counted had simple or zero onsets. Although many details are glossed over here, it is clear that this kind of syllable structure is most consistent with a fairly regular wave-like alternation of amplitude peaks and valleys. The occurrence and the timing of this pattern have been suggested to be related to a natural frequency of jaw movement (MacNeilage, 1998), which can be approximately equated with a comfortable mastication rate. However, as our parents rightly insisted, this does not mean that we *were* meant to talk and eat at the same time.

4.4   There is paradigmatic contrast

If moderately rapid alternation of amplitude peaks and valleys is a natural characteristic of speaking, perhaps as a result of synchronizing to a rhythm of the jaw, a natural segmentation in time emerges between those elements which form the amplitude peaks and those which form amplitude troughs, yielding essentially C and V positions. Unless a variety of qualitatively different sounds are available to fill these positions, it is not possible to create a vocabulary and to build the other components that make it possible to encode in sound a usefully rich enough range of messages (Studdert-Kennedy, 1998). The elements that go into these positions have been studied from several different universal perspectives. Two of these concern overall patterns of segment inventories, and the overall range of possible segments, respectively. The universal set of possible segments is more clearly constrained by "mechanical" considerations (at least in part), but patterns in the structure of segment inventories have usually been viewed as emerging from interactions of factors viewed in an "ecological" perspective. There are two old favorites in this realm, ease of articulation and ease of discrimination. The joint maximization of these factors, or related ways of expressing the importance of both motoric and auditory/perceptual encoding, have been implemented in models using an adaptive strategy. These fairly successfully predict the preferred patterns in vowel inventories of different sizes as observed in large cross-linguistic surveys (Lindblom, 1986; Schwartz *et al.*, 1997). More intriguing still are the successes in replicating these predictions when similar factors are attributed to sets of virtual robots in an interacting population (Berrah and Laboissiere, 1997; de Boer, 2000). In these latter experiments, different roles of the factors in acts of "speaking" and "listening" can be represented. A general feature of all these models is that they investigate the structure of systems with a given number of elements – for example, given a system of five vowels, they will select the particular arrangements of these in vowel space which cause the least offense to articulatory ease and discriminability. They approach the question of the optimal solution for a vocabulary of size *n*, but not the issue of what is an appropriate size for *n*, or "How much contrast is enough?"

Total segment inventory size clusters around a mean of 27 segments, but how large a vocabulary of distinct items can be generated in actual languages is in fact relatively little determined by the size of their segment inventory, given how much other variables, such as suprasegmental properties and word structure, contribute. Nonetheless, an apparently widely believed pseudo-universal holds that segment inventories display internal compensatory strategies to constrain "excessive" contrast. For example, an idea that seems as durable as the Great Eskimo Vocabulary Hoax is that a language with a small number of distinctive vowel contrasts will necessarily have a large number of consonants (and possibly vice versa although this seems to be less often insisted on). We can re-visit this idea from the vantage point of the expanded UPSID sample, which gives a good idea of how many consonants typically occur and what the range of variation is. As the histogram in Figure 4.3 shows, considerably over half the languages in the entire sample have consonant inventories containing between 15 and 24 segments. The mean falls at 22.5. A curve approximating the normal distribution is superimposed. The range of values shown on the figure is limited to 0–50 for comparability with Figure 4.4, but the percentages and the curve shown are calculated over the full range (only 6 languages in the set have more than 50 consonants). The most common size of a vowel system is 5 vowels, so those with fewer than 5 may be considered to be small. Figure 4.4 gives the histogram of the consonant inventories of just the 48 languages in the sample with 4 or fewer vowels. An even higher proportion of these inventories fall within the limits 15–24, and the mean is 22.4. None of these languages has more than 50 consonants. There is absolutely no tendency for languages with few vowels to have larger than average consonant inventories.

4.5   *There are constraints on segments*

Perhaps the most discussed type of phonetic or phonological language universal relates to segments. Here, there are both universal frameworks to consider, and patterns of relationship between segments. There is space for only very brief commentary here. An attempt to survey all the segmental contrasts known to occur was offered in *The Sounds of the World's Languages* (Ladefoged and Maddieson, 1996), with the overt suggestion that this provided a good approach

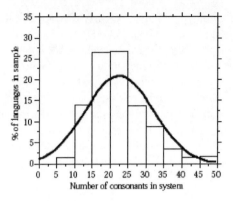

Figure 4.3   Histogram of number of consonants in expanded UPSID sample;
$n = 451$ languages.

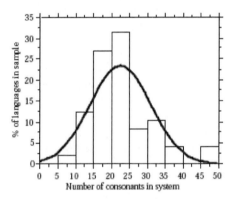

Figure 4.4   Histogram of number of consonants in languages with less than
5 vowels; $n = 48$ languages.

to the universe of possible contrasts. Phonological feature systems in most cases
also assume that there is something like a universal set of possible segments
or contrasts, and aim to restrict the descriptive power of the system so that
elements outside this set are excluded. This is particularly clear in the "feature
geometry" model of feature relations (e.g. Clements and Hume, 1995). Phonetic
and phonological approaches may have important differences, particularly in
assumptions about the "categoricity" of the elements concerned, but what is
common is that they provide a set of terms or features and a limited number of
ways of combining them. Segments that cannot be described using these terms
and combinations are assumed not just to be unknown but not to be possible
linguistic elements.

The sources of any restrictions noted are obviously diverse, and the interest lies in trying to understand their origins. Some are "mechanical" (hence, for example, the absence of pharyngeal nasals or velar clicks). Others relate to "ecological" factors like adequacy of contrast, both in acoustic output and representation as motor programs (e.g. no distinction is made between labiodentals with the lower lip slightly in front, just below, or slightly behind the upper teeth). Neither type of consideration rules out combining linguo-labial place with lingual trill manner so there is no reason to consider such to be impossible linguistic sounds, even though unattested. It is not, however, clear that they rule out what I called "Donald Duck" cheek sounds either. These use pulmonic air squeezed through a narrow lateral aperture so as to generate a vibration somewhat like the voicing vibration of the vocal folds. The fundamental frequency and other characteristics of this vibration can be varied, and the timbre modified by varying the configuration of the lips, the cheeks, and so on. This system is quite efficient: the sound output is quite loud and requires neither great effort of the articulators (which are in close to the same position as for ordinary laterals) nor high volume of air flow. In short, here is an apparently good oral source of acoustic energy which human language seems to neglect entirely (except for cartoon voices). Our phonetic classificatory system has no labels for this source (it's not a lateral trill because trills by definition have a low enough rate of vibration for each cycle to be heard as a separate beat). And neither is it modeled in any of the computational vocal tract models I have seen. So it is effectively dismissed without evaluation in most studies using an emergent paradigm. Kohler (1998) suggests we should understand the limits on possible speech sounds as arising from the fact that "speech is . . . an adaptation of the pre-existent anatomy and physiology of the vegetative system" used for "breathing, protection of the breathing system, stabilization of the rib cage, swallowing, sucking, chewing," and hence language can use "only those noise productions . . . that are related to the basic mechanisms already used for these non-speech functions." My sense is that the sound source I am talking about here is no more remote from these basic vegetative functions than, say, a tongue-tip trill.

Other segmental universals concern relations of segments within systems, including holistic patterns of distribution within subsets of segments, such as vowel systems. Many segmental universals concern relations expressed as "markedness," between segments or between the attributes of segments (Greenberg, 1966; Ferguson, 1966). There are some well-known universals of this type concerning voicing in different classes of segments: in obstruent classes, voiceless segments occur more frequently in consonant inventories than voiced ones; in sonorant classes, voiced segments are more frequent. Moreover, there is a strong implicational relationship such that, in general, the less frequent type will only be found in an inventory if the more frequent one appears there. Some phonological feature theories reflect this distribution as two different ways of marking the voiced/voiceless contrast: in obstruents, as presence or absence of the feature [voice], in sonorants, as the absence vs. presence of [expanded glottis], the feature used to distinguish aspirated from unaspirated obstruents. Thus, both the less frequent types are given a more complex structure with an additional feature present. It is certainly possible that this is a reasonable analog to the way the categorical information on these segments is stored in the brain, but the universals related to voicing are more nuanced than the two-way representation allows. The ratio of voiceless to voiced fricatives is much higher than that of voiceless to voiced plosives, and the ratio of voiced sonorants to voiceless sonorants is higher still. Moreover, a number of significant interactions between voicing and place of articulation have been noted. I will revisit just one of these. Considering just the three major places of articulation, bilabial, dental/alveolar, and velar, in a series of voiced plosives the velar place is more likely to be "missing" than either of the other two, but in a series of voiceless plosives the bilabial place is more likely to be missing. In the sample of 451 languages in UPSID, there are 40 inventories (including Temne, Ket, Thai, Pomo, and Huave) which lack /g/ when it might have been expected (because there are other velar segments and other voiced stops), and 38 (including Yoruba, Ket, Arabic, Warao, and Yareba) which lack /p/ when it might have been expected. For comparison, there are 15 "missing" cases of /d/, 9 of /b/, 3 of /k/, and 1 of /t/. The "missing /g/" and "missing /p/" cases seem to be frequent enough and sufficiently widespread across languages families and geographical areas for them to represent more than a chance pattern. Thus, while voiced plosives are less preferred in general, there seems to be something extra which disfavors /g/, and similarly something which makes /p/ less preferable than voiceless plosives at the other principal places.

Analysis of the structure of the speech organs, air-flow patterns in the vocal tract, the functioning of the auditory system, and other components of the overall human organism often provide a basis for understanding the directionality of such preferences (e.g. Ohala, 1983), each considered in isolation. To understand why voiceless fricatives are preferable to voiced ones, we can appeal to the fact that, to generate both voicing and frication, two separate ratios of air pressures have to be maintained within fairly critical limits (among other requirements). We may conclude that voiced frication is a difficult maneuver to perform, and hence tends to be avoided on "ease of articulation" grounds. Or we may argue that, given typical human performance limitations, the criticality of the requirements means that intended voiced fricatives will often lose voicing or frication. It matters little, since several lines of reasoning all concord in suggesting that voiced fricatives are indeed an inferior type of linguistic sound to voiceless fricatives. But we are a long way from being able to integrate individual explanations into a larger picture, where the relative importance of inherent effort, performance limitations, and all the other relevant considerations are taken jointly into account. This wonderful theory of the future will explain both why voiced fricatives are more frequent than voiceless sonorants, and why "missing" /g/ and /p/ are about equally frequent!

4.6   *There are patterns in phonetic detail*

A good many very strictly phonetic universals pertaining to segments have also been noted. These universals concern details of production, acoustics, etc., having little to do with the basic contrastive structure of phonological systems. These include "local" patterns of timing and fundamental frequency (e.g., closure duration for bilabial plosives is generally a little longer than for velar ones under matching conditions, and high vowels have a slightly higher F0 than low vowels, other things being equal). Others of the same sort are described in Maddieson (1997). These universals cannot yet be based on large samples, since the necessary data are not available for many languages. This argues for caution in accepting their universality. It also increases the uncertainty about their appropriate formulation. For example, the two mentioned above are sometimes expressed as general correlations between closure duration and a scale of frontness of stop articulation, or between F0 and a scale of vowel height. A scalar relationship might well be appropriate for the F0 / vowel height relationship, although it remains difficult to show, but is more doubtful in the case of closure duration and frontness of articulation, since stops at places in between velar and bilabial have very varied durations.

Some phonetic universals are so well understood that we no longer think of them as empirical observations about languages, but simply as part of an overall phonetic theory. It is a universal that vowel formants are typically lower in the immediate vicinity of a bilabial consonant than elsewhere. Since this follows from general acoustic principles incorporated into our understanding of articulatory/acoustic relations, no-one is likely to find it a good use of their time to conduct a survey of this phenomenon. However, we do not have a good understanding of why plosive closure durations should vary with place, or F0 with vowel height. In such cases, surveys are more obviously valuable so that the nature of the pattern can be reliably established before attempts at explanation are made.

Duration and fundamental frequency have important distinctive roles in language, e.g. for contrasts of quantity and tone respectively, and the "local" effects are superimposed on top of much larger contrastive differences. Superimposition of place-related duration differences on a single/geminate stop distinction is illustrated in Figure 4.5. Since the mean closure durations for geminates are much longer than for singletons, it is obvious that closure durations can be "voluntarily" adjusted over wide ranges; yet, within a quantity, they are not

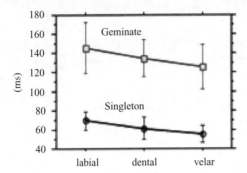

Figure 4.5 Closure durations of intervocalic plosives in Berber; means of four speakers. See Louali and Maddieson (1999) for details.

adjusted to be equal at different places of articulation. We can note that the *absolute* difference in mean duration between single and geminate pairs at different places is more uniform (70–76 ms) than the *ratio* of the differences (2.09–2.49), meaning that an additive model is better than a multiplicative one for predicting these geminate durations. Whatever causes the place-related differences is not perturbed by this addition, suggesting that it might relate to built-in delays in the implementation of motor commands to the different articulators, rather than to, say, differences in their natural frequencies. More and deeper studies on duration and timing would help clarify issues such as these, and where the divisions between universal and language-particular phenomena fall.

4.7   There is variability

The final class of phonetic universals to be mentioned here concern the systematic use of variation. Position in prosodic units, intended clarity of speech, and relative redundancy of information conveyed are among factors shown to contribute to controlled variation within repetitions of the same word. Such transformations (Lindblom *et al.*, 1992; Lindblom, 1998) of the same linguistic material illustrate the adaptive flexibility of speaking. Some particular transforms noted include lengthening in phrase-final position, more energetic articulation in initial position, and more coarticulation in low-information contexts. The fact of plasticity which this reflects is itself an important language universal. However, which particular transforms are truly widespread is something we will only know when more data are in. Increased coarticulation in low-information contexts looks likely to be more general than, say, phrase-final lengthening, since the phrase-final position is in many languages a position of extreme reduction marked by vowel shortening, devoicing, or deletion (e.g. in Ciluba).

5   Final remarks

This chapter has only lightly scratched the surface of what might be said about phonetic and phonological universals. I have emphasized the importance of basing universals on a sample of a sufficient number of diverse languages, but stressed also that universals are not so much subjects of importance in themselves but are the preface to the formulation of ideas. A fruitful – in fact, necessary – perspective for formulation of many ideas concerning the origin of language universals is the placing of language in its biological setting, considering both the context of its early evolution and the capacities and limits of the human organism as it exists today.

5   Morphological universals

Andrew Spencer

1   Introduction

The history of morphology in grammatical theory is somewhat checkered. For the American structuralist tradition, morphology was central. In the Chomskyan generative tradition, syntax is central and morphology has been either relegated to phonology and syntax or expelled from linguistics altogether. There is thus a good deal of controversy about the status of morphology itself. It is not even entirely clear what the subject matter of morphology is. Informally, we tend to think of the domain of morphology as the word, but the concept of *word* is notoriously difficult to pin down and it is clear that the pre-theoretical notion corresponds to several distinct and partially independent technical notions (see Dixon and Aikhenvald, 2002a, for a recent review of the issues). On the other hand, for American structuralists such as Bloomfield (1933), morphology seems to have been about morphemes. However, the morpheme concept is no more secure than the word concept, and the utility of the morpheme has been flatly denied by many recent theorists.

Even without these conceptual uncertainties, we must be careful to distinguish typological claims about morphology (words or morphemes) from claims about other aspects of grammar which are often reflected in morphology. Consider the expression of number: oversimplifying considerably, we can say that if a language has a trial number it has a dual; if a language has a dual number it has a singular–plural distinction (Corbett, 2000, 38f.). This universal applies mainly to morphological systems but number can be represented suppletively on pronouns ($I \sim we$) and can be expressed in Noun Phrases by means of particles, clitics, or other auxiliary elements (pp. 136f.), rather than by inflected word forms. Therefore, the Number Hierarchy is not a universal about morphology specifically but rather about grammaticalized feature systems which are often, but not always, realized morphologically.

I shall discuss claims for universals governing the form of words, without specifying precisely what I mean by "word." In most languages, there will be a

The final version of the chapter was written while I was in receipt of a Leverhulme Trust / British Academy Senior Research Fellowship. I am grateful to both organizations for their support.

core set of expressions which differ from phrases and which can be recognized as "words" by linguists and by naive native speakers alike. The core universals should therefore be stated over such expressions. After that, it will be possible for researchers to consider the borderline cases to determine whether or not the universals are more generally valid. Nonetheless, it has to be admitted that there are difficulties in establishing universals of word structure when there is so much room for disagreement about wordhood, and when individual descriptive grammars are not entirely consistent.

This chapter is organized as follows. First, I summarize the main questions in morphological typology and universals. Next, in Section 3, I discuss some key concepts in morphology. A number of notions which are sometimes taken for granted turn out to be problematical and this inevitably complicates the search for universals. I then look at some of those problems which are most relevant for the search for universals, first conceptual problems, Section 4, and then problems of segmentation at the level of morphological substance, Section 5. In Section 6, I turn to the topic which has generated most discussion within morphological typology, the ordering of morphological units. The final section presents brief summary conclusions.

Much of the discussion will be about morphology, not about universals. I make no apology for this. First, there remains widespread ignorance outside morphological circles of some of the conceptual unclarity surrounding morphology, and, second, it is impossible to understand most of the controversy surrounding morphological universals without understanding the controversies surrounding morphological structure generally.

2   Approaches to universals

2.1   *Traditional approaches to morphological typology*

The search for linguistic universals is intimately connected with the search for a global typology of languages and language structures, and so I shall begin by mentioning the earliest such attempts at typology. Textbooks generally draw the following traditional distinctions among languages in terms of their word structure:

- isolating – analytic constructions only;
- agglutinating – one:one relation between form and meaning (see below);
- inflectional (fusional) – several inflectional morphosyntactic properties "fused" into one form or distributed across several parts of the word form (deviations from agglutination);
- polysynthetic (Noun-incorporating) – the language permits Noun–Verb compounds with a finite verb, giving expressions such as *he-bear-killed* (*with a spear*).

As pointed out in Spencer (1991, 38f.), there are problems with such a typology (though Plank, 1999, presents an interesting and sophisticated defense of certain aspects of it). Perhaps the fundamental difficulty is that it seems that it is morphological subsystems which have these properties, rather than languages. For instance, Chukchee has agglutinating derivation, fusional inflection, and productive Noun-incorporation (polysynthesis). However, in addition it has many analytic constructions, more characteristic of isolating languages.

A further problem with this typology is that it presupposes that we have a prior characterization of "word form" for all languages and a prior characterization of "morpheme." A notion of *word form* is required in defining "isolating language" in order to ensure that we can distinguish, say, a tightly bound syntactic construction consisting of tense auxiliary and verb from a verb with a tense prefix (or proclitic). Similarly, to characterize polysynthetic languages, we need to distinguish a N–V compound from a tightly knit phrase consisting of a single noun word and a verb form. In many cases where such languages have been studied, these questions become very controversial. The problems associated with the morpheme concept will be touched upon below.

2.2   Other approaches

There are several aspects of morphological organization which have attracted the attention of linguists interested in universal claims, though not all of these research traditions have been explicitly couched in the framework of universals or typology research. The most effort has been devoted to investigating principles for the ordering of morphemes and I discuss this in detail in Section 6 below.

A smaller number of studies have investigated the structure of (inflectional) paradigms. Particularly important has been the work of Carstairs (1987). In many languages there are inflectional classes, so that, say, the genitive plural form of a Noun might have one of three different markers depending on whether it belongs to declension 1, 2, or 3. Now, if all the markers for a given declension are different it's obvious that we're dealing with distinct classes, but in many cases there is overlap. How do we distinguish different inflectional classes? Suppose that one feature set, say, accusative plural, has three distinct markers, a, b, c. This means that there must be at least three different inflectional classes. If there are no other feature combinations with more than three markers, then three is the smallest number of inflectional classes we can have for this language. Now suppose that the language has the following markers: nominative singular – d, e; nominative plural – f, g; and accusative singular – h, i. Clearly, this set gives us the possibility of a large number of classes (twenty-four in fact). However, Carstairs argues that languages always have exactly the minimum number of classes, in this case, three (his Paradigm Economy Principle).

Carstairs also studied languages in which a word is inflected with several affixes in a string. If we think of affixes being added one by one from the stem outwards then we might expect conditioned allomorphy to be local, in the sense that it is sensitive to the form of the last added affix but not, say, to the form of the next affix to be added. This is the Peripherality Constraint. Interestingly, there are a number of counter-examples to this condition, some of which Carstairs analyzes in depth. However, it is probably fair to say that the Peripherality Constraint hasn't won widespread acceptance amongst students of inflectional morphology, and Stump (2001, 163) provides explicit arguments against it.

In more recent work, Carstairs-McCarthy[1] has proposed a "No Blur Condition" (see Carstairs-McCarthy, 1994; Cameron-Faulkner and Carstairs-McCarthy, 2000), which states that every word form either serves to identify its word class uniquely or gives no information about lexical class. In the latter case we would say that the word form exhibits default marking, that is, the most general marking within the lexical class for that particular set of features. Thus, a given genitive plural form would either be uniquely identifiable as, say, the gen. pl. of the third declension, or would be the most general gen. pl. form, occurring in several declensions. However, in order to get this to work, it is necessary to make a number of controversial assumptions about what affixes "mean." Moreover, there are a number of inflectional systems, such as the Noun class systems of certain Daghestan languages, which seem to be counter-examples both to Paradigm Economy and to the No Blur Condition (see Stump, 2005).

One recent study (Baker, 1996) is unusual, in that it takes some of the questions raised in traditional typology and casts them within the framework of Principles and Parameters syntax. Baker argues that there is a specific group of languages which show productive Noun-incorporation and that these languages all exhibit a cluster of apparently unrelated morphosyntactic properties: they show no subject–object asymmetries, they don't have proper reflexives, they don't have quantifiers which modify Noun Phrases directly (D-quantifiers), and they do not use adpositional phrases as arguments. In addition, their verbs have no non-finite (non-agreeing) forms that can take arguments, and only allow causatives to be formed, if at all, from unaccusative verbs. Remarkably, Baker is able to link all these properties to a single polysynthesis parameter: "Every argument of a head element must be related to a morpheme in the word containing that head", where "related to" means by agreement or by incorporation (p. 14).

In simplified terms, the polysynthesis parameter means that some languages pack essentially all their syntactic relations into the word form, so that phrases external to the Verb are adjuncts or modifiers rather than arguments. This is

---

[1] The Carstairs of Carstairs (1987) and the Carstairs-McCarthy of the later references are the same person.

a bold and ingenious hypothesis, though it is unclear how exactly it can be made compatible with recent versions of Principles and Parameters theory arising from Chomsky's (1995) Minimalist Program. Some of the properties are also found, of course, in other languages which are not polysynthetic, which raises the question of what exactly the polysynthesis parameter is a parameter of. Finally, in at least two of Baker's polysynthetic languages it seems that there are infinitives which can take arguments (Chukchee, see Spencer, 1999; and Rembarrnga, Nordlinger and Saulwick, 2002), so these would be clear counter-examples to one part of the parameter. Nonetheless, Baker's work is very thought-provoking and it would be interesting to know what, if anything, lies behind the correlations he discusses.

Turning to more mainstream typological literature, there have been relatively few recent studies devoted specifically to morphological typology, though a number of the chapters in the second volume of Booij, Lehmann, Mugdan, and Skopetas' *Handbook* (2004), deal with typology, and several of the chapters in Haspelmath *et al.* (2001) discuss the typology of predominantly morphological phenomena. Discussion of some of the history of morphological typology can be found in these references. In addition, there have been a number of studies of primarily morphological phenomena which have established interesting correlations and proposed hierarchies of various sorts to account for the observed tendencies. These include agreement (Corbett, 1983; Barlow and Ferguson, 1988), gender (Corbett, 1991), number (Corbett, 2000), tense and aspect (Dahl, 1985), and action nominalizations (Koptjevskaja-Tamm, 1993).

The Konstanz Universals database[2] (Plank and Filiminova, 2000) contains a number of putative morphological universals, and the Surrey Morphology Group[3] under Greville Corbett is engaged on a number of important typological projects, including syncretisms and agreement. Further details of the Konstanz and Surrey projects can be found on their websites.

3   Some basic concepts

3.1   Morpheme concept

In a tradition which dates back at least to the work of Baudouin de Courtenay, it has been common to assume that words are made up of morphemes, that is, roots and affixes which serve as Saussurean signs: the arbitrary pairing of form and meaning. This is relatively uncontroversial in the case of roots. For affixes, such as the English plural suffix, it means that we must assume that there is a

---

[2] Konstanz Universals Archive: http://ling.uni-konstanz.de/pages/proj/sprachbau.htm.
[3] Surrey Morphology Group: www.surrey.ac.uk/LIS/SMG/.

lexical entry along the lines of (1) telling us the pronunciation, meaning, and combinatorial possibilities of the plural marker:

(1)   MOR /z/: {z, ɪz, s}
       SYN Nroot____
       SEM PLURAL[N]

In this entry, I've given the basic form and various phonologically conditioned allomorphs (though even this analysis is not uncontroversial). The strongest claim to make about morphemes is that all grammatical properties expressed by single word forms correspond to a morpheme. This is the essence of (2):

(2)   *Agglutination Principle*:
       A morphologically complex word is a sign such that
       (a) the MOR component results from compounding the MOR
           components of the lexical entries of component morphemes and
       (b) the SEM component is the unification of the SEM values of the
           lexical entries of component morphemes.

Given (2) and the obvious lexical entry for CAT we get (3) as a partial representation of *cats*:

(3)   MOR kat + s
       SEM PLURAL[CAT]

3.2   Inflection and derivation

Inflectional morphology gives rise to the set of word forms which express purely grammatical concepts such as agreement, tense, number, and so on. Inflections are usually obligatory for a word class. For instance, all nouns in English are supposed to have a plural and all verbs are supposed to have a past tense.

Derivational morphology serves to create new words by combining a bound morpheme with a root morpheme. We might say that *driver* is the MOR component of a word meaning (informally) [PERSON WHO [DRIVES]], and that it has a suffix-*er* whose lexical entry is (4):

(4)   MOR er
       SEM PERSON WHO [*VERBS*]

The entry in (4) is not that of a word proper and so *driver* differs in structure from compounds such as *delivery boy*.

3.3   Lexeme concept

The term *word* is multiply ambiguous. For instance, we can say that the set {dog, dogs} consists of two words, but in another sense we could say that these are just two distinct forms of a single word, DOG. This latter notion of "word," corresponding to the ordinary notion of "dictionary entry," is usually denoted by the term "lexeme." Thus, {dog, dogs} are the singular and plural forms respectively of the lexeme DOG.

3.4   Affixation, compounding, and cliticization

Compounding results from concatenating two existing words into an expression that has the properties of a word rather than a phrase. Affixes are bound forms and never occur unless attached, directly or indirectly, to a root. Affixes attach only to specific classes of root – for instance, only to noun roots. Their placement is therefore determined by selectional principles which appeal to such lexical classes. Clitics, however, attach "promiscuously" to words of any class. Their placement appeals to syntactic categories, such as "the right edge of a Noun Phrase," as in the English possessive clitic: *[the Queen of England]'s hat.*

4   Some conceptual problems in morphology

4.1   Morphemes and lexemes

The brief characterizations given in the preceding section are extremely simple and well known from any introductory textbook of linguistics. Moreover, they seem to be fairly obvious concepts, scarcely in need of justification. It is therefore a little disturbing to find that, on the one hand, they are all extremely controversial and, on the other hand, they are mutually incompatible. In particular, the morpheme concept is incompatible with the lexeme concept and the related inflection/derivation distinction. The reason is that all morphology is a kind of compounding if we accept the Agglutination Principle. Thus, we can"t say that *cats* is a form of a lexeme CAT, any more than we can say that the expression *two cats* is the dual number form of a lexeme C A T. The only difference between the plural /z/ or the /er/ suffix on the one hand, and words such as *cat* or *drive* on the other, is that *cat/drive* can occur on their own. However, in many languages even this would not be true: namely, in those languages where all roots are bound and have to be inflected to form a word.

4.2   The lexeme concept

The lexeme concept fits in well with the inflection/derivation distinction: inflected forms are word forms of a lexeme, while derivation creates new lexemes. However, the inflection/derivation distinction is very difficult to draw. One difficulty arises when we assume, as many linguists seem to do, that inflections themselves have a meaning. If the meaning of the form *cats* is in some sense [PLURAL[CAT]], then why don't we say that [PLURAL] is the SEM value of a separate lexeme, in the same way we would presumably call CAT-LIKE a separate lexeme: [SIMILAR-TO[CAT]]. Booij (1994, 1996) argues that there are two sorts of inflection, contextual inflection and inherent inflection. Contextual inflection is determined entirely by the syntax, as in the case of Adjective–Noun agreement. Inherent inflection is inflection which seems to have a meaning of its own, such as plural number or past tense. This allows us to distinguish contextual inflection from derivation in a principled way, but it is still very difficult to find a principled distinction between inherent inflection and derivation. For instance, in English we would normally regard a word form such as *re-write* as the result of derivational morphology, with the prefix adding the meaning of [AGAIN[VERB]] or some such. However, what is to stop us saying that *re-write* is actually the Iterative Aspect form of the Verb WRITE? Unfortunately, most inflection seems to be of the inherent type (and even agreement inflection can sometimes give the impression of bearing meaning).

These problems are related to the difficulty of individuating lexemes. By what criteria do we say that RE-WRITE is a different lexeme from WRITE (albeit a related lexeme)? Questions also surround compounding and the lexeme concept. Is *train driver* a single lexeme or two lexemes? If it is one lexeme, how does it relate to the apparently syntactic expression *driver of trains*? If it is two lexemes, should we not treat compounding more as a special kind of syntax? Similarly, is the *broke* in *Tom broke the vase* and *The vase broke* a form of the one lexeme or two closely related ones? How can we tell in a principled fashion?

4.3   The morpheme-as-sign concept

In the strictest interpretation of the morpheme concept, any occurrence of a morpheme in a word should express just one meaning or feature value, and any meaning or feature value expressed within a word should be expressed by just one morpheme. However, it is well known that languages (including so-called "agglutinating" languages) frequently show deviations from this one:one pairing of form and meaning. The logically possible deviations are listed in (5):

(5)   Deviations from agglutination (one:one mapping between form and meaning)
   • cumulation: one:many
   • extended exponence: many:one
   • zero exponence: zero:many
   • meaningless morphs: many:zero

Cumulation is found when a single affix conveys two or more feature values/meanings. For instance, in Spanish *como* "I eat," the *-o* ending signals simultaneously 1sg, Present (vs. Preterite), "Indicative" (vs. Subjunctive). Extended exponence is found when a single feature specification is realized jointly by two or more affixes or by an affix and root allomorph combination. In *comía* "I was eating," the Imperfect tense is signaled by the *-i* suffix, but the person/number agreement also serves to indicate that the tense is Imperfect. (In addition, *-i* cumulates "Imperfect" with "2nd or 3rd conjugation.") In zero exponence, we find no affix where we would expect one, given the rest of the paradigm. Russian Nouns inflect for case and number. The genitive plural of *stol*, "table" is *stolov*, while the genitive plural of *nasekomoe* "insect" is *nasekomyx*. However, the Class 2 word *lampa* "lamp" has a genitive plural with no ending: *lamp*. Thus, a zero ending signals simultaneously "genitive," "plural," and "2nd declension." Finally, it is not uncommon to find morphemes to which absolutely no meaning can be given. A simple example occurs with certain sorts of compound in many languages. Thus, English has so-called "neo-classical" compounds built up out of Latin and especially Greek elements. In most cases, the two components are separated by a formative *-o-*, an intermorph, whose only function is to serve as a linker. It conveys no meaning of its own: *cyt-o-phage, phag-o-cyte*.

An example of the kind of non-agglutinating morphology that we encounter in inflection is given in (6), a form of the Spanish Verb *comer* "eat":

(6)   *comería* "I/he/she would eat"
        com   e   r   í   a
        EAT   2nd conj inf impf. (2/3 conj)   1sg/3sg (1 conj?)

Clearly, given the usual interpretations of the component morphemes, we can't build up the feature composition of the whole word by unifying the features of the morphemes. In particular, we would have to answer the following questions:
- Why does a finite form contain an infinitive morpheme?
- Why does a conditional mood form have an imperfect tense morpheme?
- Where does the specification of conditional mood come from, given that none of the individual component morphemes can be said to "mean" conditional mood?

The same situation is found in derivational morphology, as witnessed by the English examples in (7):

(7)   *Derivation*
        Form: understand = under + stand (cf. *understood*)
        Meaning: understand ≠ under + stand (cf. *understood*)
        Cf. undertake ≠ under + take, withhold ≠ with + hold, withstand ≠ with + stand, and so on.

The problem with the examples in (6, 7) is that we have non-compositional morphology: the meaning or feature content of the whole cannot be predicted from any sensible characterization of the meaning of the parts. These words behave therefore like idioms in syntax and the "morphemes" *under*, *stand*, and so on are actually cranberry morphs (or cranberry morphemes). In point of fact, most of the commonly cited derivational morphology of languages such as English tends to be non-compositional (though this fact is sometimes obscured because linguists often downplay the degree of non-compositionality). What this means is that a great many "morphemes," in inflection or derivation, have no readily identifiable "meaning/function" (see also Spencer, 2000).

Frequently occurring compounds show a strong tendency to develop special lexicalized meanings which make them at least partly non-compositional. Thus, in the case of *blackbird*, *textbook*, *nervous system*, and perhaps thousands of other English examples we can discern a semantic "head" element of the compound, which contributes its meaning in a compositional fashion: *bird*, *book*, *system*. But the modifier element is not semantically compositional. A blackbird doesn't have to be black, and it is very difficult to see what *text* can refer to in *textbook*. As for *nervous* in *nervous system*, this is an almost unique usage (cf. **nervous fiber*, **nervous ending*, **nervous transmitter*, **nervous potential*, **nervous spike*, **nervous clamp*, **nervous synapse*, etc., etc., as compared with *nerve fiber* and so on).

Interestingly, it turns out to be difficult, if not impossible, to identify cases of cumulation, extended exponence, and zero forms in uncontroversial instances of compounding. This suggests that inflectional/derivational affixation is not really the same as compounding.

The conclusion drawn by many, if not most, morphologists is that the morpheme concept is inappropriate except as a crude approximation. Instead, students of inflectional systems, in particular, adopt a realizational approach to morphology. On this approach, morphemes are taken to be markers serving to realize some feature specification or collection of features. They are not listed lexical entries in their own right. In this respect, we can say that all morphemes (not just intermorphemes such as *-o-* or cranberries such as *under + stand*) are, strictly speaking, meaningless, in the sense that their grammatical representation does not include a specification of a semantics or feature content. Such realizational models are "top-down" models in the sense that we start with a complete feature characterization of the word form we wish to generate and then apply a set of articulated rules which tell us how to construct an appropriate word form for a given lexeme or lexical class. This contrasts with the "bottom-up" morpheme-based account in which morphemes and their meanings are combined and the meaning of the whole computed from its parts.

Realizational models are often associated with the notion of *paradigm*. A paradigm is a set of forms associated with the various permitted combinations of feature values found in a language. The paradigm itself is therefore a derived concept, though a useful one. Another important concept, related to that of the paradigm, is that of *default realization*. A given feature set often has several possible realizations depending on the lexical class. All but one of these can be thought of as "special cases" and the remaining realization is then the general or default case. For instance, Spanish verbs are either irregular or fall into one of three conjugation classes. The endings of irregular verbs and verbs of the 3rd and 2nd conjugation can all be thought of as "special cases" in varying degrees, while the endings of verbs of the 1st conjugation are the "default" case. Varying degrees of generality are handled by nested defaults. Thus, we might wish to say that, by default, if a verb has an infinitive form *V-er* or *V-ir* then its 1sg present indicative form is *V-o*. However, there is a subgeneralization for verbs in *-cer/-cir*: *conocer* "know" ~ *conozco*, *merecer* "deserve" ~ *merezco*. This 1sg form in *-ozco/-ezco* can be thought of as a sub-default. This itself can be overridden, as in *cocer* ~ *cuezo* or *mecer* ~ *mezo*. Some endings are valid for nearly all Verbs, as is the case with the 1pl *-mos* ending. The rule governing *-mos* suffixation therefore just needs to mention the features "1pl" and does not need to specify tense, mood, or conjugation features.

In a language like English, paradigm structure can help solve conceptual puzzles which arise from morpheme-based theories. Thus, in order for a strict morpheme theory to be able to label the form *cat* as a singular form, it is necessary to assume a zero singular morpheme (presumably a suffix). Such zeros have been considered suspect since they were first proposed. In a paradigm-based theory, however, we can say that the paradigm has two cells, one for singular, one for plural. The plural cell is accounted for by the *-s* suffixation rule, but there's no special rule for singular. We therefore have to resort to the default form, which for English is the bare root. Thus, *cat* as an uninflected word form is interpreted as filling the "singular" cell of the Noun paradigm, without the need for any other stipulation and without the need for dubious zeros (see Stump, 1998, 41, for discussion of the problem of zeros in the context of a recent theory which seeks to defend the morpheme concept).

4.4   Inflection and derivation

There are well-known difficulties in drawing the distinction between inflection and derivation (see Plank, 1994, for a summary). The difficulties which are relevant for the subsequent discussion are summarized here.

Inflection is supposed to be obligatory, but there are numerous cases where it is difficult to define what we mean by "obligatory," and we often find that words lack inflected forms which they ought to have. First, there are semantic or lexical restrictions. For instance, it is generally said that mass terms have no plural form while *pluralia tantum* nouns such as scissors have no singular form. The Verb *forgo* lacks past tense and past participle forms: **forgoed, *forwent*. Defective paradigms are actually quite common in morphologically rich languages, often without any obvious phonological or semantic justification (see Morin, 1997, for a detailed discussion of this in French). Quite commonly, we see inflectional relics from earlier stages of the language but only for a small number of lexical items. For instance, of all Verbs in English, only the Verb BE retains separate forms for person and number in the present tense and for number in the past tense.

We normally think of a lexeme as belonging to a single word class (Noun, Verb, Adjective, and so on). If inflection provides forms of a single lexeme, then we do not expect inflectional morphology to change word class. However, we often encounter transpositions, that is, morphology which serves solely to change word class. The most well-known types are action nominalizations and participles from Verbs (v $\Rightarrow$ N and v $\Rightarrow$ A), but in principle all three major categories can be transposed into each other (for discussion, see Beard, 1995; Haspelmath, 1996; Spencer, 2005). Quite often the resulting transposed category retains some of the morphosyntactic properties of the original category, to the extent that it is very difficult to know just how to label the derived word form. An example of this is provided in the Spanish nominal infinitive *al comer las manzanas* "eating the apples," where a Verb form which takes a direct object nonetheless takes a definite article and is the object of a Preposition, as though it were a Noun. Linguists tend to be divided on whether to call such morphology "inflection," "derivation," or something else.

There are many instances of morphology which has the appearance of being inflectional but which seems to create new lexemes, by adding a semantic predicate to the basic lexeme. Argument structure alternations are a rich source. A typical array of such alternations is found in the Bantu languages, exemplified here from Swahili (Ashton, 1944, 214f.):

(8)   Swahili argument structure derivatives
        funga   "bind, tie"
        fungia   "bind for someone" (applicative)
        fungwa   "get bound" (passive)
        fungika   "be bound" (neuter, stative)
        fungisha   "cause to bind" (causative)
        fungana   "bind each other" (reciprocal)
        (and others, *fungama* "be in fixed position," *fungua, funguka*
        "untie," etc.)

Some of these forms, for instance the causative, seem to add lexical content (and, indeed, add a participant, the causer). On the other hand, the passive seems to be like the English participial passive in being solely a valency-altering device which does not change the lexical meaning at all. The neuter/stative form is interesting. This is comparable in its semantics and its morphosyntax to the English middle construction (*These shirts wash easily*). Now arguably the English (and Dutch) middle constructions *do* add lexical content (see Ackema and Schoorlemmer, 1994, on Dutch/English) and this would appear to be true of Romance and Bantu languages, too.

Bantu verbs often have a reciprocal form distinct from the ordinary reflexive. The reflexive is generally expressed by a reflexive pronominal object prefix (*ji* in the case of Swahili). Mchombo (1993) shows that in Chichewa the reflexive prefix *zi* is effectively an incorporated pronominal which realizes a syntactically represented reflexive object. In this respect, the reflexive construction looks inflectional (in the same way that agreement morphology is inflectional). On the other hand, the reciprocal suffix behaves rather more like a derivational form: there is no evidence that the reciprocal suffix realizes a syntactically active reciprocal Pronoun.

Finally, many languages distinguish grammatical aspects in the verb morphology. In Spanish conjugation, aspect is intimately bound up with tense, and it is not possible to separate out tense and aspect markers in synthetic Verb forms. By contrast, in Slavic languages we find that non-stative Verbs appear in one of two forms, a perfective and imperfective aspect. Perfective aspect forms generally convey completed events while imperfective forms convey on-going or repeated events. Linguists have therefore tried to assimilate the distinction to a telic/atelic or bounded/unbounded semantic distinction of the kind often discussed in the context of verbal lexical semantics. However, there are serious problems in doing this. As a result, linguists are divided as to whether to treat Slavic aspect as inflection or derivation. Matters get more complicated in that these languages have rich morphological resources for modifying the aspectual meaning of a Verb (so-called *Aktionsarten* or "modes of action"). Thus, we find affixes which add meanings such as inception, completion, repetition, partial action, attenuated action, excessive action, and so on (see Forsyth, 1970, for a survey of these issues in Russian). The problem is that the various criteria which have been proposed for distinguishing inflection from derivation give equivocal results when applied to Slavic "modes of action." The question is even more complex in other language groups where such "modes of action" are more firmly grammaticalized, such as Athapaskan (see Rice, 2000, for extended discussion).

I characterized derivational morphology as the creation of new lexemes from old lexemes, and so derivation implies a degree of lexical relatedness between input and output. However, there are innumerable cases in which there is no compositional semantic relationship between input and output. This was illustrated with *understand* above. From a morphological point of view, it is clear that *understand* contains the Verb form *stand*, because it shares the idiosyncratic past tense / past participle allomorphy of that base Verb: *understood*. This phenomenon is extremely common. Just consider all the Spanish Verbs with prefixes such as *con/com-*, *in/im-*, *de-*, *re-*, *pro-*, *per-*, and so on. There are large numbers of Verbs like *comprometer* which have all the morphological properties of their base Verb (in this case *prometer*) but have absolutely no semantic relationship to that base (see also Bybee, 1985, 83, and Spencer, 2000, 231f., for detailed discussion).

The conclusion reached in Spencer (2000) is that we need to distinguish various forms of lexical relatedness, including purely form-based relatedness (*stand* ~ *understand*), transpositions, argument structure alternations, purely morphological distinctions such as inflectional class markers, as well as the traditionally defined derivational relationships. In addition, we need to distinguish a set of "functional" categories that the language operates with, whether it does this by inflections, clitics, auxiliary elements, word order, intonation, or whatever. However, once we've defined all these forms of lexical relatedness and all these morphosyntactic functional features, it is not clear that we ever need to appeal explicitly in the grammar to an inflection/derivation distinction. Specifically, I know of no theory of grammar which has found the need for a feature [MorphForm: {Inflection, Derivation}]. It is probable, then, that this is just a superficial descriptive distinction, which is of use to linguists when first describing a language in general outline but which has no theoretical significance as such. The real questions to be answered are then: "what are the functional features and how are they realized?"; "what is the form of a lexical entry for a given word class in the language?"; and "what are the systematic ways in which the language relates lexical entries (lexemes) to each other?" The answer to these questions may or may not make appeal to devices we think of as "morphological."

4.5   *Interim conclusions*

From this short survey, it appears that none of the crucial concepts needed for a principled theory of morphology is without serious conceptual difficulties. For those who adopt realizational models, this has little effect on theorizing about universals. For such morphologists, the real universals will lie presumably in questions of paradigm structure. Since the paradigm is a side-effect of feature systems, the universals are actually statements about features, independently of how those features are expressed. Given those assumptions, it is not clear that there are any interesting universal statements that can be made about word structure that go beyond statements of tendencies resulting from the interaction of a variety of factors, linguistic and non-linguistic. In particular, the order in which formatives ("morphemes") occur is not in itself a very interesting question, by and large, being the result of relatively haphazard grammaticalization processes. For morpheme theorists, on the other hand, there is inevitably a strong tendency to see some kind of syntactic superstructure to morpheme orderings. We turn to that possibility in Section 6. Before then, however, I discuss some questions relating to the concrete structure of words.

5   Form-related questions

5.1   Form-related universals

There are relatively few potential universals relating to the form of words. There
is an overall tendency cross-linguistically for morphology to be expressed by
affixes rather than by changes of the form of the root (root allomorphy) or
changes in stress, tone, and so on. In general, if a language makes use of, say,
ablaut to signal a morphological property, then it will also make use of affixation.
For instance, English has a plural form *men*, but the regular plural is signaled
by the suffix *-s*. This is because ablaut formations almost always arise when an
affix triggers a phonological change in the stem and then the affix disappears
as the language changes over time. In principle, one could imagine a language
which had just ablauting inflection, though given the normal patterns of grammaticalization this would be somewhat unlikely. Nonetheless, in Vietnamese
we find an intriguing situation: this language is generally said to lack morphology other than compounding. However, it has a special type of reduplication
process, giving rise to a variety of meanings, in which some part of a monosyl-
labic root is repeated in the reduplicant, e.g. from *sạch* "clean" we get *sạch sẽ*.

It has often been noted that languages show a stronger preference for suffixing
than for prefixing (Hawkins and Cutler, 1988). However, it does not seem
possible to make this into more than a tendency: it is not true, for instance, that
a language will always have suffixes if it has prefixes, since there are languages
which just have prefixes (Athabaskan). Moreover, it is not entirely clear what
such a statement would mean, especially in the case of derivational morphology.
When making such universal claims, should we include just the productive
affixes such as the *anti-* of *anti-clerical* or should we include "etymological"
affixes, such as the *com-* and *pro-* of *compromise*?

There are a number of putative universals governing affixation which one
could postulate. It might be the case, for instance, that all languages which
have infixes also have non-infixing affixes. Similarly, some languages allow
infixation to apply to reduplicated forms, and presumably all such languages
also allow infixation to apply to non-reduplicated forms. On the other hand, it is
not clear how much the study of such universals would deepen our understanding
of language structure.

There are further obstacles standing in the way of establishing form-related
universals, however. In Section 4, I raised a variety of questions about the conceptual underpinnings of morphology. Now I turn to more practical problems
of word segmentation which can impinge seriously on the search for universals.
Two particular problems are: distinguishing short, unaccented, phonologically
dependent function words from genuine affixes; and distinguishing tightly knit
phrases from genuine compounds.

Table 5.1 *Zwicky and Pullum clitic/affix properties*

Affix	Clitic
Expresses inflectional (functional) or derivational (lexical) meaning.	Expresses inflectional (functional) meaning.
Placement with respect to stem type.	Placement with respect to syntactic position (e.g. after first constituent).
May undergo idiosyncratic allomorphy.	No idiosyncratic allomorphs.
May trigger idiosyncratic allomorphy on stem / other affixes.	Does not trigger idiosyncratic allomorphy.
Not placed externally to clitic.	Not placed internally to affix.

5.2   Clitics versus affixes

Discussion of word structure conventionally distinguishes between phonological words and morphological words. A phonological word is the domain of a particular subset of phonological processes in the language while a morphological word is a structural unit whose form is governed by word formation rules. The morphological word is generally seen as the largest object generated by word formation (or morpheme combination) rules and the smallest object manipulated by syntactic process.

The phonological word and the morphological word do not always coincide. Thus, in a sentence such as *It's a boy* the first phonological word /its/ consists of a Pronoun serving as a dummy subject and a form of the copular verb. Thus, a single phonological word straddles the boundary between subject and predicate. The reduced form of the copula is usually considered to be a clitic. In Early Modern English we would be more likely to hear *Tis a boy*, in which the Pronoun is cliticized to the Verb form. The intuition behind these distinctions, then, is that a sequence of clitics and their host in syntactic structure can behave phonologically like a single word. However, the phonological dependence of clitics makes them look somewhat like affixes. Zwicky and Pullum (1983) outlined a number of typical properties distinguishing clitics from affixes, summarized in Table 5.1.

Useful as these criteria have proved in descriptive studies, they don't define a set of necessary and sufficient conditions for clitic- or affixhood, with one exception: where a putative affix triggers idiosyncratic allomorphy on its host it would be a perverse abuse of terminology to call it a clitic (this is no impediment to some linguists, of course!). Zwicky and Pullum developed these criteria in order to decide whether the English negative *-n't* formative is an affix or a clitic, and they concluded that it has all the properties of an affix and none of the properties of a clitic. From this they were able to conclude that negative auxiliary forms such as *won't*, *didn't*, *have not*, and so on are actually inflected forms. The argumentation seems impeccable, though one rarely sees analyses of English as a language in which negative polarity is an inflectional category.

When we come to examine other cases, however, it often turns out that these and other criteria give mixed results. A particularly intriguing situation occurs when one and the same formative seems to show the behavior of a clitic in some constructions and that of an affix in others. European Portuguese pronominal "clitics" are a case in point. These occur in groups of up to two elements, either postposed or preposed, depending on various syntactic and lexical factors. As enclitics, they have all the properties of affixes. For instance, they have to be repeated on conjoined verbs, they can occur before tense/agreement markers in the future and conditional forms ("mesoclisis"), and, crucially, they trigger completely idiosyncratic allomorphy on the Verb stem. On the other hand, as proclitics, they are loosely attached to the Verb and can be separated by one of a fixed set of elements, a single string of clitics can apply to both members of a conjoined Verb, and they fail to trigger any special allomorphy on their host (Luís and Spencer, 2005). This is illustrated in (9, 10):

(9)   Enclitics as suffixes
         dar "to give"
         da-os "gives them" < da + os
         damos "we give"
         damo-los "we give them" < damos + os (idiosyncratic stem *and*
              affix allomorphy)
         daremos "we will give"
         dar-tos-emos "we will give it to you" ("mesoclisis")

(10)   Proclitics as clitics (phrasal affixes):
         Não os damos "we don't give them"
         Não tos daremos "we won't give them to you"
         Não tos daremos o vendremos "we won't give or sell them to you"

What is important here is that the "clitic cluster" is identical in form whether it is a string of suffixes ("enclitics") or a proclitic string.

In other cases, it is simply unclear whether to treat a given formative as an affix or a clitic. Thus, consider the element *-ú/ü* that creates Adjectives from Nouns in Hungarian. This can attach to short phrases as in (11):

(11)   magyar nyelv   ⇒ magyar nyelvü
         Hungarian language   pertaining to the Hungarian language
         negy láb   ⇒ negy lábú
         four legs   four-legged

From a syntactic point of view *-ú/ü* applies to a phrase and should therefore be an independent syntactic terminal, hence, a word. From the

morphophonological point of view, however, this formative is a bound element that attaches to the right edge of a Noun and, like other bona fide affixes,
undergoes vowel harmony. Of interest is the fact that a number of other formatives in Hungarian which are generally analyzed as affixes fail to undergo
vowel harmony.

The conclusion drawn by many linguists is that there is no categorial distinction between clitics and affixes (Börjars, 1998, 84f.; see also Aronoff and Sridhar, 1983, for relevant discussion). Even Aikhenvald (2002, 42), who summarizes the differences between (canonical) clitics and (canonical) affixes, admits
that her criteria "suggest a scalar, or continuum-type, approach," which is to
say that there is no categorial difference between clitics and affixes. Formatives
traditionally described as clitics or affixes display different degrees of bound-
edness, host selectivity, and so on, and while some of these properties cluster
together to give us prototypical instances of clitics or affixes, those properties
are, in principle, and sometimes in practice, independent.

5.3   Words versus phrases

Clitics tend to be unaccented, phonologically weak elements. Affixes which
are in the domain of word stress or accent principles can often be prosodically
strong. However, even where we find a prosodically strong formative, it can be
very difficult to distinguish an affix from a syntactically independent function
word, particle, or even lexical item. The kinds of problems we encounter include
loosely cohering case suffixes which have similar properties to postpositions,
and TAM (tense/aspect/mood) auxiliaries which invariably appear adjacent to a
lexical verb and thus are difficult to distinguish from affixes or, indeed, from clitics. In many languages, an uninflected Noun argument (usually a direct object)
can appear adjacent to a Verb, sometimes in a position not normally associated
with direct objects. Sometimes, the collocation is so tight that one might wish
to treat it as a lexical compound, so that the language is treated as showing
noun incorporation. However, quite often we find that the degree of cohesion
is not quite as strong as that in less controversial cases of Noun incorporation,
such as Chukchee or Nahuatl. Miner (1986) argued that Zuni has strict Noun
incorporation and also this looser form, which he called "loose compounding."
Massam (2001) claims that Niuean and other Oceanic languages exhibit this
sort of loose compounding rather than true incorporation.

Even where prosodic, syntactic, and morphological criteria converge and we
can treat a string of words as a syntactic expression, we often find that it fulfills
a function which is effectively morphological. This occurs when periphrastic
expressions, such as finite auxiliary + non-finite participle constructions, serve
to realize inflectional properties of a Verb (Ackerman and Webelhuth, 1998).
For example, Sadler and Spencer (2001) demonstrate in some detail that the

periphrastic perfective passive in Latin has this function. The perfective passive is formed from the copular/auxiliary Verb *esse* "be" and the perfective passive participle, usually ending in *-tus*: *amatus est* "was loved." However, this construction cannot be taken to be a compositional syntactic expression. Latin has Verbs which are passive in form but active in meaning ("deponent Verbs") and they form their perfective actives using the same periphrasis: *loquitur* "speaks," *locutus est* "spoke [active]." Thus, it would be an error to derive the perfective and passive meaning of *amatus est* from the putative perfective passive meaning of the participle. Rather, the periphrasis is a (meaningless) constructional idiom, the whole of which serves conjointly to express the features "perfective passive." Arguably, this is the best way to analyze all periphrases which express inflectional ("functional") features, including constructions such as the English perfect and progressive aspect. In the case of Latin, Sadler and Spencer (2001) argue that the periphrasis actually occupies cells in the *morphological* paradigm of the verb, thus complicating the relationship between morphology and syntax.

5.4   Summary

Discussion of universals often presupposes certain morphological concepts which, I have argued, can be problematical. This is summarized in the following list:

Morpheme concept	unviable
Inflection/derivation	problematical
Wordhood	unclear
Affixation ~ cliticization distinction	unviable
Compound ~ phrase distinction	problematical
Lexeme concept	problematical
Lexical relatedness	still requires proper characterization
Inflectional (functional) feature	still requires proper characterization

The central concept, perhaps, is that of the morpheme. Many typological studies of morphology and most of the work conducted in the search for universals ask questions about the mapping between form and meaning, but generally presuppose that there's a one:one relationship to begin with – that is, such studies generally investigate the properties of classical morphemes. But it is precisely this concept that is questioned in paradigm-based approaches to morphology. Therefore, a large proportion of the discussion of morphological universals has to be rejected in its current form by a significant number of morphologists.

6   Some universals

6.1   *Morphotactics – universals in the order of "meaningful elements"*

The most effort in the search for morphological universals has been directed towards establishing principles of morpheme order. One obvious point is that the most recently grammaticalized affixes will tend to occur externally to the older affixes. This was enshrined in the theory of Level (or Stratal) Ordering (Siegel, 1974) which became incorporated into Lexical Phonology (Kiparsky, 1982). For English, it is claimed that there are two classes of affix, Class I and Class II, distinguished in that only the Class I affixes trigger idiosyncratic allomorphy and lexical stress shifts. According to the theory, all Class I affixes have to be internal to all Class II affixes. However, this cross-cuts the inflection–derivation divide, because irregular inflections are Class I affixes (for instance, the *-en* past participle ending of, say, *written*) while regular inflections are Class II (e.g. the *-ed* of *talked*).

The Level Ordering hypothesis attracted considerable criticism even from Lexical Phonologists (see Booij, 1987), and Fabb (1988) argued that, even for English, the theory fails for morphological reasons. Other, related approaches to ordering are the Atom Condition (Siegel, 1977) and the Right-hand Head Rule (Williams, 1981). Both these approaches suffer conceptual difficulties and are disconfirmed by too many counter-examples for them to influence current thinking.

A significant research effort has looked at the ordering of individual morphemes cross-linguistically. An important, if generally unstated, assumption in this research is that not only do classical morphemes exist, but that there exist past tense morphemes, perfective aspect morphemes, interrogative mood morphemes, and 1pl subject agreement morphemes, and that these are comparable across all languages. The best one can say about this assumption is that it has yet to be defended properly. Nonetheless, there are probably enough relatively clear cases for generalizations of various kinds to emerge.

An important starting point is found in the final subset of Greenberg's (1966) original list of universals, morphological universals 26–45. Now many of these (30, 32, 34, 36–38, 43–45) seem to involve markedness relations over feature systems and so are not specific to morphology (cf. what I said above about number universals). Some of the universals relate morphology to word-order type (27, 31, 33, 40, 41). Only six seem to concern pure morphology (e.g. 28: derivation is nearer the root than inflection; 29: inflection implies derivation; 39: number markers are nearer the root than case markers). A similar picture is found from the Konstanz Universals Archive (Plank and Filiminova, 2000).

Much subsequent research has concentrated on establishing principles governing the ordering of individual morphemes within a word form. However, another strand has attempted to impose ordering restrictions on types or classes of morphemes, most notably, inflectional vs. derivational morphemes. I shall discuss those studies first and then turn to the morpheme ordering studies. One of the intriguing conceptual issues underlying this research concerns the question of the viability of the morpheme: in realization (paradigm-based) theories, in which the classical morpheme plays no role as a "meaningful element," how can you speak about "morpheme ordering"?

6.2   Inflection, derivation, compounding

The standard view is that inflectional morphemes are placed outside derivational morphemes, in the sense that inflections occur further from the lexical root than derivational affixes. This makes sense, given that derivation creates a new lexeme while inflection creates a form of that lexeme. The order of morphemes is thus seen to mirror the logical order of the two types of process. Similarly, a compound word is generally inflected "externally," on its head if it has one, so that we would not expect to see inflection inside a compound.

Claims about the relative ordering of inflection and derivation are difficult to maintain, of course, in any theory which denies such a distinction. As we have seen, it is not clear how to reconstruct the inflection/derivation divide in a thorough-going morpheme-based theory. It is therefore somewhat ironic that the distinction should be viewed as important by those who work within a morpheme-based architecture, while those who work in a realizational approach, for whom an inflection/derivation distinction is a natural one, tend to deny that there is a universal ordering.

Given a little reflection, the idea that inflection is always external to derivation has little to recommend it. Much, however, hinges on how we characterize a derived word. For example, by any reasonable definition of word formation, the Spanish *irse* "go away" has to be derived from *ir* "go" by addition of the reflexive clitic. This makes the clitic a derivational morpheme. But this clitic is a relatively free element and appears external to Auxiliary Verbs, leave alone inflection: *se han ido*. More "standard" instances of morphology pose no less serious problems. Many languages have Preverbs (early Indo-European, Georgian, Hungarian, and many others) or Particle Verbs (Germanic, including English) which give rise to discontinuous lexemes in which the Preverb or particle is separated from the main word form, as in *She made the story up*. Even where the Preverb is always fixed to the Verb stem morphologically we find interesting cases of inflection between the Preverb and the Verb. The so-called Greek augment is a case in point. In Table 5.2, we see examples of present and past tense Verb forms (Holton, *et al.*, 1997, 161f.).

The tense prefix is *e-* but the derivational prefixes *epi-*, *sim-*, *ana-* appear external to that tense marker. In the Athapaskan languages, derivational preverbs

Table 5.2 *Greek augment*

Present	Past imperfective
grafo "write"	e-grafa
epivalo "impose"	ep-e-vala
sim-veni "happen"	sin-e-vi
ep-ana-lamvano "repeat"	ep-an-e-lava

are firmly fixed to the Verb form, yet they appear outside inflectional prefixes in all Verb forms in which they occur (see discussion of Rice, 2000, below). In Hungarian, the Preverbs are generally separated from the Verb stem in the syntax, much like German separable prefixes, but they function as genuine prefixes when the lexeme undergoes derivation, as demonstrated in detail by Ackerman and LeSourd (1997).

The idea that inflection can never occur within a compound has a certain appeal for endocentric compounding. Thus, we speak of *book shelves* but not a **books shelf* even if the shelf is for several books. However, plurals are not particularly uncommon inside compounds in English, and in languages such as Latvian and Finnish we often find number- and case-marked nouns inside compounds. When we turn to exocentric compounding, then it's quite common to find what Stump (2001, ch. 4) calls "headed inflection" in which the internal member of the compound is inflected. An example is Breton compound plurals of the form *kizhier-koad* "squirrels," literally "cats-wood" (Stump, 2001, 108).

I conclude, therefore, that there is no way in which we can maintain the idea that inflection and derivation are ordered relative to each other or relative to compounding processes.

6.3   Morpheme ordering

There are several universalist approaches to morpheme ordering, with complex relationships between them. Some approaches assume the ordering is the result of semantic constraints, while others assume that syntax is responsible. Rice's (2000) approach appeals to a notion of *semantic scope*, couched in syntactic terms.

6.3.1   The Relevance Hierarchy

One of the most important typological studies of morpheme order was Bybee, 1985 (see also Bybee *et al.*, 1994). Bybee argued that morpheme ordering tendencies within verb forms arise from semantics: morphemes whose meaning is closer in some sense, or more "relevant" to the basic meaning of the Verb, will appear closer to the Verb. Thus, argument structure alternations, such as passives or causatives, are more intimately connected to verb lexical semantics than, say, evidential mood marking. Sure enough, there is an extremely strong tendency for argument structure markers to appear closer to the verb than mood markers. Bybee (1985) enshrined this in her influential Relevance Hierarchy, the basic form of which is shown in (12) (where "<" means "is external to"):

(12)   MOOD < TENSE < ASPECT < VOICE

Strictly speaking, however, it would be a mistake to think of this as a purely morphological claim. After all, the English auxiliary system respects exactly this hierarchy: *has been seen* Tense/Aspect – Voice, *has been walking* Tense/Aspect – Aspect, *might have been seen* Mood – Aspect – Voice.

The Relevance Hierarchy captures a robust statistical typological generalization and as such demands some sort of explanation. It is not without counter-examples. If *se* is a passive marker in Spanish reflexive passives, then (13) is such a counter-example (and how would a morpheme theorist committed to the existence of a Voice functional head analyze *se* otherwise?):

(13)   *Estos libros se han leído.*
        these books *REFL* have been read
        "These books have been read."

In a number of languages, however, the reflexive-marker-turned-passive-marker has become a genuine affix, but has become frozen in word-final position. Thus, in Russian we have passive word forms such as (14):

(14)   *Statja   pere-pis-yva-l-a-s'*
        article   re-write-IMPFV-PAST-FEM.SG-REFL
        "The article was being re-written."

Similar constructions are found in Scandinavian and in the Baltic languages. Similarly, in Latin the passive morpheme *-(u)r* is external to all other verb suffixes.

A further difficulty is that of identifying the meaning of a given affix or formative. Tense and aspect are notoriously difficult to tell apart, for instance. Moreover, grammaticalization often gives an entirely "wrong" meaning to a form without any change in morpheme order. Thus, impersonal passive forms are often co-opted as modal constructions of various sorts, perfect aspect forms become evidentials, and so on. More generally, as we saw in example (6), Verb forms often turn out to be non-compositional. In that case, it is simply impossible to discuss the order of the meaningful elements, because the elements are not meaningful.

6.3.2   Morphology and antisymmetry

In the wake of the "split-infl" approach to inflection advocated by Pollock (1989), a number of linguists proposed a purely syntactic analysis of inflectional morphology for the Verb Phrase (e.g. Ouhalla, 1991) and the Noun Phrase (e.g. Ritter, 1991). In this approach, a lexical head moves into the position of a functional head to "pick up" Voice, Tense, Agreement, etc., morphemes. This means that the order of affixation (*modulo* the suffix/prefix distinction) can be reflected in the hierarchical syntactic order of those heads, an instantiation of Baker's Mirror Principle.

The original versions of these ideas received what is perhaps the shortest and most complete refutation in the history of linguistics when Joseph and Smirniotopoulos (1993) pointed out in a ten-page squib that the whole approach is refuted by the mere fact of affixal allomorphy (see also Spencer, 1992, for a refutation of the doctrine with respect to nominal inflection). Independently, the quaint, but incoherent, metaphor of a head "picking up" an affix was then abandoned by Chomsky (1993) in favor of a notion of *feature checking*. Nonetheless, the basic idea remained at the heart of Distributed Morphology (Halle and Marantz, 1993) and has been resuscitated within the framework of Kayne's (1994) theory of antisymmetry. Ironically, two of the features which most strongly motivated original versions of the theory, namely subject agreement and negation, are deliberately left out of the more recent syntactic accounts, because of the recognition that these features do not obey any obvious universal principles of ordering.

Cinque (1999, 106) considerably extends the scope of Bybee's (1985) proposals. He takes as his starting point syntactic (word order) restrictions on strings of adverbials in English and Italian and uses this to expand the original hierarchy to include a couple of dozen positions, mostly with adverbial meanings:

(15)   Cinque's hierarchy

$\text{MoodP}_{\text{speech act}} > \text{MoodP}_{\text{evaluative}} > \text{MoodP}_{\text{evidential}} > \text{ModP}_{\text{epistemic}} >$
$\text{TP(Past)} > \text{TP(Future)} > \text{MoodP}_{\text{irrealis}} > \text{ModP}_{\text{necessity}} >$
$\text{ModP}_{\text{possibility}} > \text{AspP}_{\text{habitual}} > \text{AspP}_{\text{repetitive(I)}} > \text{AspP}_{\text{frequentative(I)}} >$
$\text{ModP}_{\text{volitional}} > \text{AspP}_{\text{celerative(I)}} > \text{TP}_{\text{(Anterior)}} > \text{AspP}_{\text{terminative}} >$
$\text{AspP}_{\text{continuative}} > \text{AspP}_{\text{retrospective}} > \text{AspP}_{\text{proximative}} > \text{AspP}_{\text{durative}} >$
$\text{AspP}_{\text{generic/progressive}} > \text{AspP}_{\text{prospective}} > \text{ModP}_{\text{obligation}} >$
$\text{ModP}_{\text{permission/ability}} > \text{AspP}_{\text{Completive(I)}} > \text{AspP}_{\text{PlCompletive}} > \text{VoiceP} >$
$\text{AspP}_{\text{celerative(II)}} > \text{AspP}_{\text{repetitive(II)}} > \text{AspP}_{\text{frequentative(II)}} >$
$\text{AspP}_{\text{CSgCompletive(II)}}$

If I understand him correctly, these positions are supposed to be "innately specified" in some sense. He establishes these positions by careful consideration of the pairwise ordering of grammaticalized elements in a large sample of diverse languages. Now, most of these orderings turn out to be what you would expect on the assumption that semantic adverbial scope is reflected in surface left-to-right linear order (or perhaps one should say the first-to-last temporal order for spoken language). Where these meanings are grammaticalized as Verb affixes, the anchor point is the Verb root, so that outer affixes take scope over inner affixes. For instance, an interrogative mood operator will always, apparently, appear "higher" in the clause (further away from the Verb root) than an evidential marker. This corresponds to the fact that it is reasonable to ask about an event which your addressee has not witnessed, but it is impossible to interpret the notion of the evidential form of a question: "I hereby reportedly ask whether . . ." is gibberish. An inspection of Cinque's orderings suggests that this simple semantic property accounts for nearly all the observed orderings. Cinque is aware of this counter-argument, of course, but offers only a very unconvincing response to it (Cinque, 1999, 134f.).

There may well be counter-examples, however. Example (13) and Balto-Slavic and Latin passives are just as problematical for Cinque as they are for the Relevance Hierarchy. Mithun (1999, 34) describes a phenomenon in Yup'ik which may be a counter-example when analyzed in Cinque's terms (that is, endorsing an unreconstructed version of the morpheme concept). From (15) we can see that past tense should be higher than (external to) future tense. This is true of the example in (16):

(16) *ayakatallruunga.*
      ayag-qatar-llru-u-nga
      go-IMM.FUT-PAST-IND.INTR-1SG
      "I was going to go."

However, the opposite order is also possible:

(17) *ayallruciqua.*
      ayag-llru-ciqe-u-a
      go-PAST-FUT-IND.INTR-1SG
      "I will have gone."

Example (17) would therefore seem to be a counter-example to (15). (The orders *ayag-ciqe-llru-u-nga* or *ayag-llru-qatar-u-a* are ungrammatical.)

The orderings are supposed to be operative over just one clause, so that, if another clausal domain is started, then we could in principle get apparent violations. But this represents something of an equivocation over the notion of *clause*. For instance, Yup'ik has grammaticalized clause structure within a single Verb form (Mithun, 1999, 38). Predicates of speaking or thinking take the form of suffixes: *-ni* "claim that," *-yuke* "think that," *-nayuke* "think that maybe":

(18)   *ayallrunillruat.*
ayag-llru-ni-llru-a-at
go-PAST-say-PAST-IND.TR-3PL/3SG
"They said he had left."

On the other hand, there is evidence that a whole clause can be part of a
morphological paradigm. In Bulgarian, there are no infinitives and subordinate
clauses are often introduced by the complementizer *da* (Spencer 2001, 2003a):

(19)   *Ivan iska   pisma da   piše.*
Ivan wants   letters DA   writes
"Ivan wants to write *letters*."

(Note the focused extraposed object of the embedded clause.) The *da*-clause
starts its own clitic domain (clitics are shown below in bold italics):

(20)   *Ne   **ste**   **li** vie iskali da   **mu**   **gi**   pokaža?*
NEG   AUX   Q   you want   DA   to.him them   I.show
"Don't you (reportedly) want me to show them to him?" or
"Haven't you been wanting me to show them to him?"

Now, the simple future tense is formed by adding the (invariable) future
particle ("clitic") *šte* to the present tense or present perfect form of the Verb:

(21)   *Te   šte   pišat   pismoto.*
They FUT write.3PL the.letter
"They will write the letter."

A non-future tense form is negated by a clitic/particle *ne* which appears at
the beginning of the clitic cluster. This was seen in the main clause of example
(20). However, future tenses have to be negated by means of a special impersonal negative auxiliary, *njama* (homophonous with the portmanteau Verb "not
have"), which takes a (finite) *da*-clause. Thus, the negation of (21) is (22):

(22)   *Te   njama da   pišat   pismoto.*
They NJAMA DA   write.3PL the.letter
"They will not write the letter."

It's very unclear what Cinque's system would make of such constructions
in which a whole clause is grammaticalized. If there is any doubt about what
constitutes a clause, and hence the order domain for verbal morphemes, then
the theory can make no worthwhile predictions.

Bulgarian provides an instance of another puzzle (Spencer, 2001). That language has a special evidential (renarrated) mood. For 1st/2nd persons the form is
the same as that of the indicative perfect, being formed with the Auxiliary "be"
and the *l*-participle form of the main Verb (example [20] above is an instance

of this). However, the two paradigms differ in the 3rd person, because the evidential, but not the perfect, has no auxiliary precisely in 3rd person forms. It is difficult to see how such a fact can even be accommodated in a system such as Cinque's.

Finally, it is not uncommon to find modal and temporal/aspectual features signaled by mobile particles. Although Cinque does not discuss conditional mood forms explicitly, they presumably have to have their own functional head. In that case, it is very unclear how to handle Russian conditionals, which are formed by placing a particle, *by*, more or less anywhere in the clause (Spencer, 2001).

6.3.3   *Morphology and syntax: Mirror Principle (Baker, 1985, 1988)*

The approach of Cinque illustrates the application of the Mirror Principle: the order of morphological operations reflects order of syntactic operations. This principle was first claimed by Baker (1985) for valency alternations and some agreement processes. The idea is that the order of morphemes in a word form mirrors the order of syntactic operations underlying the word form. This makes sense if it actually is the syntactic processes which construct the word forms. Now, as Grimshaw (1986) points out, the facts certainly do not demand a syntactic analysis of word formation. Moreover, it can be very difficult to test the theory because it is not always obvious how to constrain the order of syntactic operations (assuming this temporal metaphor has any meaning in such cases). In the case of the Noun Phrase domain, it is possible to argue that there is an inherent ordering of syntactic relationships. Thus, consider a language that marks both possessor agreement and case. Possessor agreement, as when "my house" is expressed by a 1sg agreement affix on "house," is a purely NP-internal matter. Case marking of "my house," however, is determined externally (e.g. by a case-selecting Preposition or Verb). Therefore, case markers should always be external to possessor agreement markers. In Spencer (1992), I show that this prediction – and a number of similar predictions – is not universally true. One response to this kind of problem is to argue that case and agreement are "purely morphological" and are added to the word form in more or less any order (Halle and Marantz, 1993).

However, there's also ample evidence from valency alternations that the Mirror Principle is false. Hyman (2003) discusses the rich set of valency alternations found throughout Bantu. He shows that there is a pervasive ordering illustrated in (23):

(23)   CARP template
        Stem – Causative – Applicative – Reciprocal – Passive

This ordering tends to be respected even if it goes against the natural order of syntactic processes. Thus, in a sentence such as *The hare caused the lion*

to dance for the hyena we would have an applicative Verb, *dance-for*, which
is causativized: *make (Y) [dance-for (Z)]*. Nonetheless, the order of suffixes
would normally be Stem-Causative-Applicative.

Intriguingly, some languages manage to violate both the Mirror Principle and
the CARP template. Thus, in Zulu, we find examples such as (24) (Doke, 1973
[1927], 138):

(24)   *ku-ya-zond-wa-na*   *lapha.*
         CL: 10-ASP-hate-PASS-RECIP   here
         "There is mutual hatred here."

This is literally the passive of the reciprocal: *X and Y hate each other* ⇒ *it is
hated each other*. It can not be formed by applying the reciprocal to the passive
form because reciprocals can not be formed from intransitive predicates. Now
the CARP template order is what you would expect, given the Mirror Principle,
so the observed order violates both principles. A similar case is seen in the
closely related language Xhosa (Kirsch *et al.*, 1999, 153):

(25)   *Ku-ya*   *kutheth-wa-na*   *ngomvuzo.*
         CL: 10-ASP   talk-PASS-RECIP   salary
         "Salary is negotiable." (= "there will be talking with each other
         about salary")

A somewhat different approach to morpheme order is taken by Rice (2000).
She bases herself on a very detailed study of a single group, the Athabaskan
languages. These languages are unusual in that they are strictly SOV languages
in their syntax but they are also almost exclusively prefixing. Rice argues that
there is generally a straightforward correlation between linear order and semantic scope: the prefix to the right tends to take the prefix to the left in its scope.
This is odd, in that it means that in most cases an internal prefix takes an external
prefix in its scope. In fact, the whole system is roughly the reverse of what we
would normally expect from the Relevance Hierarchy. Rice expresses scope in
terms of syntactic structure rather than semantic structure as such, and there are
a number of technical problems with her syntax-based solution (see Spencer,
2003b, for details), but overall it seems to be the case that linear order defines
semantic scope.

7   Conclusions: morphological universals and grammaticalization

Morphological patterns are the result of processes governing grammaticalization. In one sense, this is all there is to morphology, and so any search for
morphological universals is likely to be closely linked to the search for a theory
of grammaticalization. I have argued that other approaches which are based on a
purely syntactic view of morphology and word structure cannot work. However,

it is very unclear what a theory of grammaticalization would look like or even whether such a thing is possible (Lightfoot, 1999). A great many factors, some linguistic, others extralinguistic, govern the way that patterns get grammaticalized and, as yet, no one has discovered with certainty any overriding factor.

If we think of morphology as the study of word structure, we are greatly hampered by the fact that we have no really good understanding of what could constitute a universal characterization of morphological wordhood. There may be clear criteria for wordhood in individual languages, but we have no clear-cut set of criteria that can be applied to the totality of the world's languages to decide whether a given expression is a word, a tightly knit phrase, a word + particle combination, an idiom, or something else. There is no clear boundary between clitics and affixes, or between compounds and phrases. This makes it very difficult to speak about any kind of universal.

Of the few good candidates for purely morphological universals, those based on the "order of meaningful elements" have been very popular objects of investigation. However, morphologists are increasingly turning to paradigm-based realizational models (so-called "Word-and-Paradigm" models) to describe morphology and even some aspects of syntax, and those models deny the classical concept of the morpheme. But if there is no morpheme, then how can we talk about the ordering of morphemes, as "meaningful elements"? This is an interesting challenge. Perhaps the correct solution is the simplest and, in a way, the least interesting. Even if it should turn out that morphemes do not play a formal role in morphological theory, it is certainly the case that we can very often detect clear and frequent correspondences between form and meaning within word structure. To a first approximation it is quite natural to say that the -s of *cats* means "plural" and the -ed of *walked* means "past." No doubt such simple mappings are widely available to the language learner. So perhaps all we are seeing in morpheme order generalizations is the operation of a strong tendency for semantic scope to be reflected in the linear order of those elements that most transparently reflect the meaning. But it is not obvious that much more than this can, or needs to, be said.

6 Syntactic typology: just how exotic ARE European-type relative clauses?

Bernard Comrie

1   General considerations

My aim in this chapter is first to present an overview of my assessment of the state of the art in syntactic typology, and then to illustrate the general points in Section 2 by means of the investigation of one particular phenomenon, namely the syntactic typology of relative clauses, with particular regard to areal characteristics of European languages in comparison with other languages of the world.

What distinguishes the typological approach to syntax, or indeed to grammar as a whole, from other approaches? One feature of typological work, indeed arguably the defining characteristic of such work, is the serious attention paid to cross-linguistic diversity. In order to understand Language, it is essential to understand languages. Although all approaches that consider themselves general-linguistic in orientation at least pay lip-service to the cross-linguistic applicability of their tenets, it is the typological approach that sets out to examine data from as wide a range of languages as possible, in order to ensure that we have the best basis possible for deciding what logical possibilities are actually attested among the languages of the world, and thus for assessing how wide-ranging our characterization of the phenomenon in question must be. It is not sufficient for an approach to handle English but not Japanese, or vice versa. And indeed, in Section 2 of this chapter, I will be taking data from a fair range of languages, backed up by data from far more languages in the overall typological literature on relative clauses, in order to draw certain specific conclusions about the typology of relative clauses.

One way of characterizing the difference is to describe the typological approach as primarily data-driven – typologists are interested in languages, in cross-linguistic variation, and therefore the accounts that they come up with are driven by the cross-linguistic data rather than by aprioristic assumptions about what should be the case – in contrast to approaches like Generative Grammar that are primarily theory-driven: if generative grammarians turn to another language, this is primarily in the knowledge, expectation, or hope that they will find a particular theoretically interesting point in this language. Like many absolute contrasts, this one is a caricature if taken to its logical extreme – for instance, typologists certainly often have expectations as they approach a new language – but it nonetheless serves to highlight a clear difference in emphasis between the two approaches.

Related to these differences is another one, namely that typologists tend to eschew abstract analyses, while many other approaches to syntax and grammar are wedded to such analyses. If a typologist finds a piece of data that appears to be a counter-example to a hypothesized generalization, then the typologist's first inclination is – or at least should be – to treat it at face value as a counter-example, whereas a generative grammarian's first inclination might well be to try and find an abstract analysis of the data that makes it not an exception. Consider the possible initial reactions of a typologist and a generative grammarian to the observation that some languages have the basic constituent order Verb – Subject – Object (v s o), as it relates to the claim that all languages have in their clause structure a Verb Phrase (v p) node that includes the Verb and object to the exclusion of the subject. A typologist's initial conclusion would probably be to reject the v p hypothesis, on the grounds that there is no way of grouping together Verb and object to the exclusion of subject in a linear order v s o. By contrast, a generative grammarian's initial reaction might well be to propose that the v s o order is superficial, and that at a more abstract level of representation the constituent order is actually some other, for instance s v o, in which Verb and object are adjacent. Again, this absolute contrast between the two approaches is something of a caricature, although it does serve to highlight a difference in emphasis between the two approaches. Indeed, in Section 2, I will try to show that the typologist does sometimes need to analyze a construction, going beyond what is immediately observable to the eye or ear, in order to provide an adequate typological characterization of that construction. Conversely, the best Generative Grammar takes seriously the need to justify abstract analyses; see, for instance, the contributions to Carnie and Guilfoyle (2000) on v s o languages, some of which come to conclusions other than the assumption of a different underlying constituent order.

There are two specific aspects of the general points made in the foregoing that I would like to return to. The first is the question of whether the typologist's search for cross-linguistic data is likely indeed to provide a characterization of the range of cross-linguistic possibilities. Clearly, the typologist only has access to certain languages, maximally to all languages spoken today and all extinct languages that were sufficiently well documented to provide relevant data; in practice, given, *inter alia*, the simple fact that not all languages currently spoken have been sufficiently well documented to be a source of reliable data, the number of languages available is likely to be considerably smaller. While one can devise sophisticated methods of sampling existing languages, there is no guarantee that these are indeed representative of the human language potential. It might be that, quite by chance, certain possibilities are in fact not included in the set of languages that are available to us. Twenty years ago, I was reasonably optimistic that this might not be a serious problem, and that the set of languages available to us might indeed be a representative sample of the human linguistic potential, given the extraordinary range of variation that is found within this set of languages. More recently, colleagues have succeeded in convincing me that there is no strong reason for this confidence, and indeed that there might be some arguments against it, a point to which I return below.

Do the considerations at the end of the previous paragraph mean that the typologist's insistence on empirical cross-linguistic research is misplaced? After all, if the languages available do not constitute a representative sample anyway, why bother trying to examine a large number of them? I think that the typologist's approach is nonetheless justified. While we cannot be sure that the possibilities identified by the typologist exhaust all the possibilities made available by the human language potential, we do nonetheless know that whatever general linguistic account we construct must be able to account for all the variation that typologists have uncovered. So a theory that disallows a particular phenomenon still needs to be confronted with all the data we have at our disposal.

The second specific aspect that I want to consider briefly relates to a topic that is of great interest to typologists and will be a major factor in Section 2 of this chapter, but which nonetheless turns out to play an important role in the evaluation of reliability of language samples. It is the question of the independence of one language from another. Clearly, if two languages are genealogically related,[1] descended from a common ancestor, then properties that they share might simply be properties of their common ancestor that they have inherited from that common ancestor. From the fact that English, Dutch, and Swedish all have a word *man* denoting an adult male human being, we would not conclude that this is a universal property of language, because we know that these languages are all related within the Germanic branch of the Indo-European language family and inherited this word from their common ancestor, Proto-Germanic; other languages have different words, like Spanish *hombre*. Given that English, French, and German all share the word *religion* (with slight variations in pronunciation and spelling) meaning "system of faith and worship," we should not be led to the conclusion that this is the only possible expression to denote this concept. We know that these three languages have been in close contact, an areal phenomenon, and that they have borrowed words from one

---

[1] Most linguists would say *genetically related*. Give that the words *genetic* and *genetically* are now associated, at least by non-linguists, primarily with genetics, some linguists prefer other terminology, such as *genealogical(ly)*.

another and from a common source, Latin. Indeed, in this case we know that all three languages have taken the word from Latin *religio*; and other languages can have quite different words, such as Czech *náboženství*.

The problem in the examples in the previous paragraph is that they are not independent of one another, because the languages in question are related either genealogically or areally. In the particular cases discussed, it was possible to counteract this effect by finding another language that is independent in the relevant respect. This is usually possible in the case of the relation between the sound and meaning of a lexical item, given the conventional (in Saussurean terminology: arbitrary) nature of this relationship. However, in other areas it can be quite problematic, as shown by the work of Dryer (1989) on the identification of large linguistic areas that can cover whole continents or more. Suppose, for instance, that one wants to choose two languages that both, independently, have front rounded vowels, in order to test hypotheses about other linguistic properties that might correlate with such vowels. At first sight, choosing French and Cantonese might seem a good idea. The two languages are genealogically unrelated (or about as unrelated as two languages can be, for those who believe that all human languages are ultimately related genealogically). The two languages are also spoken in geographically completely different parts of the world, namely western Europe and southern China. But are they? If we look at the distribution of languages with front rounded vowels in the languages of Eurasia, then we can trace an almost unbroken line (and before the expansion of Slavic, especially Russian, it probably was an unbroken line) of languages with front rounded vowels from French through Germanic, Uralic, Turkic, Mongolic, and other Sinitic (Chinese) languages to Cantonese. Although French and Cantonese have not had any direct contact relevant to the occurrence of front rounded vowels in the two languages, it cannot be excluded that each of them has had significant contact with relatives or neighbors which have had contact with relatives or neighbors, and so on, until an unbroken chain of contact is built up. A similar problem occurs when comparing most verb-final languages of Eurasia with one another. Much as in the discussion of the previous paragraph, and indeed the general considerations of sampling discussed above, from the fact that one can identify properties common to even large groups of languages, it is dangerous to generalize these as principled universals, unless one can take the most stringent precautions to ensure that one is indeed dealing with a sufficient range of independent phenomena. On the other hand, where one identifies differences, then it is clear that the general account of the phenomenon in question must be capable of providing for these differences, thus bringing us back to our general conclusions that the typological approach is invaluable in showing us what needs to be included, but less reliable in showing us what needs to be excluded.

In order to come close to understanding the effects that areal contact can have on the distribution of typological variants, it is important to study particular examples in as much detail as possible, trying to ascertain the genealogical and areal distribution of variants, and the extent to which they can be considered independent of one another, which in turn may require investigation of the historical bases of the present-day distribution. In Section 2, I attempt to do some of this in the case of one particular construction, namely relative clauses.

2   Relative clauses in Europe and beyond

A topic of recurrent interest to syntacticians, from traditional grammarians to generativists and typologists, has been the relative clause. On the typological side, this includes a major monograph, C. Lehmann (1984), that attempts to characterize the range of known cross-linguistic variety in this construction.

2.1   *The relative pronoun strategy*

Of the various types of relative clause that are found across the languages of the world, there is one that turns out to be particularly characteristic of the languages, especially the major literary languages, of Europe. It is illustrated in (1) for a rather literary variety of English, and in (2) for Russian, a language whose standard variety essentially allows only this possibility.[2]

(1)   English
    (a) $_{NP}$[the man $_S$[whom I saw yesterday]$_S$]$_{NP}$ left today
    (b) $_{NP}$[the man $_S$[to whom I gave the book yesterday]$_S$]$_{NP}$ left today

(2)   Russian
    (a) *mal'čik,   [kotorogo ja   videl]*
        boy.NOM REL.ACC I.NOM saw
        "the boy whom I saw"

    (b) *mal'čik,   [kotoromu ja   dal   knigu]*
        boy.NOM REL.DAT I.NOM gave book.ACC
        "the boy to whom I gave a book"

I will call this kind of relative clause construction the Relative Pronoun strategy. What are the characteristics of this relative clause construction?

First, this construction is externally headed, i.e. the head Noun *man* in (1) or *mal'čik* in (2) stands outside the relative clause. Contrast this with (3), from

---

[2] In order to facilitate the reading of the representation of relative clauses, the subordinate clause is enclosed in square brackets.

Diegueño, in which the head Noun *ʔwa:* "house" is inside the relative clause (Gorbet, 1976, 43–44). A literal translation of (3) into English would be something like "I will sing in the [I saw house yesterday]."

(3)   Diegueño
        [tənay   ʔwa: ʔwu:w]-pu-L ^{Y} ʔciyawx.
        yesterday house I.saw-the-L O C I.will.sing
        "I will sing in the house that I saw yesterday."

Second, within the relative clause in the Relative Pronoun strategy, the head Noun is taken up again inside the relative clause by a Pronoun showing the semantic or syntactic role that the notional head Noun plays inside the relative clause; depending on the language, and sometimes on the particular syntactic/semantic role in question, this will be done by marking the Pronoun by means of case (e.g. the accusative case in [1a] and [2a], the dative case in [2b]), or by an adposition (Preposition or Postposition), as in (1b). One can contrast this with an alternative construction in English, illustrated in (4), where, if indeed the item *that* is to be analyzed as a Pronoun, it does not show case: it has no separate accusative, and unlike (other) Pronouns cannot be preceded by a Preposition.

(4)   English
        (a) the man [that I saw yesterday]
        (b) the man [that I gave the book to yesterday]

Third, the Pronoun in question (or the phrase containing it) is preposed to the beginning of the clause. In English, objects normally follow the Verb, whether Nouns or Pronouns (cf. *I gave it to him*), but in (1a) the direct object *whom* appears at the beginning of the relative clause, and in (1b) the same applies to the indirect object *to whom*, in which case the whole Prepositional Phrase including the Pronoun moves to the front of the relative clause.[3] Contrast this with Persian example (5), in which there is a Pronoun in the relative clause (the third person singular Pronoun *u*, as part of the Prepositional Phrase *be u*), but this Pronoun is not preposed in the relative clause.

---

[3] Given that different languages have different constituent order possibilities, one might wish to generalize this somewhat by specifying not that the Relative Pronoun must be preposed, but rather that it must be moved to some specified position; this possibility will become relevant in Section 2.5. Although I formulate the third characteristic feature of the Relative Pronoun strategy in terms of movement, this should not be interpreted as a necessary commitment to a literal movement analysis; what is crucial is that the linear position of the object in a relative clause like (1a) is different from the linear position of a corresponding direct object in the corresponding simple clause, in this case *I saw the man yesterday*.

(5)   Persian
        zan   [ke Hasan be u   sibe zamini dâd]
        woman that Hasan to her potato   gave
        "the woman to whom Hasan gave a potato"

These features of the Relative Pronoun construction are summarized in (6).

(6)   (a) The construction is externally headed.
        (b) Within the relative clause, the head is taken up by a Pronoun
             showing its semantic/syntactic role in the relative clause (by
             case marking, adposition).
        (c) This Pronoun (or the phrase containing it) is preposed to the
             beginning of the clause (or, in principle, to any specific
             predefined position).

In a number of recent works, including in particular Comrie (1998), I have
argued that the Relative Pronoun strategy is, by and large, if not exclusively,
restricted in its areal coverage to languages spoken in Europe, plus languages
that have been in areal contact with languages of Europe. Although most languages of Europe belong to the Indo-European family, and although the Relative Pronoun strategy in European languages almost certainly first arose within
Indo-European – see, further, Section 2.2 – it is important to note that the distribution of the Relative Pronoun strategy is better characterized in areal than in
genetic terms. Non-European Indo-European languages typically do not have
the Relative Pronoun strategy, for example Persian (see [5]), which uses the
so-called Pronoun-retention strategy, and Vedic (see Section 2.2), which uses
the so-called correlative strategy (as in [9]). Conversely, some of the few non-
Indo-European languages of Europe do have the Relative Pronoun strategy, for
example Hungarian, illustrated in (7).

(7)   Hungarian
        a   fiú   [aki-t   láttam]
        the boy who-ACC I.saw
        "the boy whom I saw"

As implied in the previous paragraph, the Relative Pronoun strategy seems to
have spread by means of language contact, among both Indo-European and non-
Indo-European languages of Europe, and also to some non-European languages
that have been in contact with European languages. The sentences in (8) are from
Ewenki, a Tungusic language spoken in Siberia and in contact with Russian; the
examples are cited from Kolesnikova (1966, 200, 227). Sentence (8a) illustrates
the traditional relative clause construction of Ewenki, in which the relative
clause contains no overt representation of the notional head, the so-called gap

strategy; a literal translation into English would be something like "he went into the house [my friend lived]."

(8)   Ewenki
        (a) *tar gulə-lə*   *ī-rə-n*   *[girkī-w   injə-rī-lə-n].*
            he house-into go-AOR-3SG   friend-my live-PTCPL-into-3SG
            "He went into the house where my friend lived."

        (b) *amakān*   *julədū-wun*   *gūləsəg*   *icəw-rə-n*
            soon   in.front-IPL   village   appear-AOR-3SG
            [anti-wa   *bu*   *ə-cə-wun*   *sā-rə].*
            which-ACC   we   NEG-PST-IPL   know-CONNEG
            "Soon in front of us appeared a village which we did not know."

In contrast, sentence (8b), which reflects an innovatory construction in Ewenki that arose under Russian influence, has the relative clause introduced by a Relative Pronoun (as in Russian, identical to one series of interrogative Pronouns) that is case-marked for its syntactic role in the relative clause.

The main question that I want to try and answer in this section is whether indeed the Relative Pronoun strategy is restricted to languages of Europe and other languages that have been in contact with them. However, in order to answer this question, it will first be necessary to examine a fair range of data that might be considered to illustrate the Relative Pronoun strategy outside Europe, but which I will argue in nearly every case is best analyzed in some other way. This will be the theme of Sections 2.2–2.5.

Before turning to these data, however, I want to clarify certain points relating to the term *Relative Pronoun strategy* that have sometimes caused confusion, through the failure to realize that the conditions set out in (6) are necessary and sufficient for the characterization of this construction. First, it is not necessary that the Relative Pronoun be formally distinct from other kinds of Pronouns, indeed it is more frequent than not that the Relative Pronoun is identical either to an interrogative Pronoun (as with English *who*, *which*) or to a demonstrative Pronoun (as with German *der*), though there are sometimes differences in form – for example, the Latin interrogative and Relative Pronouns are identical in most case–number combinations, but not in the nominative singular masculine (interrogative *quis*, relative *qui*), or in the nominative–accusative singular neuter (interrogative *quid*, relative *quod*). Second and conversely, the fact that a Pronoun is restricted to relative clauses, and is therefore reasonably referred to as a Relative Pronoun, does not qualify its construction as an instance of the Relative Pronoun strategy if the conditions in (6) are not met. As will be seen in Section 2.3, example (12), Modern Standard Arabic has a Pronoun that occurs only in a relative clause, but that does not satisfy the conditions for the Relative Pronoun strategy because its case is determined not by its syntactic/semantic role in the relative clause, but rather by its syntactic/semantic role in the matrix clause (in fact, it agrees in case with its head Noun in the matrix clause).

2.2   The correlative strategy

A relative clause strategy that bears some resemblance to the Relative Pronoun strategy is the correlative strategy, illustrated by the Vedic sentence in (9). A more literal translation into English would be something like "Oh Soma, [which aids of you are beneficial to the worshipper], with them be a helper to us."

(9)   Vedic (*RV* 1, 91, 9)
        sóma [yás   te   mayobhúva
        soma which.NOM.PL.F of.you beneficial.NOM.PL.F

        ūtáyaḥ   sánti dāśúṣe]   tắbhir   no
        aids.NOM.PL.F are   to.worshipper with.those to.us

        vítắ   bhava.
        helper you.be
        "Soma, be a helper to us with those of your aids that are beneficial to the worshipper."

Crucial to this construction is the presence of coreferential nominal elements in both relative and main clauses. Although the literal translation of (9) into English sounds somewhat strange, to say the least, one does find somewhat similar constructions with indefinite relatives, of the type *whoever said that, let him keep quiet*, with coreferential *whoever* and *him*.

The similarity between the Relative Pronoun strategy and the correlative strategy is not accidental, nor the fact that both occur under different circumstances in English, since it is very likely that the Relative Pronoun strategy developed out of the correlative strategy, in the historical development of certain Indo-European languages; see, for instance, the discussion in W. P. Lehmann (1974, 61–68, 243–245) and references cited there – examples (9–11) here are adapted from this source. One can see different stages in the development in examples (10) and (11) from Hittite. Sentence (10) is a canonical correlative construction (with the exception that, following general principles for the omission of unstressed Pronouns, there is no coreferential Pronoun in the matrix clause); note in particular that in (10), as in the Vedic sentence in (9), the two clauses are simply ordered one after the other; a more literal translation into English would be "Which omen appears, we report it to the king and queen."

(10)   Hittite (*KBo* XVII 1 IV 9)
        [kwis   sagai-s   kisari]   ta   LUGAL-i
        which.NOM.SG   omen-NOM   becomes   CONN   king-DAT

        SAL.LUGAL-ya   tarweni.
        queen-and   we.say
        "We report to the king and queen the omen that appears."

In sentence (11) by contrast, although the internal structure of the relative clause is not significantly different from that in (10), its relation to the matrix clause is; no longer does it stand separate from the matrix clause, rather it is inserted into the matrix clause, being positioned crucially immediately after the head Noun "house"; it is this shift in linear order, perhaps not so great a change in languages with constituent order as free as in the early Indo-European languages, that marks the shift from correlative clause strategy to Relative Pronoun strategy. In other words, an example like the Hittite sentence in (11) already has all the characteristics of the Relative Pronoun strategy.

(11)   Hittite (*HG* I §50)
        mān   URUArinna   11 ITUa-s   tizzi   nu   apēl
        when   Arinna   11 month-NOM begins   CONN   he.GEN.SG

        É-ZU   [kwel-a   GISeyan   ask-i-ss-i
        house-3SG   which.GEN.SG-CONN eyan.tree gate-LOC-3SG-LOC

        sakuwān]   arāuwan.
        visible   tax.free
        "When in Arinna the eleventh month begins, then his house [at the gate of which the eyan tree is visible] is exempt from tax."

Note that the observations of this section add a further historical dimension to the Relative Pronoun strategy in European languages. They suggest that this strategy arose as a modification of the correlative strategy that is widespread in early Indo-European languages. Given that this modification is a specific historical event, it may well have occurred only once in the prehistory of European languages (with Europe being notionally extended somewhat to include Anatolia, where Hittite was spoken). It might subsequently have spread by contact.

2.3   Pronouns with case determined by matrix clause

It will have been noted that the drift of the present discussion is to examine relative clause constructions that bear some resemblance to the Relative Pronoun strategy but differ in crucial respects, in order to refine the limits that should be placed on the definition of the Relative Pronoun strategy. In this subsection, the topic of discussion will be constructions that look like the Relative

Pronoun strategy, but in which the case of the pronominal element in question is determined not by its role in the relative clause, but rather by its role in the main clause.

The canonical example of this construction is from Arabic, more strictly from Classical or Modern Standard Arabic, since the vernaculars have lost all or almost all case marking. Example (12) is from Modern Standard Arabic (Cantarino, 1975, 163). As already noted at the end of Section 2.1, the pronoun found in the relative clause of (12) is restricted to relative clauses, and is therefore properly called a Relative Pronoun, but does not satisfy the definition of the Relative Pronoun strategy (see [6]) since its case is determined by its role in the matrix clause. In (12), the Relative Pronoun *(i)llað-aani* is in the nominative, agreeing with the head Noun in the matrix clause, although the role of the notional head in the relative clause is as a direct object, as can be seen in the accusative form of the coreferential Pronoun *-humaa* cliticized to the Verb (i.e. Arabic, like Persian in example [5], illustrates the Pronoun-retention strategy, albeit a typologically somewhat unusual variant thereof).

(12)   Arabic (Modern Standard) (only construction available, case
         determined by main clause)
         'al-yulaam-aani   *l-musiiqiyy-aani*   *[llað-aani*
         the-boy-DU.NOM   the-musical-DU.NOM   REL-DU.NOM

         'arsala-humaa   *siiraanuu]*
         sent.3sG-them.DU   Cyrano.NOM
         "the two boy musicians whom Cyrano sent"

Two further points should be made concerning this Arabic construction before moving on. First, case marking of the Relative Pronoun is highly restricted in Arabic, being found in the dual number only; but in the dual, the distinction is robust. Second, this is the only construction that Arabic has involving an introductory Pronoun in the relative clause, i.e. one does not find equivalent constructions in which the case of the Pronoun is determined by the role of the notional head in the relative clause, which would then be an instance of the Relative Pronoun strategy.

One can contrast this with the situation in Ancient Greek. In Ancient Greek, in most instances the case of the Relative Pronoun is determined by its syntactic/semantic role in the relative clause, as in sentence (13).

(13)   Ancient Greek
         hoi   *ándres*   *[hoùs*   *eîdes]*   *apêlthon.*
         the.PL.NOM   man.PL.NOM   which.PL.ACC   saw.2sG   went.3PL
         "The men whom you saw went."

The word *ándres* "men" is nominative as subject of the matrix clause; the coreferential Relative Pronoun *hoús* (in non-pausal position, *hoùs*) is accusative as direct object of the relative clause.

Under certain circumstances, however, one finds that the case of the Relative Pronoun is not determined by the role of the notional head in the relative clause, but rather agrees in case with the head Noun in the matrix clause. This is the usual (but not invariable) construction when the head Noun is in the genitive or dative and the expected case of the Relative Pronoun would be the accusative, as in (14).

(14)   Ancient Greek (Xenophon, *Anabasis*, 1, 7)
        áksioi   tês   eleutherías   [hês   kéktēsthai]
        worthy the.GEN freedom.GEN which.GEN you.have.gained
        "worthy of the freedom that you have gained"

In (14), the Relative Pronoun functions as object of the transitive Verb of the relative clause, but nonetheless appears in the genitive case, the same as the head Noun in the matrix clause (as object of the Adjective *áksioi* "worthy"). This might then seem to parallel the Arabic construction in (12), and thus to fall outside the scope of the Relative Pronoun strategy.

However, Ancient Greek has another, much less frequent kind of relative clause in which, instead of the case of the head Noun expected from its role in the matrix clause, one finds the head Noun agreeing in case with the Relative Pronoun, which latter does have the case that would be expected from its role in the relative clause. An example is given in (15).

(15)   Ancient Greek (Xenophon, *Hellenica*, 1, 4)
        élegon   hóti pántōn   [hôn   déontai]
        they.said that all.GEN.PL which.GEN.PL they.need

        pepragótes   eîen.
        having.done they.are.OPT
        "They said that they had done all things which they needed."

The Verb of the relative clause, *déomai* "I need", governs the genitive case, so that the genitive of the Relative Pronoun is as expected. However, the Verb of the matrix clause, "do", is a straightforward transitive Verb that governs the accusative case, so that the word "all" would have been expected to be in the accusative case. In fact, it is in the genitive. The accusative would have been possible here, though the construction as in (15) is also found, with attraction of the case of the antecedent to that of the Relative Pronoun.

The formulation just given provides a hint to an alternative analysis of (14). If Ancient Greek more generally has the possibility of case attraction between antecedent and Relative Pronoun, then one might expect that this could go in the direction of attracting the antecedent to the Relative Pronoun, as in (15), or in the inverse direction, attracting the Relative Pronoun to the antecedent, as in (14). Consideration of a fuller range of constructions in Ancient Greek, in particular the fact that attraction is never obligatory and can in principle operate in either direction, suggests that the better analysis of Ancient Greek is not to posit an Arabic-like construction (cf. [12]), but rather to say that Ancient Greek has the Relative Pronoun strategy, on top of which is overlaid the possibility of case attraction. Although Ancient Greek (14) looks like Arabic (12), its place within the broader context of Ancient Greek syntax suggests a different analysis. As pointed out in Section 1, typology does not mean lack of analysis!

2.4   Preposing

In (6), it was noted that one of the necessary conditions for a construction to count as an instance of the Relative Pronoun strategy is the preposing of the Relative Pronoun within the relative clause. But it turns out that we need to be a little more specific about exactly what is meant by preposing here. We can illustrate this by considering relative clause formation, in relation to simple clauses, in colloquial Czech.[4] Examples are provided in (16).

(16)   Czech (colloquial)

    (a) *to   děvče uhodilo toho   muže.*
         that girl   hit   that.ACC man.ACC
         "That girl hit that man."

    (b) *to   děvče ho   uhodilo.*
         that girl   him   hit
         "That girl hit him."

    (c) *muž, co   ho   to   děvče uhodilo*
         man REL him   that girl   hit
         "the man whom that girl hit"

Sentence (16a) illustrates the neutral order in Czech of a sentence containing Subject, Verb, and Object when both subject and object are or include nouns, and this order is Subject–Verb–Object. However, as in many European languages, unstressed Pronouns, which are clitics, show a different linear order; in Czech, they occupy the so-called Wackernagel position, immediately after the first major constituent of the clause. In (16b), therefore, the accusative clitic Pronoun *ho* occurs immediately after the clause-initial subject. In colloquial Czech, relativization on the direct object involves an unmarked relativizer *co* and resumption of the head Noun in the relative clause by means of a clitic Pronoun, as in (16c), which thus illustrates the Pronoun-retention strategy. Note that the relativizer *co* counts as the initial major constituent of the clause, so that the clitic Pronoun occurs immediately thereafter. Since Czech clitic Pronouns are enclitic, cliticizing to the preceding constituent, phonologically

---

[4] Standard written Czech has a classical European Relative Pronoun strategy construction similar to Russian (2).

co-ho is a single unit. This single unit occurs initially in the relative clause, and is case-marked (accusative) for its role within the relative clause, and would thus seem also to satisfy the definition of the Relative Pronoun strategy. However, there is a crucial difference between an example like (16c) and one like (1a). In (16c), the position of the accusative-marked *co* follows automatically from principles that are needed independently in the grammar of Czech, namely the fact that unstressed Pronouns occupy the Wackernagel position; note that this is needed even in simple sentences like (16b). By contrast, in English a specific rule is needed in relative clauses to prepose the Relative Pronoun. If we therefore impose an interpretation on (6) that the preposing must be a specific rule of preposing, rather than a general preposing required independently of relative clauses, then we can include examples like (1a) as instances of the Relative Pronoun strategy while excluding examples like (16c). Once again, analysis is required, in particular the comparison with other constructions of the language, to determine the typological classification of a construction.

Since colloquial Czech is also a European language, the question whether its relative clause construction is classified as an instance of the Relative Pronoun strategy or as an instance of Pronoun retention might seem irrelevant to our general areal concerns. Two comments are in order. First, in the discussion in Section 2.1, I noted in passing that the Relative Pronoun strategy is characteristic, in particular, of standard, literary varieties of European languages. Non-standard varieties of these languages often prefer other constructions, in particular Pronoun retention (and under certain circumstances the gap strategy), so the behavior of colloquial Czech, if analyzed as having Pronoun retention, fits into a pattern that is consistent with the behavior of many other colloquial varieties of European languages.

Second, the same problem as has been noted with colloquial Czech also occurs with a number of languages spoken outside Europe. Modern Hebrew, for instance, has as its basic construction for relativizing objects of Prepositions the Pronoun-retention construction as in (17a), in which the combination of Preposition and unstressed Pronoun occurs in the usual position for prepositional phrases used as object of a Verb, namely after that Verb. An alternative construction, more formal than the (a) variant, preposes the combined Preposition and Pronoun to form one word with the relative marker, as in (17b) (Glinert, 1989, 365).

(17)   Modern Hebrew
        (a) *ha-báyit   še-hityaxásta   elav*
            the-house REL -you.referred to.it

        (b) *ha-báyit   še-elav   hityaxásta*
            the-house REL -to.it you.referred
            "the house to which you referred"

It should be noted that the Modern Hebrew relative marker *še-* is proclitic, attaching phonologically to whatever full word immediately follows it, be this the Verb as in (17a) or a prepositional phrase as in (17b). The fact that (17a) is possible alongside (and, indeed, stylistically more neutral than) (17b) provides an additional piece of evidence in Modern Hebrew against a Relative Pronoun analysis, not available in colloquial Czech (where clitic Pronouns cannot follow the Verb, unless it happens to be the first major constituent of the clause, which will never be the case in a relative clause introduced by *co*).

The same pattern is found in a language from a completely different part of the world, namely Ute (anonymous, 1980, 195).[5] The normal constituent order in Ute is Subject–Object–Verb, and this is the order we find in (18a), with the comitative Noun Phrase between the subject and the Verb in the relative clause; this is an instance of the Pronoun-retention strategy (more literally "the woman that the man worked with her"). An alternative, less frequent order, preposes the postpositional phrase within the clause, thus providing a close typological parallel to Modern Hebrew.

(18) Ute
(a) *mamácai̱*   *'u*   *[ta'wáci   'uwáy   pṵ́-wa   wṵ́ṵka-na̱]*
    woman.NOM ART.NOM man.OBL ART.OBL PRO-with work-REL.NS

(b) *mamácai̱*   *'u*   *[pṵ́-wa   ta'wáci   'uwáy   wṵ́ṵka-na̱]*
    woman.NOM ART.NOM PRO-with man.OBL ART.OBL work-REL.NS
    "the woman with whom the man is working"

A more complex case is provided by Berber, illustrated here by Figuig Berber (though the pattern is similar across all Berber languages), as presented in Kossmann (1997). Berber has Prepositions occurring before the Noun Phrases that they govern, in which case one finds the forms shown in the left-hand column of (19b). Special forms of the Prepositions are used before personal Pronouns (which are suffixed to the bound Preposition stem), as indicated in the second column of (19b); note that, at least for the most common Prepositions, the pre-pronominal forms are often quite different from those occurring before full Noun Phrases, and even make a distinction not found in the latter, between "with" and "about." How is relativization on the object of a Preposition constructed, as in (19)? Yet another form of the Preposition is used, as given in the third column of (19b), this time closely related to that found with pronominal suffixes, and this element is preposed within the relative clause, as in (19a) – under other circumstances, a prepositional object or adjunct would normally follow the Verb.

---

[5] The grammar was compiled as the result of cooperation between linguist T. Givón and a large group of speakers of the Ute language. Note that the nominative case of Nouns in Ute is indicated by devoicing the final vowel, indicated in the orthography by means of underlining; the oblique case lacks this devoicing. The subjects of relative clauses stand in the oblique case.

(19)   Figuig Berber
        (a) *tiddart [deg   immut]*
            house   in.REL he.died
            "the house in which he died"

        (b) before noun before pronoun in relative clause
              i   *di-*   *deg*   "in"
              l   *yr-*   *yer*   "to"
              s   *zzi-*   *zzeg*   "with"
              s   *xf-*   *xef*   "about"

   Unfortunately, the idiosyncratic relations among the three columns of Berber
forms in (19b) make it difficult to decide on an unequivocal analysis. Given that
the forms in the third column are so similar to those in the second, and given
that they nonetheless occur as separate words rather than as bound stems, one
analysis would claim that they are simply irregular combinations of Preposition
and Relative Pronoun (since these forms are unique to Relative Pronouns); since
they mark the syntactic/semantic role of the notional head in the relative clause
and are preposed within the relative clause (and given that the head is external
to the relative clause), this analysis satisfies all requirements of the Relative
Pronoun strategy. An alternative analysis would say that the items in the third
column are simply allomorphs of the Prepositions, with no added Pronoun –
note that the forms for "to" and "about" provide no evidence of a pronominal
element where one would expect it, namely at the end (although, conversely,
the forms for "in" and "with" could be analyzed as having a suffixed *-g*) –
and that these prepositional forms are preposed in the relative clause; but since
they are not case-marked Pronouns, they would not satisfy the definition of
the Relative Pronoun strategy.[6] I am not aware of any further evidence that
would resolve the issue, and must therefore leave the question open. Note that
if Berber is analyzed as having the Relative Pronoun strategy, then it is adjacent
to the European area, especially given the importance of contacts around the
Mediterranean. The position of Berber may also be relevant in the discussion
of Songhay, to be taken up in Section 2.6.

2.5   *Verb marking*

Is there a distinct Verb-marking strategy of forming relative clauses, in which
different Verb forms are used to indicate the syntactic/semantic role of the
notional head within the relative clause? Although various colleagues have
tried to persuade me over the years that there is, I have until recently resisted

---

[6] I am grateful to Orin Gensler for discussion of the Berber material. Gensler favors the second
analysis, and notes that a construction more transparently paralleling this second analysis for
Berber is found in Old Irish. See also the discussion of Songhay in Section 2.6.

the idea, although I have now come round to accepting that, in certain instances, one must recognize the existence of such a strategy. Moreover, this strategy turns out to be relevant to drawing the precise boundaries of the Relative Pronoun strategy, perhaps surprisingly so, given that the Verb-marking strategy is at first sight so different from it.

First, however, it will be useful to consider the kind of reason why, for so long, I was reluctant to accept the existence of the Verb-marking strategy. Consider the Malagasy relative clauses in (20d–f). Example (20d) relativizes the agent, "the woman," (20e) relativizes the patient, "rice," while (20f) relativizes the beneficiary, "the children." In each example, the Verb has a different form, traditionally called active in (d), passive in (e), and circumstantial in (f). This seems prima facie evidence for a Verb-marking strategy, with the Verb coding the semantic role of the notional head Noun within the relative clause.

(20)   Malagasy
    (a) *nividy   ny vary ny vehivavy.*
        bought.ACT the rice the woman
        "The woman bought the rice."

    (b) *novidin'   ny vehivavy ny vary.*
        bought.PASS the woman   the rice
        "The rice was bought by the woman."

    (c) *nividianan'   ny vehivavy ny vary ny ankizy.*
        bought-CIRC the woman   the rice   the children
        "?The children were bought rice by the woman."

    (d) *ny vehivavy [izay nividy   ny   vary]*
        the woman   REL buy.ACT the rice
        "the woman who bought the rice"

    (e) *ny vary [izay novidin' ny vehivavy]*
        the rice REL buy.PASS the woman
        "the rice that was bought by the woman / that the woman bought"

    (f) *ny ankizy   [izay nividianan' ny vehivavy ny vary]*
        the children REL buy-CIRC   the woman   the rice
        "the children for whom the woman bought rice / ?that were bought rice by the woman"

However, the voice distinction found in (20d–f) is found not only in relative clauses, but also in simple sentences like (20a–c), where it functions as a voice system, with (20a) corresponding in form to the English active, (20b) to the passive, and (20c) to the somewhat marginal alternative passive given as the English translation to this example. In other words, the different Verb forms exist independently of the relative clause construction. Moreover, the distribution in relative clauses can be explained without making any special claim, bar one, about relative clauses: namely, that Malagasy only allows relativization of subjects. In the active, this is the agent. In the passive, it is the patient. In the circumstantial, it is the beneficiary. The distribution of forms in (20d–f), and also the fact that Malagasy has no alternative literal equivalents of "the rice that the woman bought" or "the woman by whom the rice was bought", means that, in Malagasy, one has not a distinct Verb-marking strategy, but simply the interaction of a rather rich voice system and a constraint that only subjects can be relativized. (In terms of the classification of relative clause constructions, Malagasy has a straightforward gap strategy.)

But now consider the Turkish examples in (21). In Turkish, two different Verb forms are used in relative clauses; while terminology varies, I will call them the present participle (in -an, with morphophonemic variants) and the nominalization (in -dig, again with morphophonemic variants). While the precise delimitation of the boundary between the use of the two is quite complex (see further, for instance, Kornfilt, 1997, 57–60), roughly speaking one can say that the present participle is used for relativizing subjects (as in [21a]), while the nominalization is used for relativizing non-subjects (as in [21b–c]).

(21)   Turkish
        (a) *[üniversite-de   hukuk oku-yan]*   *kız*
            university-LOC law   study-PRS.PRT girl
            "the girl who is studying law at the university"

        (b) *[yaz-dığ-ım]*   *mektup*
            write-NMZ-1SG   letter
            "the letter which I wrote"

        (c) *[çık-tığ-ımız]*   *kapı*
            emerge-NMZ-1PL   door
            "the door from which we emerged"

Although in one sense Turkish has the gap strategy, since there is no nominal element in the relative clause that indicates the syntactic/semantic role of the notional head inside that clause, a distinction is made in terms of the morphology of its Verb. Turkish should thus be analyzed as simultaneously exhibiting the gap strategy and the Verb-marking strategy; these are two independent parameters, and a language can be independently characterized on both.

It is not the aim of this chapter to discuss the Verb-marking strategy in detail, though a few other examples will be cited, and references given to a few more. Berber shows a distinction between the Verb form used for relativizing subjects and that used for relativizing non-subjects. Although Malagasy was argued above not to be an instance of Verb marking, several other Austronesian languages do illustrate this type – for instance Kambera (Klamer, 1998, 316–337), with *ma-* (or *na-* with past time reference) used to mark Verbs of relative clauses where the subject (22a) or the possessor of the subject (22b) is relativized, and *pa-* where an object (22c) is relativized (including applicative objects, instruments [22d], comitatives, and locatives [22e]).

(22)

    Kambera

    (a) *ku-ita-yana*   *na*   *tau*   *[na ma-pàpu*   *watar].*
         1SG.NOM-see-3SG.ACC ART person ART REL.SBJ-pluck corn
         "I see the person that plucks corn."

    (b) *ita-nggu-nya*   *na*   *tau*   *[na na-meti*
         see-1SG.GEN-3SG.DAT ART person ART REL.SBJ-die

         kuru uma-nya].
         wife-3SG.GEN
         "I saw the man whose wife died."

    (c) *na*   *njara [na pa-kei*   *memang-na-nya]*
         ART horse ART REL.OBJ-buy immediately-3SG.GEN-3SG.DAT
         "the horse that he immediately bought for her"

    (d) *na*   *huru*   *[na pa-nga-wà-nggu*   *uhu]*
         ART spoon ART REL.OBJ-eat-use-1SG.GEN rice
         "the spoon with which I eat rice"

    (e) *na*   *uma*   *[na pa-beli-nggu]*
         ART house ART REL.OBJ-return-1SG.GEN
         "the house to which I returned"

    Other Austronesian languages that have Verb-coding relative clauses include Tukang Besi (Donohue, 1999, 367–385) and Nias (Brown, 2001).

    Lhasa Tibetan clearly has the Verb-marking strategy, although different sources (for instance, Genetti, 1992, with data from Scott DeLancey and acknowledgments to Myung-Hee Kim), and Tournadre (1996, 331–332) give slightly different distributions of the forms, no doubt reflecting dialectal variation within Lhasa Tibetan. The distribution given by Tournadre is shown in Table 6.1, where the abbreviations S, A, and P stand for intransitive subject, agent-like argument of a transitive Verb, and patient-like argument of a transitive Verb, respectively; the form used for locatives is also used for datives and beneficiaries. Examples are given in (23), with (23a) relativizing S, (23b) relativizing A, (23c) relativizing P, (23d) relativizing an instrument, and (23e) relativizing a locative.

Table 6.1 *Verb marking in Lhasa Tibetan relative clauses*

	Imperfective	Perfective
A	*-mkhan*	*-mkhan*
S	*-mkhan*	*-pa*
P	*-yag*	*-pa*
Instrument	*-yag*	*-yag*
Locative	*-sa*	*-sa*

(23)   Lhasa Tibetan

(a) *[dering   phebs-mkhan-gi]   blama*
today   come-REL.S-GEN   lama
"the lama who comes today"

(b) *[stag gsod-mkhan] mi   pha=gi red.*
tiger kill-REL.A   man   that   be
"That is the man who killed the tiger."

(c) *[kho-s   bsad-pa]   stag*
he-ERG   kill-REL.PFV.P tiger
"the tiger which he killed"

(d) *[tshal   gtub-yag-gi]   gri*
vegetable cut-REL.INS-GEN knife
"the knife with which one cuts the vegetables"

(e) *[kho sdod-sa-'i]   khang=pa*
he   stay-REL.OBL-GEN house
"the house where he stays"

A number of languages in the Americas show the Verb-marking strategy. Ute makes a distinction between relativizing on subjects and on non-subjects. In the examples in (18) cited above, the Verb form is marked for relativizing a non-subject, while there is pronoun-retention of the comitative, i.e. the construction combines Verb marking and Pronoun retention; relativizing subjects and direct objects involves no Pronoun retention, but rather the gap strategy, but with Verb marking (anonymous, 1980, 182–203). Cuzco Quechua makes a distinction between relativizing subjects and non-subjects (Lefebvre and Muysken, 1988, 166–197). The examples in (24) illustrate Verb marking in another South American language, Macushi, the data being drawn from Abbot (1991, 93–96). Note that Macushi distinguishes one set of forms used for relativizing subjects (as in [24a] and [24b] – these forms also encode varying combinations of tense–aspect, number, and transitivity), one form for relativizing direct objects (as in [24c]), and one for relativizing obliques (including instruments, locatives, and temporals) (as in [24d]).

(24)   Macushi
   (a) *[to'   era'ma-i   iipî'-san   wanî-'pî]   mutti*
        they   get-PURP   come-NMZ.SBJ.PST.PL   be-PST   mutti

        moropai   bode.
        and   bode
        "The ones who came to get them were Mutti and Bode."

   (b) *[pena-ron-kon   yan-pîtî-tîpon]*   *mîîkîrî.*
        long.ago-NMZ-COLL   eat-ITER-NMZ.SBJ.PST.TR he
        "He is the one who repeatedly ate the old ones."

   (c) *seni [a-nyo'   n-arima-'pî]   sararu.*
        this 2-husband NMZ.OBJ-send-PST meat
        "This is the meat your husband sent."

   (d) *[u-we'na-to']   pata'-se   mîrîrî.*
        1-sleep-NMZ.OBL place-POSS that
        "That is the place where I sleep."

Yet a further South American language to show Verb encoding is Apurinã (Facundes, 2000), with a distinction between forms for relativizing subject, and object in the presence of a subject, and object in an actorless construction, and a special form where a third person subject is relativized and the object is first or second person.

What is the specific relevance of Verb marking to our present concern with the Relative Pronoun strategy? The question arises because of the suggestion by Facundes (2000), specifically with regard to Apurinã but extendible to other Verb-marking languages, that Verb marking is simply the equivalent of the Relative Pronoun strategy in a language that uses non-finite Verb forms as its basic means of joining clauses into complex sentences. To take a relatively straightforward example like Turkish: where English uses conjunctions to introduce subordinate clauses, Turkish makes use primarily of non-finite forms, as in *gel-ince* "when he comes," with a converbal (gerundial) form of the Verb *gel* "come." By the same token, where English uses Relative Pronouns to introduce a relative clause, such languages use non-finite Verb forms. Moreover, just as English (especially the more literary variety) uses different forms of the Relative Pronoun depending on whether one is relativizing a subject, a direct object, etc., so too languages with Verb-marking relative clause constructions make use of different non-finite Verb forms depending on which syntactic/semantic role is relativized.

I consider this an interesting idea, and have indeed myself toyed with the proposal that the differential marking of subject and non-subject relativization in Turkish – which is unusual in Turkic languages as a whole – might be a response to the fact that neighboring Indo-European languages differentiate relativizing different syntactic/semantic roles (Comrie, 1997). Nonetheless, there are also substantial differences between the Relative Pronoun strategy and Verb marking. In particular, the Relative Pronoun strategy normally enables a distinction to be made between a range of different syntactic/semantic roles that can be relativized, whereas Verb marking typically makes only a handful of distinctions, the range of distinctions being much more like what is found in a voice system than what is found with the Relative Pronoun strategy. The Relative Pronoun strategy closely follows the range of distinctions made by means of cases and/or adpositions in simple clauses, while Verb marking often merges or cuts across such distinctions. Etymologically, the forms used in Verb marking are often nominalizations, and therefore the distinctions they make tend to be the distinctions made in nominalizations, such as subject vs. object (e.g. English *employer* vs. *employee*) or special forms for instruments, such as the Arabic *miCCaaC*, e.g. *miftaah* "key" – cf. the Verb *fataha* "open." The range of distinctions made by Verb marking is more similar to the range of diathesis distinctions made in nominalizations, and also shares some of the same idiosyncrasies. So, despite the parallels, there seem also to be structural reasons to keep the Relative Pronoun strategy and Verb marking apart.

And perhaps areal reasons too. As noted repeatedly, the Relative Pronoun strategy is areally highly restricted. By contrast, the Verb-marking strategy, once recognized, is widespread across the languages of the world, having been identified even in the limited treatment in this chapter on the periphery of Europe, in North Africa, in the heart of Asia, in the Indonesian archipelago, in North America, and repeatedly in South America. The Relative Pronoun strategy is certainly not a cross-linguistically normal way of encoding the syntactic/semantic role of the notional head within the relative clause in languages with finite subordinate clauses, in the way that Verb marking does seem to be a normal means in languages that use non-finite clauses.

2.6   *The Relative Pronoun strategy without European influence*

Having proceeded so far by looking at constructions that might be instances of the Relative Pronoun strategy and showing that they either definitely, or probably, or possibly are not, it is now time to ask more directly whether there are, on the basis of sampling of the languages of the world, attested cases of the Relative Pronoun strategy outside of Europe. It will be recalled that so far the only language (or rather, group of languages) that I have not explicitly tried to exclude is Berber. In Comrie and Kuteva (2005), three languages were uncovered that seem indeed to provide instances of the Relative Pronoun strategy in languages that neither are spoken in Europe nor developed their relative clause construction (as far as we can tell) under European influence. They are Coast Tsimshian, Karok, and Koyra Chiini, and it is to these that we now turn.

My source for Coast Tsimshian (Sm'algy<u>a</u>x) is Mulder (1994, 140–143). In this language, the only positions that can be relativized are S, A, and P. There are two relativization markers, *in* and *gu*. The former is used for relativizing A, the latter for relativizing S and P, i.e. the system is ergative–absolutive. The element *gu*, but not *in*, may be omitted. As can be seen in the examples in (25), these elements appear clause-initially in the relative clause.

(25)   Coast Tsimshian (Sm'algy<u>a</u>x)

    (a) *t'apxadool-tga   hana'<u>a</u>ng-t   [in   waay   Hatsenas]*
        two-CN.ADJ   women-3A   REL.A   find   Hatsenas
        "the two women who had found Hatsenas"

    (b) *n-ts'm-waab-t-ga*   *[gu   haytg-it*
        POSS-in-house-3POSS-CN.PREP   REL.S/P   stand-3S

        gi-sga   na-süül-ga   t'aa]
        DEM-CN.PREP   POSS-middle-CN.POSS   lake
        "in his lodge which stood in the middle of the lake"

    (c) *na-waa-t*   *[gu   nah   k'yinam-s*
        POSS-name-3POSS   REL.S/P   PST   give-CN.PRED

        nagwat-gas   'niit]
        father-CN.PREP   3SG
        "the name which his father had given to him"

This certainly looks like the Relative Pronoun strategy, in that the initial element in the relative clause shows a formal distinction depending on the syntactic role relativized. There is, nonetheless, one potential difference, relating to a point that has hitherto not been emphasized in discussing the definition of the Relative Pronoun strategy given in (6). This definition specifies that the clause-initial element in question must be a Pronoun. I know of no evidence that *in* or *gu* in Coast Tsimshian are Pronouns; indeed, given the heavy constraints on relativization in Coast Tsimshian – restricted to S, A, and P – it is not clear how one could expect these items to show pronominal behavior, since they cannot be governed by Prepositions. Moreover, for what it is worth, the independent pronouns in Coast Tsimshian make no distinction in form between S, A, and P (Mulder, 1994, 66). So, Coast Tsimshian seems a good candidate for having the Relative Pronoun strategy, but some uncertainties still remain.

Karok, whose relative clauses are described by Bright (1957, 130–131), is a stronger candidate. In Karok, relative clauses are introduced by means of an element *pa*, which Bright identifies as a nominalizer, to which are attached the same clitics as are attached to Noun Phrases to indicate syntactic/semantic role, as in the examples in (26):

(26)   Karok
    (a) *[payê · m   pa='î · n   'imússaruktihap]   va ·   nanitíppah.*
         now   NMZ-ERG   is.visiting.you   that   my.brother
         "The one who is visiting you now is my brother."

    (b) *kâ · m   vuhvúha   'ukyâ · ti   [pa=kúθ*
         upriver   deerskin.dance   he.is.making   NMZ-BENEF
         'ivúrayvutih].
         you.are.wandering.around

         "The one for whose sake you are wandering around is performing a deerskin dance upriver."

The only thing that one might worry about with respect to Karok, other than the extreme paucity of examples of relative clauses, is that all those given are headless, so that one does not know how a headed relative clause would be formed.[7] Nonetheless, the range of data that we have available points strongly in the direction of Karok having the Relative Pronoun strategy, since relative clauses are introduced by an element that is clearly pronominal in nature, to the extent that it can take the same case clitics as ordinary noun phrases.

Our last example is Koyra Chiini, a variety of Songhay spoken in Timbuktu and neighboring areas and whose relevant relative clauses are described by Heath (1999, 192). Since Koyra Chiini lacks case marking, the relevant examples are those with Postpositions. Such relative clauses have two possible constructions, as illustrated in (27a–b):

(27)   Koyra Chiini
    (a) *baŋgu [kaa hari   si   hun   a   ra   tamba]*
         swamp REL water   IPV.NEG   leave   it   from   quick
         "a flooded area, in which water doesn't recede quickly"

    (b) *baŋgu di yo [kaa ra   na   hari d(i) o   ta   hun]*
         swamp the PL REL LOC FOC water the IPV TOP leave
         "the flooded areas, in which the water has receded"

In (27a), the relative clause is introduced by the invariable relative clause marker *kaa*, while the role of the notional head Noun within the relative clause

---

[7] This is a frequently encountered feature of descriptions of relative clauses in indigenous languages of the Americas, suggesting that it is not just an artifact of particular descriptions, but that this really is the preferred kind of relative clause across a number of languages. The nature of the descriptions often makes it impossible to tell whether headed relative clauses were actually impossible.

is indicated by means of the Pronoun *a* governed by the Postposition *ra* "from." In other words, this is a straightforward Pronoun-retention construction. There is no evidence in this construction that *kaa* is nominal. Example (27b), however, is more intriguing. Given that *ra* is a Postposition, one analysis would be that it remains a Postposition in (27b) and is governing the element *kaa*, which is thus, whatever its status in (27a), clearly behaving as a Pronoun.[8] Under this analysis, (27b) would illustrate the Relative Pronoun strategy. Alternatively, one might try to analyze the Koyra Chiini construction along the lines of the second analysis suggested for Berber construction (19a) above, treating sentence (27b) as having movement of the Postposition to (nearly) clause-initial position, as proposed to me by Orin Gensler – an analysis that gains in plausibility when one recognizes that Songhay and Berber are in areal contact, and which would also not require *kaa* to be analyzed as a Pronoun in (27). So the Koyra Chiini evidence is not unequivocal, but there is at least as good a case to be made here for the Relative Pronoun strategy as in Berber.

To sum up this section, there is certainly prima facie evidence that the Relative Pronoun strategy is found very occasionally in languages outside Europe that have undergone no relevant contact with a European language – none of the three languages discussed in this section has relative clauses that are in other respects like those found in languages of Europe – but in each of our three cases there are at least some reasons for questioning the Relative Pronoun strategy analysis, with Karok being the strongest candidate.

3   Conclusions

In this chapter, I have tried to take the reader through one of the kinds of things that typologists do. This kind of work certainly does not exhaust typology, since I have paid little attention, for instance, to providing a principled justification of the typology of relative clauses that I have used. What I do, however, hope to have shown is how one can take a plausible hypothesis about the restricted areal distribution of the Relative Pronoun strategy for forming relative clauses, test this against a range of languages, find that the hypothesis is in general borne out, learn a lot about relative clauses in various languages along the way, and finally realize that there are some instances that may be counter-examples and, perhaps even more importantly – since humility is arguably a virtue in a scientist – that there are some cases that still defy a clear answer.

---

[8] One might compare non-standard English examples like *the man that's dog ran away*, which seem to instantiate declension of *that* introducing a relative clause, apparently treating it as a pronoun.

7   Some universals of Verb semantics

Robert D. Van Valin, Jr.

1   Introduction

Most of the work on universals of human languages has been concentrated on the phonological, morphological, and syntactic properties of languages, with much less attention being devoted to the semantic side of language. The purpose of this chapter is to contribute to the investigation of universals in the realm of semantics, specifically Verb semantics. It will be argued that there is a fundamental set of distinctions which inform the Verb systems of all languages, and a system of semantic representation will be proposed to capture these distinctions.

The discussion will proceed as follows. In Section 2, the set of distinctions will be introduced and justified, and in Section 3, a formal system of semantic representation to capture them will be proposed. In Section 4, evidence of the widespread validity of these distinctions will be put forward, and in Section 5, conclusions will be presented.

2   *Aktionsart* and the organization of verbal semantics

The fundamental insight comes from Vendler (1967), who proposed a classification of Verbs into states, achievements, accomplishments, and activities. Examples of English Verbs from each of the *Aktionsart* classes are given in (1).

(1)   a. States: *be sick, be tall, be dead, love, know, believe*
       b. Achievements: *pop, explode, shatter* (the intransitive versions)
       c. Accomplishments: *melt, freeze, dry* (the intransitive versions);
         learn
       d. Activities: *march, walk, roll* (the intransitive versions); *swim,*
         think, snow, write

States depict static situations which are inherently temporally unbounded (atelic), and both achievements and accomplishments express changes of state, which are inherently temporally bounded (telic), or they express onsets of actions (not found in English but see Section 4 below): achievements are punctual, while accomplishments are not. Both of these types of change of state

Verb yield a result state; that is, the result state of something freezing is that it is frozen, and the result state of something shattering is that it is shattered. Activities are dynamic, inherently temporally unbounded (atelic), states of affairs.

There is one important non-Vendlerian *Aktionsart* class, namely semelfactives (Smith, 1997). Semelfactives are punctual events which have no result state. Examples are given in (2).

(2)   a. The beacon flashed.
       b. Kim sneezed.
       c. The tree branch tapped on the door.
       d. Chris glimpsed Dana.

Semelfactives differ from achievements in lacking a result state, and this can be seen in their inability to be used as adjectival modifiers expressing a result state, e.g. *the shattered window* vs. **the flashed light*, *a burst blood vessel* vs. **a glimpsed person*.

There is an important derivational relation between two classes, namely that between activities and what are called Active Accomplishments, the telic use of activity Verbs. This general pattern relates activity Verbs of motion (e.g. *run*), consumption (e.g. *eat*), and creation (e.g. *paint*) to the corresponding active accomplishment Verbs. This is illustrated in (3) for English.

(3)   a. The soccer players jogged in the park.   Activity
       a'. The soccer players jogged to the park.   Active Accomplishment
       b. Pat drank beer.   Activity
       b'. Pat drank a beer.   Active Accomplishment
       c. Leslie wrote (for several hours).   Activity
       c'. Leslie wrote a poem.   Active Accomplishment

These classes can be characterized in terms of four features, [± static], [± dynamic], [± telic], and [± punctual].

(4)   a. State: [+ static] [− dynamic] [− telic] [− punctual]
       b. Activity: [− static] [+ dynamic] [− telic] [− punctual]
       c. Achievement: [− static] [− dynamic] [+ telic] [+ punctual]
       d. Semelfactive: [− static] [± dynamic] [− telic] [+ punctual]
       e. Accomplishment: [− static] [− dynamic] [+ telic] [− punctual]
       f. Active   [− static] [+ dynamic] [+ telic] [− punctual]
          accomplishment:

The most fundamental distinction is that between static and non-static Verbs, which differentiates Verbs which code a "happening" from those which code a "non-happening." In other words, with respect to some situation, one could ask, "what happened?" or "what is happening?" If, for example, a sentence like

Sally just walked in the door could be the answer to this question, then the Verb *walk* is [− static]. On the other hand, a sentence like *Bill believes that UFOs are real* could not be the answer to this question, because nothing is taking place. Hence *believe* is a [+ static] Verb. By this criterion, activities, achievements, semelfactives, accomplishments, and active accomplishments are [− static]. States, however, are [+ static].

The feature "dynamic" relates to whether the state of affairs involves action or not. Activities and active accomplishments both entail action, as indicated by the fact that these Verbs can be modified by Adverbs like *violently*, *vigorously*, *gently*, *strongly*, and *energetically*. States, achievements, and accomplishments are non-dynamic and do not occur with Adverbs like these. Some semelfactive Verbs appear to be dynamic, e.g. *sneeze* as in *She sneezed once violently*, while others do not, e.g. *glimpse* as in *He glimpsed the intruder strongly*.

The feature "telic" is concerned with whether a Verb depicts a state of affairs with an inherent terminal point or not. States and activities do not have inherent terminal points. For example, a sentence like *Tom is clever* makes no reference to a temporal boundary, and consequently is non-telic (atelic). In *The earth is orbiting around the sun*, for example, there is a reference to an activity, but orbiting need not terminate. This is not due to the progressive aspect; in *the ice is melting on the roof*, the Verb *melt* entails that there is a terminal point at which the ice will be melted. Therefore, *orbit* is [− telic], while the intransitive Verb *melt* is [+ telic]. Active accomplishments are telic: in *Pat drank a beer*, there is an inherent terminal point, namely the point at which the beer is completely consumed. Similarly, in *Bill jogged to the park*, the inherent endpoint is when Bill arrives at the park. Achievements also have terminal points; if a bomb explodes or a window shatters, the terminal point is the moment of the explosion or the shattering. An achievement is a transition between one state of affairs (the bomb is unexploded, the window is whole) and a new state of affairs (the bomb is exploded, the window is shattered). Hence these Verbs are [+ telic] as well. Semelfactives, on the other hand, are pure events with no transition between one state and the next. In, e.g., *The light flashed once*, the light is in exactly the same state after the event as it was before it; there is no change of state, as with an achievement, hence no transition. Consequently, they are considered to be [− telic]. Therefore, states, activities, and semelfactives are unbounded (atelic), while achievements, accomplishments, and active accomplishments are bounded (telic).

The final feature, [± punctual], differentiates events with internal duration from those which lack it. The Verbs *melt* and *pop* both involve changes of state, as in *the ice melted* and *the balloon popped*, but they differ in that the former takes place over a time span, while the latter is instantaneous, for all practical purposes. Hence, achievements are punctual, while accomplishments are not. Semelfactives are also punctual, since they denote events without much temporal duration. Since states and activities are atelic, they must by definition involve temporal duration, and therefore they are always [– punctual].

Each of these six classes has a causative counterpart, as exemplified in (5).

(5)   a. State: The girl is scared.
       a′. Causative state: The tiger frightens/scares the girl.
       b. Achievement: The balloon popped.
       b′. Causative achievement: The dog popped the balloon.
       c. Semelfactive: The pencil tapped on the table.
       c′ Causative semelfactive: The teacher tapped the pencil
                                                on the table.
       d. Accomplishment: The snow melted.
       d′. Causative accomplishment: The hot sun melted the snow.
       e. Activity: The ball bounced around the room.
       e′. Causative activity: The boy bounced the ball around
                                                the room.
       f. Active accomplishment: The soldiers marched to the park.
       f′. Causative active   The sergeant marched the soldiers
            accomplishment: to the park.

There are a number of syntactic and semantic tests for determining the class of a Verb. A list of possible tests for the Verb class is given in Table 7.1; the

Table 7.1 *Tests for* Aktionsart *classes*[1]

Criterion	State	Achieve	Accmp	Activity	Active Accomp	Seml
1. Occurs with progressive	No*	No*	Yes	Yes	Yes	No*
2. Occurs with Adverb like *vigorously, gently*, etc.	No	No	No	Yes	Yes	Some*
3. Occurs with Adverb like *quickly, slowly*, etc.	No	No*	Yes	Yes	Yes	No*
4. Occurs with *X for an hour, spend an hour Xing*	Yes*	No*	Irrelevant*	Yes	Irrelevant*	Yes*
5. Occurs with *X in an hour*	No	No*	Yes	No	Yes	No*
6. Can be used as stative modifier	Yes	Yes	Yes	No	Yes	No
7. Has causative paraphrase	No	No	No	No	No	No

---

[1] It should be noted that it is necessary to adapt the tests to the features of the language under investigation. For example, one of the tests Dowty (1979) gives to differentiate states from the non-states is "has habitual interpretation in simple present tense," which is clearly an English-specific test.

causative classes will be discussed below. The "*" means that certain compli-
cations arise with this test, which will also be discussed below.

Test 1 is useful only in languages like English and Icelandic which have
a progressive aspect; it can occur with activities (6d), accomplishments (6b),
active accomplishments (6e), but not with most states[2] (6a, a′) or achievements
with a singular subject (6c). When it occurs with semelfactives, it necessarily
results in an iterative reading (6f); this is also the case when the progressive is
added to an achievement with a plural subject.

(6)   a. *Dana is being tall / fat / a doctor.
       a′. *Pat is knowing the answer / believing that today is Wednesday.
       b. The ice is melting.
       c. *The firecracker is popping (cf. The firecrackers are popping).
       d. Kim is dancing/singing/running/talking/crying/sleeping.
       e. Chris is walking to the park.
       f. The light is flashing (*once).

This test is marked "No" for semelfactives, because if an Adverb like *once*
or *one time* is added to make an iterative reading impossible, the progressive
is unacceptable. As noted earlier, the progressive with a semelfactive Verb (or
an achievement Verb with a plural subject) yields a Verb which patterns like an
activity Verb.

Test 2 involves the ability to co-occur with Adverbs that code dynamic
action, e.g. *vigorously*, *gently*, *dynamically*, etc. This is a test for the feature
[dynamic].[3]

(7)   a. *Max is vigorously tall / fat / a linguist.
       a′. *Max vigorously knows the answer / believes that today is
           Wednesday.

[2] There is an additional complexity with the progressive test. Some stative predicates, such as *sit*,
stand, and *lie*, may occur with the progressive under certain circumstances, as in (i).

(i)   a. The book is lying on the table.
       b. The city lies / *is lying at the base of the mountains.

Carlson (1977) calls the statives in (ia) *stage-level* predicates, because they depict a situation
which is not necessarily permanent. When the situation is necessarily permanent, as in (ib), the
progressive is impossible. Carlson refers to statives representing permanent states or attributes
as *individual-level* predicates.

[3] There is an important caution relevant to this test. It is crucial to avoid Adverbs which require
a controlling subject, e.g. *deliberately*, *carefully*. While they are incompatible with states and
achievements, they are also incompatible with activity Verbs which have subjects which refer to
non-agentive participants in the action, e.g. *shiver* as in *the dog shivered violently / *deliberately
in the cold*, or *shake* as in *the house shook violently / *carefully during the earthquake*. Hence, in
selecting Adverbs for this test, it is necessary to test their compatibility with involuntary Verbs
like *shiver*, and with Verbs like *shake* which can have an inanimate subject. If a language lacks
Adverbs of this kind, then other kinds of adjunct Verbal modifiers can be used, e.g. PPs like *with
great force*, *in a vigorous way*, which express the same thing as these Adverbs.

  b. *The snow is melting / melted vigorously.

  b′. *The window shattered vigorously.

  c. Mary is dancing/singing/running/talking/crying vigorously/ actively.

  c′. The house is shaking violently/vigorously/forcefully.

  d. Pat ran energetically to the park.

  e. Chris coughed once violently.

  e′. *Chris caught sight of the intruder forcefully/strongly/ energetically.

Test 3 is relevant only to non-stative Verbs and distinguishes non-punctual from punctual Verbs. Adverbs like *quickly*, *rapidly*, and *slowly*, which will be called "pace" Adverbs, can occur with events with temporal duration, regardless of whether they entail dynamic action, e.g. *the snow is melting slowly/??vigorously, John slowly/*vigorously realized his mistake*. The "*" on the "No" in the achievement and semelfactive columns means that pace Adverbs indicating very short temporal intervals are marginally acceptable with these Verbs, e.g. *the bomb exploded instantly, the light flashed instantly*. Hence, with achievement Verbs, it is necessary to use pace Adverbs which indicate a relatively slow process, e.g. *the bomb exploded *slowly/gradually*, for the test to be effective. Again, with semelfactive Verbs these Adverbs only make sense with an iterative interpretation of the Verb, and consequently adding *once* should make them unacceptable, e.g. *??The tree branch tapped slowly on the window once*.

Tests 4 and 5 differentiate telic from non-telic Verbs. Test 4 isolates the property of having duration in time; it shows that states, accomplishments, activities, and active accomplishments all have temporal duration, but achievements do not. Semelfactives can take a *for* PP expressing very short duration, as in (8f). Test 5 focuses on terminal points. If something is done *in* ten minutes, then explicit reference is being made to the termination point of the event. In other words, the event began at a certain time and finished ten minutes later. If something is done *for* ten minutes, the same event could still be going on at a later time. All the *for*-phrase indicates is that an event went on for a certain amount of time, without any indication when it started or when it ended. So in *he read the book in an hour*, the event began and ended in the space of one hour, with the subject having finished reading the book, whereas in *he read the book for an hour*, there is no indication of when the action began or ended, and the same event could still be going on at a later time. In general, states and activities readily take *for*-phrases, while achievements and accomplishments take *in*-phrases. Because achievements are punctual, however, they are only compatible with *in*-phrases referring to an exceedingly short period of time, e.g. *in the blink of an eye, in an instant, in a fraction of a second*. They are incompatible with *in*-phrases referring to temporal periods longer than this, e.g. *in ten seconds, in a minute*, and *in an hour*, unless they have an iterative reading, and accordingly they are marked "No*" in Table 7.1.

(8)   a. Max was tired/ill/happy for/*in an hour.
       a'. Max liked Susan for/*in an hour.
       b. The snow melted in/for an hour.
       c. The window shattered in/*for a fraction of a second.
           (*The window shattered in an hour.)
       d. Mary danced/sang/cried/talked/slept for/*in ten minutes.
       e. Tom drank the glass of beer in/*for an hour.
       e'. Tom drank beer for/*in an hour.
       f. The light flashed once for/??in an instant.
       f' *The light flashed once in/for an hour.

State predicates which denote inherent properties do not normally take *for* phrases, e.g. **Tom was tall/thin/short/fat for an hour*. Hence there is an asterisk on the "Yes" signaling that this test is problematic for some state predicates (cf. footnote 2). Some accomplishments and active accomplishments can co-occur with *for*-phrases, e.g. *the dishes dried for ten minutes* or *Chris jogged to the park for five minutes*, which follows from their being non-punctual, which is the main point of test 3. Hence the occurrence of *for*-phrases with accomplishments is really redundant and indicates nothing new about accomplishments or active accomplishments. Therefore, it is marked as "irrelevant" in Table 7.1 for them.[4]

Test 6 serves primarily to distinguish the two punctual types from each other. As noted earlier, semelfactives have no result state, and accordingly they cannot serve as stative modifiers, e.g. **the tapped window, *the flashed light*. Achievements, on the other hand, do entail a result state and therefore can function as stative modifiers, e.g. *the shattered window, the burst blood vessel*. This is related to the fact noted earlier that semelfactives can have an iterative interpretation with a singular subject, while achievements can only have such a reading with a plural subject. Because the subject of an achievement undergoes a change of state, it cannot undergo it again, and therefore a different referent is required for the action to repeat, whereas, because the subject of a semelfactive Verb does not undergo a change of state, it can repeat the action, hence the possibility of an iterative reading with a singular subject. This contrast could be used as an additional test for differentiating achievements from semelfactives. There is

---

[4] Finally, there is an additional co-occurrence which must be noted. Achievements, semelfactives, and activities do co-occur with *in*-phrases, e.g. *The bomb will explode in one hour, Mary will sing in ten minutes*; these phrases refer to the time until the onset of the action or event, not to the temporal duration of the event itself and are therefore irrelevant to these tests. Thus, it is not sufficient simply to ascertain the type of temporal phrase that a Verb can occur with; it is, rather, necessary to pay attention to the meaning of the sentence as well.

no simple syntactic test to determine whether a Verb is inherently causative or not, but paraphrases can be useful, as illustrated in (9). This is test 7.

(9)   a. The tiger caused the girl to be afraid.
        b. The dog caused the balloon to pop.
        c. The hot sun caused the snow to melt.
        d. The boy caused the ball to bounce around the room.

It is important to make sure that the paraphrases have the same number of NPs as the original sentence being paraphrased; that is, "Pat causes Chris to come to have the book" is an appropriate paraphrase of *Pat gives the book to Chris*, but "Leslie causes Leslie/herself to run" is not a possible paraphrase of *Leslie runs* (it is at best a paraphrase of *Leslie made herself run*). This means that this test cannot apply to single argument Verbs, i.e. Verbs that have one argument in their basic form, because it would be impossible to make a causative paraphrase with a single participant. It must be emphasized that the claim here is not that *The dog scared the boy* and *The dog caused the boy to be afraid* mean exactly the same thing; rather it is that if *The dog scared the boy* is true, then *The dog caused the boy to be afraid* is also true; the converse need not hold.[5]

Furthermore, the causative relation intended here is exactly the same one that is signaled by causative morphology in many languages.

When the causative versions of the classes listed in Table 7.1 are included, the result is as given in Table 7.2.

The "*" for achievements and semelfactives, as well as their causative counterparts, with respect to tests 3 and 5 is the same as discussed above, as is the "*" for test 4 with state predicates. Causative states present some interesting complexities with respect to tests 1 and 2. Specifically, the more active the causing state of affairs is, the better the progressive and dynamic Adverbs are with causative state predicates. Consider the following contrasts.

(10)   a. Your attitude upsets / ?is upsetting me.
        a′. Your boorish behavior upsets / is upsetting me.
        b. Your clothes nauseate / ?are nauseating me.
        b′. The smell of your clothes nauseates / is nauseating me.
        c. The clown's funny hair amuses / ?is amusing the children.
        c′. The clown's zany antics amuse / are amusing the children.

The first sentence in each pair presents a rather static situation as the cause of the state of affairs, while the second presents a more dynamic causing state of

---

[5] In discussions of Verb semantics and paraphrases, it has often been pointed out that there are situations under which *John caused Bill to die* would be true but *John killed Bill* would not be. This is correct but irrelevant. The crucial point is that, in all circumstances in which *John killed Bill* would be true, *John caused Bill to die* would also be true. This is the paraphrase relation that is essential for this test.

Table 7.2 *Tests for determining predicate classes*

Class	Test 1 prog.	Test 2 dynamic	Test 3 duration	Test 4 *for*-PP	Test 5 *in*-PP	Test 6 stat.mod.	Test 7 cause
State	No	No	No	Yes*	No	Yes	No
Activity	Yes	Yes	Yes	Yes	No	No	No
Achievement	No*	No	No*	No*	No*	Yes	No
Semelfactive	No*	Some*	No*	Yes*	No*	No	No
Accomplishment	Yes	No	Yes	Irrelev.*	Yes	Yes	No
Active accomplishment	Yes	Yes	Yes	Irrelev.*	Yes	Yes	No
Causative state	Yes*	Yes*	No	Yes	No	Yes	Yes
Causative activity	Yes	Yes	Yes	Yes	No	Yes	Yes
Causative achievement	No	Yes*	No*	No	No*	Yes	Yes
Causative semelfactive	No*	Yes*	No*	No*	No*	No	Yes
Causative accomplishment	Yes	Yes*	Yes	Irrelev.*	Yes	Yes	Yes
Causative active accomplishment	Yes	Yes	Yes	Irrelev.*	Yes	Yes	Yes

affairs. While none of the combinations is impossible, the progressive is better with the more dynamic causing state of affairs and worse with the more static one. Dynamic Adverbs also force a dynamic reading for the causing state of affairs. For example, the sentence *the clown actively amused the children* could only be a report about the state of affairs described by (10c′), not (10c).

The "Yes*" for Test 2 for causative achievements, semelfactives, and accomplishments reflects the fact that this type of Adverb is not always acceptable with these Verbs. It modifies the causing activity. Because they are sometimes acceptable, causative accomplishments differ little from causative active accomplishments in terms of these tests. But there are important differences. First, there should always be at least some dynamic Adverbs which they are compatible with, and, because there are two activities, the causing activity and the caused activity, there may be ambiguity as to which one is being modified, something which is not the case with causative accomplishments. Second, causative accomplishments are ultimately related to a state predicate, whereas causative active accomplishments are ultimately related to an activity predicate. That is, the non-causative form of a causative accomplishment should be an accomplishment, which should involve a specific result state. The non-causative form of a causative active accomplishment, on the other hand, should be an active accomplishment, which should involve a specific activity. It should also be noted that causative accomplishments are much more common than causative active accomplishments, and therefore, in unclear cases, it is more likely that the Verb would be a causative accomplishment, rather than a causative active accomplishment.

3   A system of semantic representation

The distinctions elaborated in Section 2 are fundamental to the organization of Verbal systems, and therefore it is necessary to have a representational scheme which expresses them directly. Following the general approach (albeit not the specifics) in Dowty (1979), Verbs are analyzed in terms of a lexical decomposition system in which state and activity predicates are taken as basic and the other classes are derived from them. States are represented as bare predicates, e.g. **know′** (x, y), **dead′** (x). Activity Verb representations all contain the element **do′**, e.g. **do′**(x, [**cry′**(x)]) "cry," **do′**(x, [**eat′**(x, y)]) "eat." All other classes are built upon state or activity predicates plus one or more operators and connectives. Achievements, which are punctual changes of state or onsets of activity, are represented as a state or activity predicate plus an INGRessive operator, e.g. INGR **shattered′**(x) "shatter [INTR]." English lacks lexical Verbs meaning a punctual onset of an activity, but other languages have such Verbs. In Russian, *plakat'* "cry" is an activity Verb, and *zaplakat'* "burst out crying" is an achievement, i.e. INGR **do′**(x, [**cry′**(x)]); note the translation using the punctual expression *burst out*. Semelfactives likewise can be built on states or activities, e.g. *glimpse* would have the representation SEML **see′**(x, y), while *cough* would have the representation SEML **do′**(x, [**sneeze′**(x)]). This captures the fact that only semelfactives based on activities have an activity reading when iterative, e.g. *Dana is sneezing* vs. **Pat is glimpsing Sandy*. This also accounts for their differential behavior with dynamic Adverbs: semelfactives derived from activities can co-occur with such Adverbs, e.g. *He coughed once violently*, while those derived from states cannot: **He glimpsed her vigorously*. Accomplishments, which are non-punctual changes of state or onsets of activity, are represented as a state or activity predicate plus a BECOME operator, e.g. BECOME **frozen′**(x) "freeze [INTR]". Russian also provides an example of a non-punctual onset of activity Verb: *govorit'* "talk, speak" is an activity Verb, and *zagovorit'* "start talking" is an accomplishment, i.e. BECOME **do′**(x, [**speak′**(x)]). Causative Verbs have a complex structure consisting of a predicate indicating the causing action or event, usually an activity predicate, linked to a predicate indicating the resulting state of affairs by an operator–connective CAUSE, e.g. [**do′** . . .] CAUSE [BECOME/INGR **pred′** . . .].[6]

Accomplishment Verbs like *freeze* and *melt* involve both a process that takes place over time and an inherent endpoint of the process leading to a result state.

[6] Treating causatives as all having the same "CAUSE" element is a gross oversimplification for many reasons, only one of which will be mentioned here. First, there is a contrast among three basic types of causality: (i) *Pam made Sally go* [Direct (Coercive)]; (ii) *Pam had Sally go* [Indirect (Non-coercive)]; and (iii) *Pam let Sally go* [Permissive]. Both direct and indirect causality will be represented by "CAUSE," and permissive causality will be represented by "LET" in logical structure. English Verbs like *let*, *drop*, and *release* would have LET instead of CAUSE in their logical structure. Virtually all the examples to be discussed involve direct or indirect causality.

Achievement Verbs like *pop*, on the other hand, have no process, only a punctual event leading to a result state. Thus, an accomplishment can be analyzed as a process plus an achievement, if the final moment of the process is equated with the punctual event of the achievement. There is no direct representation of such a process in this decomposition system. It is not the same as an activity, since it is not dynamic, i.e. such processes do not co-occur with the Adverbs of test 2 in Table 7.2. This can be seen in English when Verbs like *melt* occur in the progressive, which isolates the process from the endpoint, as in (11).

(11)   a. The ice is melting.
         b. The ice is melting slowly/*vigorously.

There are languages in which Verbs directly express processes with no necessary implication of an endpoint and result state, unlike English Verbs like *melt* and *dry*. The following examples are from Mparntwe Arrernte, an Aboriginal language of central Australia (Wilkins, 1989).

(12)   a. *Ayenge   irrernte   ne-ke.*
             1sgNOM   cold   COP-PAST
             "I was cold."

         b. *Ayenge   irrernt-irre-ke.*
             1sgNOM   cold-PROC-PAST
             "I got colder/cooler/*cold."

         b′. *Ayenge   iparrpele/*tyepetyepele   irrernt-irre-ke.*
             1sgNOM   quickly/energetically   cold-PROC-PAST
             "I got colder quickly/*energetically."

         c. *Ayenge   irrernte-arle-irre-ke.*
             1sgNOM   cold-RES-PROC-PAST
             "I got cold."

The crucial contrast is between (12b) and (12c): the suffix *-irre* added to the stative stem *irrernte* "cold" means "become colder" or "become cooler" but not "become cold," i.e. it signals a change from less cold to more cold without entailing that the process has reached the endpoint of being cold. Like (11b) in English, a dynamic Adverb like *tyepetyepele* "energetically" is impossible with a process. In order to signal the reaching of the endpoint, the suffix *-arle* "result" must be added, as in (c), to indicate that the process reached its termination, yielding a result state. Hence, in Mparntwe Arrernte it is necessary to represent processes independent of a possible endpoint and result state. In order to do this, it is necessary to introduce an operator PROC for "process."

The decompositional representation for the examples in (12) would be as in (13).

(13)   a. **cold'**(1sg)   *irrernte*
         b. PROC **cold'**(1sg)   *irrernte + irre*
         c. PROC **cold'**(1sg) & INGR **cold'**(1sg)[7] *irrernte + arle + irre*

Thus, BECOME with a state predicate is decomposable into PROC & INGR.[8] However, it will continue to be used with Verbs like English *melt* and *dry*, because they normally entail both a process and a result state.[9] Unlike INGR, SEML, and BECOME, PROC does not occur with activity Verbs. The other three entail an event or transition which is the onset of the activity, and because PROC has no event or transition entailment, it could not be used to characterize some kind of pre-onset process.

As shown in (3), active accomplishments are made up of an activity predicate plus a change of state which makes them telic. There are two types of active accomplishments: those involving Verbs of motion, as in (3a′), and those involving Verbs of consumption and creation in (3b′,c′). With the first type, the change is a change of location, namely the motion is completed when the subject arrives at a particular location. Hence the decompositional representation of (3a′) would be as in (14a). With respect to Verbs of consumption and creation, on the other hand, the result state is either the consumption or creation of an object, which involves a change of state rather than location. The representations for the examples in (3b′,c′) are given in (14b,c).

(14)   a. **do'**(soccer players, [**jog'**(soccer players)]) & INGR **be-at'**(park, soccer players)
         b. **do'**(Pat, [**drink'**(Pat, beer)]) & INGR **consumed'**(beer)
         c. **do'**(Leslie, [**write'**(Leslie, poem)]) & INGR **exist'**(poem)

Because active accomplishments are composed of an activity + termination with result state, they are more accurately characterized as "active achievements". However, they will still be referred to as "[active] accomplishments", since this is the standard term for them in the literature.

These decompositional representations of Verbs are termed LOGICAL STRUCTURES [LS], and the schemata for the classes are given in Table 7.3.

Following the conventions of formal semantics, constants (which are normally predicates) are in boldface followed by a prime, whereas variable

---

[7] The INGR operator here is not directly signaled by the Verbal morphology, which indicates a process plus a result state. The existence of a result state necessarily entails a change of state leading to the result, hence the INGR.

[8] "&" is a connective meaning "and then"; see Dowty (1979, 74–75).

[9] The effect of the progressive on Verbs like this can now be easily expressed: progressive + BECOME **pred'**(x) yields PROC **pred'**(x). In other words, the progressive cancels the INGR component of BECOME, leaving only PROC. This follows from the incompatibility of the progressive and achievements, as expressed in test 1.

Table 7.3 *Lexical representations for* Aktionsart *classes*

Verb class	Logical structure
STATE	**predicate′**(x) or (x,y)
ACTIVITY	**do′**(x, [**predicate′**(x) or (x, y)])
ACHIEVEMENT	INGR **predicate′**(x) or (x,y), or INGR **do′**(x, [**predicate′**(x) or (x, y)])
SEMELFACTIVE	SEML **predicate′**(x) or (x,y), or SEML **do′**(x, [**predicate′**(x) or (x, y)])
ACCOMPLISHMENT	BECOME **predicate′**(x) or (x,y), or BECOME **do′**(x, [**predicate′**(x) or (x, y)])
ACTIVE ACCOMPLISHMENT	**do′**(x, [**predicate′**$_1$(x, (y))]) and INGR **predicate′**$_2$(z, x) or (y)
CAUSATIVE	α CAUSE β, where α, β are LSs of any type

elements are in normal typeface. The elements in boldface + prime are part of the vocabulary of the semantic metalanguage used in the decomposition; they are not words from any particular human language, despite their obvious similarity to English words. Hence the same representations are used for all languages (where appropriate), e.g. the logical structure for Lakhota *t'á* and English *die* would be BECOME **dead′**(x). The variables are filled by lexical items from the language being analyzed; for example, the English sentence "the dog died" would have the logical structure BECOME **dead′**(dog), while the corresponding Lakhota sentence *šúka ki t'é* "the dog died" would have the logical structure BECOME **dead′**(šúka). Thus, the constants should be drawn from the semantic metalanguage, while the variable(s) should be filled by lexical items from the language in question. If the constants were also to be drawn from different languages as well, then the LSs would become unintelligible and impossible to compare, e.g. English BECOME **dead′**(dog) vs. German WERDEN **tot′**(Hund) vs. Lakhota UYÁ **t'a′**(šúka). The point of the semantic metalanguage is to have a common representation for the meaning of Verbs and other predicators across languages, in order to facilitate cross-linguistic comparison and generalization.

Examples of some English Verbs with their logical structure are presented in (15).

(15)   a. STATES

Sandy is a lawyer.	**be′**(Sandy, [**lawyer′**])
The cup is shattered.	**shattered′**(cup)
Chris is in the kitchen.	**be-in′**(kitchen, Chris)[10]
Leslie saw the photo.	**see′**(Leslie, photo)

---

[10] The order of arguments in the logical structure is determined by the semantic role assigned to the position in the representation; it does not correspond to the order of arguments in the syntax of any particular language. This issue will not be addressed in this chapter. See Van Valin and LaPolla (1997, 113–116, 125–127).

b. ACTIVITIES

The girls laughed.	**do′**(girls, [**laugh′**(girls)])
Carl ate pizza.	**do′**(Carl, [**eat′**(Carl, pizza)])

c. ACHIEVEMENTS

The glass shattered.	INGR **shattered′**(glass)
The balloon popped.	INGR **popped′**(balloon)

d. SEMELFACTIVES

Leslie glimpsed the photo.	SEML **see′**(Leslie, photo)
Tim sneezed.	SEML **do′**(Tim, [**sneeze′**(Tim)])

e. ACCOMPLISHMENTS

The ice melted.	BECOME **melted′**(ice)
Alice learned German.	BECOME **know′**(Alice, German)

f. ACTIVE ACCOMPLISHMENTS

Chris ran to the park.	**do′**(Chris, [**run′**(Chris)]) & INGR **be-at′**(park, Chris)
Carl ate the pizza.	**do′**(Carl, [**eat′**(Carl, pizza)]) & INGR **consumed′**(pizza)

g. CAUSATIVES

The dog scared the boy.	[**do′**(dog, Ø)] CAUSE [**feel′** (boy,[**afraid′**])]
Max melted the ice.	[**do′**(Max, Ø)] CAUSE [BECOME **melted′**(ice)]
The cat popped the balloon.	[**do′**(cat, Ø)] CAUSE [INGR **popped′** (balloon)]
Sam flashed the light.	[**do′**(Sam, Ø)] CAUSE [SEML **do′** (light, [**flash′**(light)])]
Felix bounced the ball.	[**do′**(Felix, Ø)] CAUSE [**do′**(ball, [**bounce′**(ball)])]
Mary fed the pizza to the child.	[**do′**(Mary, Ø)] CAUSE [**do′** (child, [**eat′** (child, pizza)]) & INGR **consumed′**(pizza)]

In (15g), "**do′**(x, Ø)" represents an unspecified activity.

A crucial point to be emphasized is that it is necessary to distinguish the basic lexical meaning of a Verb, e.g. *drink* as an activity Verb, from its meaning in a particular context, e.g. *drink a glass of beer* as an active accomplishment predication. The former would have "**do′**(x, [**drink′**(x, y)])" as its representation in its lexical entry in the lexicon, whereas the latter would have "**do′**(x, [**drink′**(x, y)]) & INGR **consumed′**(y)" as the representation of the Verb of the clause in which *drink* appears. A given logical structure is intended to represent a particular meaning or interpretation of a lexical item; it is not necessarily the case that there is a single logical structure underlying all of the uses of a particular verbal lexical item. It is not necessary to list each of these Verbs separately in the lexicon; rather, the activity forms would be listed and the active accomplishment use could be derived by the following lexical rules.

(16)   a. Motion Verbs:

$\mathbf{do'}(x, [\mathbf{pred'}(x)]) \longleftrightarrow \mathbf{do'}(x, [\mathbf{pred'}(x)]) \, \& \, \text{INGR} \, \mathbf{be\text{-}LOC'}(y, x)$

b. Creation/consumption Verbs:

$\mathbf{do'}(x, [\mathbf{pred'_1}(x, y)]) \longleftrightarrow \mathbf{do'}(x, [\mathbf{pred'_1}(x, y)]) \, \& \, \text{INGR} \, \mathbf{pred'_2}(y)$

There are, however, lexical active accomplishment Verbs which are not derived by one of these rules; for example, *devour* is an active accomplishment and would be represented as such in its lexical entry.

There is one important additional element that can occur in logical structures that must be mentioned, namely NOT. Consider the contrast in (17).

(17)   a.   Max put the ball into the box.
         a′. $[\mathbf{do'}(\text{Max}, \emptyset)]$ CAUSE [BECOME $\mathbf{be\text{-}in'}$(box, ball)]
         b.   Max removed the ball from the box.
         b′. $[\mathbf{do'}(\text{Max}, \emptyset)]$ CAUSE [BECOME NOT $\mathbf{be\text{-}in'}$(box, ball)]

Verbs like *remove* contain a NOT in their logical structure, which in fact licenses the occurrence of the Preposition *from* with them (see Van Valin and LaPolla, 1997, 377).

An important issue facing every system of lexical decomposition is granularity: how detailed should the decomposition be? This in turn relates to the issue of what the most primitive elements in the system should be. In the system as presented here, state and activity predicates are not decomposed any further. However, such a deeper decomposition is necessary, if the representational system is to be truly descriptively and explanatorily adequate. As Van Valin and Wilkins (1993) note, "[the Dowty (1979) system] provides only enough semantic content to allow general syntactic predictions for whole Verb classes but not enough for subtler syntactic predictions to be made for individual predicates" (p. 504). The Dowty system contrasts sharply with Wierzbicka's (1972, 1980, 1988) detailed program of semantic explication, for example. Van Valin and Wilkins explore the further decomposition of the English Verb *remember* and its equivalents in Mparntwe Arrernte. Van Valin and LaPolla (1997) investigate the decomposition of Modern English Verbs of saying. Mairal and Faber (2002) investigate the extended decomposition of Verbs of cutting in English, while González Orta (2002) examines the semantic structure of the Old English Verb *secgan* "say." All of these works take the system to a finer level of granularity than found in the Dowty (1979) system, and part of the motivation for it is to make possible predictions about the morphosyntactic behavior of individual predicates. This is the prime consideration in determining the proper level of granularity in the system: because this system of lexical decomposition is part of a syntactic theory, the decomposition should be no finer than required for the formulation of predictions and significant generalizations about the morphosyntactic behavior of lexical items. This is a very different goal from a theory of lexical semantics, for example, whose goals would call for a much finer level of decomposition would be required. Thus, at this time, it is impossible to state that a particular level of granularity is required or desirable; this can only be determined through empirical work on the syntax–semantics interface in as many human languages as possible.

This discussion has not presented all of the aspects of this decompositional system, but the parts of it relevant to expressing the *Aktionsart* distinctions from Section 2 have been introduced. Almost all of the examples so far have been from English, but the purpose of this chapter is to argue for some universals of semantic representation. In the next section, the applicability of these distinctions and this decompositional system to other languages will be investigated.

4   Cross-linguistic validity of the representational system

In many languages, Verbs in these different classes may be overtly morphologically related to each other. State predicates form the basis of change of state Verbs, achievements, and accomplishments, and these in turn form the basis for causative change of state Verbs, causative achievements, and causative accomplishments. Accordingly, there are languages which show these relationships explicitly in their Verbal morphology. These languages fall into three groups. In the first group, the base is a state predicate, either a Verb or an Adjective, and to this base a morpheme is added indicating BECOME or INGR, deriving an accomplishment or achievement. Then to this derived form is added a causative morpheme, deriving a causative accomplishment or achievement. In Qiang, a Tibeto-Burman language (Van Valin and LaPolla, 1997), the relationship is clear: *ba* "big" [state], *tə-ba* "become big" [accomplishment], and *tə-ba-z̧* "cause to become big" [causative accomplishment]. Consider the following examples from Huallaga Quechua (Weber, 1989).

(18)

State	Accomplishment	Causative Accomplishment
a. *qarwash-*	*qarwash-ta:-*	*qarwash-ta:-chi*
yellow	yellow-become	yellow-become-cause
"be yellow"	"become yellow"	"make something yellow"

b. *hanq'a-*   *hanq'a-ya:-*   *hanq'a-ya:-chi*
   above.on.slope   above.on.slope-become   above.on.slope-become-cause
   "be above with   "become higher"   "make something higher"
   respect to slope"

c. *hatun-*   *hatun-ya:-*   *hatun-ya:-chi*
   big   big-become   big-become-cause
   "be big"   "become bigger"   "make something bigger"

d. *umasapa-*   *umasapa-ya:-*   *umasapa-ya:-chi*
   big.headed   big.headed-become   big.headed-become-cause
   "be big-headed"   "become big-headed"   "make someone big-headed"

e. –   *wañu-*   *wañu-chi*
                           die   die-cause
                           "die"   "kill"

f. –   *yacha-*   *yacha-chi*
                           learn   learn-cause
                           "learn"   "teach"

In (18a–d), accomplishment Verbs are formed from state predicates by the addition of the suffix *-ya:-* "become," and causative accomplishments are formed from them by the addition of the causative suffix *-chi-*. As (18e–f) show, *-chi-* can be added to underived accomplishment Verbs as well.

In (12) from Mparntwe Arrernte (Wilkins, 1989), repeated in (19), morphemes indicating change and result can be added to a state predicate to signal two different change-of-state predications.

(19)   a. *Ayenge   irrernte ne-ke.*
          1sgNOM cold   COP-PAST
          "I was cold."

       b. *Ayenge   irrernt-irre-ke.*
          1sgNOM cold-PROC-PAST
          "I got colder/cooler/*cold."

       c. *Ayenge   irrernte-arle-irre-ke.*
          1sgNOM cold-RES-PROC-PAST
          "I got cold."

To the change of state forms in (19b,c) the causative suffix *-lhile-* can be added, yielding the causative change-of-state Verbs in (20).

(20)   a. *Kwatye-le ayenge   irrernt-irre-lhile-ke.*
          water-ERG 1sgNOM cold-PROC-CAUSE-PAST
          "The water made me cooler [but not to the point that I was cold]."

b. *Kwatye-le   ayenge   irrernte-arle-irre-lhile-ke.*
water-ERG 1sgNOM cold-RES-PROC-CAUSE-PAST
"The water cooled me down [to the point that I was cold]."

In the second group of languages, the inchoative and causative morphemes do not co-occur on the Verbs. This is exemplified in the following examples, from Tepehua, a Totonacan language of Mexico (Watters, 1988), in (21), and from Sanuma, the language of the Yanomami in Brazil and Venezuela (Borgman, 1989), in (22).

(21)   a. *ʔaknu:-y* "A is underground" *ta:knu:-y* "A goes underground"
           ma:knu:-y "B buries A"
        b. *lakčahu-y* "A is closed" *talakčahu-y* "A closes" *ma:lakočahu-y*
           "B closes A"
        c. *paša-y* "A is changed, different" *tapaša-y* "A changes" *ma:paša-y*
           "B changes A"
        d. *laqɬtiʔa:-y* "A is open" *talaqɬtiʔa:-y* "A opens" *ma:laqɬtiʔa:-y*
           "B opens A"

In Tepehua, many achievement and accomplishment Verbs carry the inchoative prefix *ta-*, while many causative achievement and accomplishment Verbs carry the causative prefix *ma:-*; states are unmarked. The relevant morphemes in the Sanuma examples are *-so* "BECOME" and *-ma-* "CAUSE."

(22)   a. *Pole a   pata.*
           dog 3sg big
           "The dog is big."

        b. *Salaka-nö pole a   pata-so-ma.*
           fish-INST dog 3sg big-BECOME-CMPV
           "The dog grew big with fish [diet]."

        c. *Salaka niha pole wa pata-ma   toti-ti-o-ma.*
           fish   LOC dog 2sg big-CAUSE good-CONT-PNCT-CMPV
           "You made the dog really big with fish [diet]."

As in Tepehua, the inchoative and causative morphemes do not co-occur in the same Verb.

The third group of languages exhibits a rather different pattern expressing the same relationships; it includes Yagua (Peru; Payne and Payne, 1989), Russian, and French.

(23)

Causative Accomplishment	Accomplishment	State
a. Yagua *-muta-* "open [TR]"	*-muta-y-* "open [INTR]"	*-muta-y-maa* "be open"
b. French *briser* "break [TR]"	*se briser* "break [INTR]"	*brisé* "broken"
c. Russian *razbit"* "break [TR]"	*razbit"sja* "break [INTR]"	*razbitij* "broken"

In these three languages, the base form of the Verb is a causative accomplishment, and the accomplishment and state forms are derived morphologically from it. The derivational relationships illustrated in (18) to (23) can be readily accounted for in terms of the proposed system of lexical decomposition. The state → accomplishment → causative accomplishment pattern found in Qiang, Huallaga Quechua, and Mparntwe Arrernte follows directly from the lexical representations, e.g., in (18c), *hatun-* (**big'**(x)) → *hatun-ya:-* (BECOME **big'**(x)) → *hatun-ya:-chi-* (. . . CAUSE [BECOME **big'**(x)]). The pattern is the same in Tepehua and Sanuma, except that the inchoative morpheme does not co-occur with the causative morpheme. The pattern in Yagua, French, and Russian also indicates a systematic relationship among these classes, but the function of the morphological markers is to cancel part of the logical structure rather than to add components to it, e.g. in (23a), *-muta-* (. . . CAUSE [BECOME **open'**(x)]), *-muta-y-* (BECOME **open'**(x)), in which *-y-* cancels the ". . . CAUSE" part of the logical structure, and *-muta-y-maa* (**open'**(x)), in which *-maa* cancels the BECOME part of the logical structure.

There is one other derivation that state predicates are involved in, namely the derivation of causative states. In Lakhota, a Siouan language of North America, the causative Verb *-ya* can be added to psychological state Verbs to derive causative psych Verbs, e.g. *iníh̨a* "be scared, frightened, amazed, awed" vs. *iníh̨a-ya* "scare, frighten, amaze, awe." Barai, a language of Papua-New Guinea (Olson, 1981), makes a systematic contrast between state Verbs of psychological and physical state – e.g. *doduae* "be thirsty," *gare* "be cool," *mae* "be happy," and *visi* "be sick" – and causative Verbs of induced psychological and physical state, e.g. *dodua-d-* "make thirsty," *gara-d-* "make cool," *ma-d-* "please," and *visi-nam-* "sicken." In Mparntwe Arrernte, the result and causative markers may be added directly to a stative base to create a causative state, as in (24).

(24) *Kwatye-le   ayenge   irrernte-arle-lhile-ke.*
      water-ERG   1sgNOM   cold-RES-CAUSE-PAST
      "The water made/kept me cold."

Thus, there are languages that explicitly mark in their verbal morphology the derivational relationships that state predicates enter into, as revealed by the system of lexical decomposition proposed in Section 3.[11]

In the system of lexical representation, activity Verbs all have **do′** in their logical structure. It might seem odd to posit such a complex structure for simple Verbs like *run* and *sing*, but in fact there are numerous languages which construct activity predications in just this way. Basque is a particularly good example of this. Almost all verbal expressions corresponding to intransitive activity verbs in languages like English are formed by combining a Noun with the Verb *egin* "do, make," as illustrated in (25) from Levin (1989); virtually all of the exceptions are loan words from Spanish.

(25) a. *Ni-k   lan-Ø   egin   d-u-t.*
        1sg-ERG   work-ABS   do   3sgABS-AUX-1sgERG
        "I worked." [Literally: "I did work"]

    b. Examples of other combinations:
        amets egin "to dream" *amets* "dream"
        barre egin "to laugh" *barre* "laugh"
        hitz egin   "to speak" *hitz*   "word"
        igeri egin "to swim"   *igeri* "swim"
        lo egin   "to sleep" *lo*   "sleep"
        negar egin "to cry"   *negar* "tear"

Inceptive Verbs, i.e. achievements and accomplishments, can be derived from activity Verbs. The example of the *za-* prefix in Russian was given in Section 3; it derives both punctual inceptive activities, e.g. *zaplakat'* "burst out crying," and non-punctual inceptive activities, e.g. *zagovorit'* "start talking." Hausa (Abdoulaye, 1992) has inceptive activity Verbs, e.g. *ruugàa* "start running." Georgian (Holisky, 1981a, b) also has Verbs of this type, e.g. *at'irdeba* "he will begin to cry" (INGR **do′**(x, [**cry′**(x)])) vs. *t'iris* "he is crying" (**do′**(x, [**cry′**(x)])), *ak'ank'aldeba* "he will begin to tremble" (INGR **do′**(x, [**tremble′**(x)])) vs. *k'ank'alebs* "he is trembling" (**do′**(x, [**tremble′**(x)])). According to Holisky, these are punctual inceptives, i.e. achievements. This same *-d-* infix can also be added to state Verbs to form punctual change-of-state Verbs. Pirahã (Everett, 1986), a language spoken in the Amazon basin in Brazil, in contrast, has distinct inceptive markers for states and activities: *-hoi* for initiation of an action and *-hoag* for the beginning of a state, e.g. *xaitá-hói* [sleep-*hoi*] "go to sleep, fall asleep," *biioabá-hóág* [tired-*hoag*] "get tired."

Activity Verbs can be causativized to form causative activities. In Tepehua, causative activities may be derived with the same *ma:-* prefix discussed earlier,

---

[11] However, I know of no languages in which a semelfactive Verb like "glimpse" is morphologically derived from the stative Verb "see."

e.g. *pu:pu-y* "x boils" vs. *ma:pu:pu-y* "y boils x," *soqo-y* "x hurries" vs.
ma:soqo:-y "y hurries x." In Lakhota, causative activities may be derived either
with the instrumental prefix *yu-*, which is treated as a general causative prefix
with activity Verbs, or by the causative Verb *-ya*, e.g. *čhéya* "cry" vs. *yu-čhéya*
"make cry" vs. *čheyá-ya* "make cry." In Mparntwe Arrernte, the causative suffix
-lhile, illustrated in (20) with change-of-state Verbs, can be added to activity
Verbs to create a causative activity, e.g. *unthe* "go walkabout, wander around"
vs. *unthe-lhile* "make someone go walkabout, make someone wander around."
In Sanuma, the same *-ma-* causative morpheme as in (22c) can be added to
activity Verbs, as exemplified in (26b).

(26)   a. *Pole   ose   wai   niha   a   inamo-ma.*
            dog   young   DIM   LOC   3sg   play-CMPV
            "He played with the little puppy."

        b. *Pole   ose   wai   niha   a   inamo-ma-ma.*
            dog   young   DIM   LOC   3sg   play-CAUSE-CMPV
            "(She) made him play with the little puppy."

Interestingly, languages like Russian and French do not use the decausativiza-
tion strategy involving reflexive morphology, illustrated in (23), to derive activity from causative activity Verbs; rather, the base form of such Verbs is the
activity form, and just as in these languages the causative activity meaning is
derived via overt causativization.

The other important alternation that activity Verbs enter into is that between
activity and active accomplishment Verbs, and there are a few languages which
mark this contrast overtly, e.g. Russian *est'* "eat [activity]" vs. *s'est'* "eat [active
accomplishment]," Georgian *c'er* "write [activity]" vs. *dac'er* "write [active
accomplishment]." Pirahã has suffixes which Everett (1986) glosses as "telic"
and "atelic," and with Verbs like "eat" they have the same effect seen in Georgian
and Russian, e.g. *xápiso xaho-aí-* [bark eat-ATELIC] "eat bark" vs. *xápiso xoho-
áo-* [bark eat-TELIC] "eat (the) bark." Like Georgian and Russian, Pirahã lacks
articles, and the contrast is coded on the Verb and affects the interpretation of
the NP, unlike English, where this contrast is signaled by the form of the object
NP with a Verb like *eat*.[12]

In some syntactically ergative languages – e.g. Dyirbal, an Australian Aboriginal language (Dixon, 1972), and Sama, a Philippine language (Walton, 1986) –
Verbs like "eat" are interpreted as active accomplishments when used in active
voice constructions, and, in order to express a pure activity reading, the Verbs
must be antipassivized. This is illustrated for Dyirbal in (27).

---

[12] These examples show that this contrast *cannot* be reduced to the presence or absence of articles,
as claimed in, e.g., Verkuyl (1973), because it occurs in languages which do not have articles.

(27)   a. *Balam   wudyu-Ø baŋgul   yaṟa-ŋgu dyaŋga-ɲu.*
        NM.ABS fruit-ABS NM.ERG man-ERG eat-NFUT
        "The man ate the fruit."

        b. *Bayi   yaṟa-Ø   dyaŋgay-mari-nu (bagum   wudyu-gu).*
        NM.ABS man-ABS eat-REFL-NFUT NM.DAT fruit-DAT
        "The man ate (fruit)."

The sentence in (27a) is the plain or active voice, and the sentence gets an active accomplishment reading; note the interpretation of the patient as "the fruit." In (27b), on the other hand, the Verb has been antipassivized by means of what Dixon calls "the false reflexive" form; the actor is now the absolutive subject, and the patient is now optional; if overt, it is construed non-specifically. Hence, (27b) has an activity reading. In languages like this, the activity reading of Verbs like "eat" is derived from the basic or active accomplishment use of the Verb via the voice system.

Thus, in this section, it has been shown that the relationships among the Verb classes proposed in Section 2 expressed in the system of lexical representation in Section 3 are overtly realized in the Verbal morphology of many languages. This is summarized in (28).

(28)   a. State →Accomplishment/Achievement
        Qiang, Tepehua, Quechua, Pirahã, Sanuma, Mparntwe Arrernte
        b. State → Causative State
        Lakhota, Barai, Mparntwe Arrernte
        c. Accomplishment/Achievement → Causative Accomplishment/
        Achievement
        Qiang, Lakhota, Quechua, Mparntwe Arrernte
        d. Causative Accomplishment → Accomplishment
        French, Russian, Yagua
        e. Causative Accomplishment → State
        French, Russian, Yagua
        f. Activity → Accomplishment/Achievement
        Georgian, Russian, Hausa, Pirahã
        g. Activity → Active Accomplishment
        Georgian, Russian, Pirahã
        h. Activity → Causative Activity
        Tepehua, Lakhota, Sanuma, Mparntwe Arrernte
        i. Active Accomplishment → Activity
        Dyirbal, Sama

In (28d,e) and (28i) the pattern of derivation is the opposite from that found in the others. This is not, however, a counter-example to the system developed in Section 3, because in, e.g., both (28g) and (28i) a systematic relationship between activity and active accomplishment uses of Verbs is captured, regardless of the direction of derivation in the particular language.

The only exception concerns semelfactive Verbs. In the system presented in Table 7.3, semelfactive Verbs are derived from either state or activity predicates, and yet no examples have been found in which semelfactive Verbs are morphologically derived from either state or activity Verbs. Clearly, more research is needed in this area.

The claim that these *Aktionsart* distinctions are universal does not entail the claim that Verbs which are translation equivalents of each other in different languages necessarily fall into the same class or enter into the same alternations. For example, the Verb "die" is punctual and therefore an achievement in some languages, and is non-punctual and therefore an accomplishment in others (see Botne, 2003). Hasegawa (1996) argues that the Japanese Verbs glossed "go" and "come" are punctual, unlike their English equivalents, and Kita (1999) makes the same argument for the Japanese Verbs meaning "enter" and "exit." Bickel (1995) shows that the same is true for the equivalent Verbs in Belhare, a Tibeto-Burman language spoken in Nepal. Thus, there is variation in terms of which classes a Verb may be assigned to. Moreover, there is variation in the alternations Verbs may enter into. In discussing lexicalization patterns across languages, Talmy (2001) has shown that manner-of-motion Verbs in, e.g., Romance languages, cannot enter into the activity / active accomplishment alternation illustrated in English in (3a,a′). That is, in Spanish and Italian, for example, one cannot use a Verb like "swim" or "fly" as an active accomplishment, e.g. "swim to the island" or "fly to the tree"; rather, it is necessary to use "go", a lexical active accomplishment, as the Verb and use the manner-of-motion Verb as a modifier, i.e. "go to the island [by] swimming." English, Spanish, and Italian all have motion activity and motion active accomplishment Verbs, but only in English can manner of motion Verbs be freely used telically. Here again, the classes are found in all of the languages involved, but the way Verbs in different languages pattern with respect to them is not necessarily the same.

5   Conclusion

This chapter has argued that the basic insight of Vendler (1967), which was formulated solely on the basis of data from English, is in fact a linguistic universal: the *Aktionsart* distinctions derived from his basic four categories are among the most important organizing principles of verbal systems in human languages. Starting from his categories in (1), a system containing twelve categories (six non-causative, six causative) was proposed, and a formal system of lexical representation was developed to capture the relationships among the classes. Data from a wide range of languages, summarized in (28), showed that these relationships are often coded overtly in the verbal morphology of languages. In addition to the languages discussed in this chapter, this system has also been shown to be central to the organization of the verbal systems of the following languages: Tagalog (Foley and Van Valin, 1984), Bonggi (Boutin, 1994), Yatye (Kwa, Nigeria; Foley and Van Valin, 1984; Stahlke, 1970), Italian (Centineo, 1996), Icelandic (Van Valin, 1991), Croatian (Dahm-Draksic, 1998), Korean (B. Yang, 1994), Japanese (Hasegawa, 1996; Toratani, 1998), and Bribri (Chibchan, Costa Rica, Tomcsányi, 1988). Weist (2002) shows that these distinctions are fundamental to the acquisition of verbal systems. Thus, the *Aktionsart* distinctions discussed in this chapter are prime candidates for semantic universals.

8 Language change and universals

Joan Bybee

1 Introduction

As traditionally understood, universals of language are cross-linguistic generalizations concerning synchronic grammars, and their explanations usually appeal to functional principles thought of in a synchronic domain. It stands to reason, however, that any synchronic pattern must have a diachronic dimension, since that pattern had to come into being in some way. One could even argue, as I did in Bybee (1988), that we cannot be sure of the validity of a functional explanation for a synchronic universal unless we can confirm that that functional consideration was applicable in the formation of the synchronic pattern. That is, all explanations of synchronic universals must have a diachronic dimension.

In the current chapter, I outline a position on the role of diachrony in universals, whose logical consequence is that the true universals of language are not synchronic patterns at all, but the mechanisms of change that create these patterns. This position is an extension of the theory of diachronic typology formulated and practiced by Joseph H. Greenberg, to whom this chapter is dedicated.[1]

In several papers, Greenberg proposed a method for the study of typology and universals which he called dynamic comparison or diachronic typology.[2] In this method, typological patterns are shown to emerge from common diachronic changes that arise in related and unrelated languages. It has become clear subsequently that what Greenberg elaborated in the many domains of language that he studied was not a comparative methodology so much as a theory of language that has great potential for explanation. His so-called method is in fact a model of linguistic evolution and change in which the grammars of individual languages are emergent from the processes of change that are operative in all languages at all times. In this view, the true universals of language are

---

[1] Other work formulated in this framework is found, for example, in Givón (1979) and Croft *et al.* (1990).

[2] This method/theory is evident in much of Greenberg's work, but Greenberg (1969) contains a particularly explicit statement of the theory, and Greenberg (1978b) illustrates the method for grammatical comparison.

the mechanisms of change that propel the constant creation and re-creation of grammar.

In this chapter, I will begin with a brief review of the theoretical status of universals in modern theories, and then briefly demonstrate Greenberg's method of dynamic comparison. I will then apply this theory to two examples: the grammaticization of tense and aspect in the languages of the world and the distribution of the phoneme /h/ cross-linguistically. In both cases, I will present the common paths of change for these elements and argue that the diachronic paths present much stronger cross-linguistic patterns than any comparison based solely on synchronic grammars. However, the story does not end here. Behind these paths of change are common mechanisms of change that occur in the process of language use and these mechanisms must be carefully examined, as they are the true universals of language.

2   Observations of cross-linguistic regularities

There are several levels at which universals of language can be formulated and incorporated into a linguistic theory. The first and most basic level is the level of observation. By comparing a number of distinct languages we can come up with a list of properties that all languages share, such as (1)–(5):

> Phonology:
> (1) All languages have vowels and consonants.
> (2) All languages have stop consonants.
> (3) All languages have a low vowel, [a]
>
> Morphosyntax:
> (4) All languages have nouns and verbs.
> (5) All languages have a negative construction.

A major problem we confront immediately is that absolute universals are disappointingly few. Missing from the lists above are any statements about the morphological categories that languages have. We cannot truthfully say that all languages have tense, aspect, or mood expressed morphologically (Bybee, 1985).

Another approach is to formulate relative statements, using the notion of *markedness*. As this term has come to be used today, it distinguishes the more usual or common member of an opposition, the unmarked member, from the less usual, less common member, the marked member. Thus a statement such as (6) can be formulated:

(6)   Oral vowels are unmarked compared to nasal vowels.

This statement covers the following facts (Greenberg, 1966):

(7)   Unmarked sounds are more common as phonemes in the languages of the world.

(8)   If a language has the marked sound as a phoneme, it also has the unmarked one as a phoneme.

(9)   Unmarked sounds occur more frequently in running text than the marked ones, in languages that have both.

All of the statements given so far are observations about what occurs in the languages of the world. No explanatory account of how or why these regularities manifest themselves in individual languages is provided by these statements. A fully elaborated theory of language must provide such an account.

3   Generative theories

Within generative theory, it is proposed that the observational statements of cross-linguistic regularities are built directly into the synchronic grammar of each language. As universals, they are taken to be part of the innate apparatus that children bring to the task of language acquisition. The Marking Conventions of Chomsky and Halle (1968) supply the unmarked value of features. Thus, the unmarked voiceless obstruents and oral vowels have their features [−voice] and [−nasal] supplied by the Marking Conventions, implying that children do not have to learn these feature values and that these values do not add complexity to the grammar. They are "free" because they are provided by universals.

Similarly, Optimality Theory (OT), which developed out of generative theory, formulates constraints as universals and hypothesizes that such constraints are given innately, and only their language-particular ordering needs to be learned by children (Prince and Smolensky, 1997). For example, a constraint formulated to account for (6) would say simply:

(10)   Vowels are [−nasal]

The facts in (6–9) are distilled into this one statement, which will be allowed to apply in derivations in languages with only oral vowels, but it will be overridden in languages with nasal vowels.

What generative theory and OT have in common is that the empirical observations about properties of synchronic states in the languages of the world are directly inserted (sometimes in a simplified form) into the innate apparatus of Universal Grammar, without any attempt being made to formulate them in such a way as to explain their existence. To say that a constraint is universal and innate is to isolate it from possible explanation on the basis of factors outside of language, and, indeed, to preclude the need for further explanation. Even those versions of OT that appeal to phonetic or functional explanations for constraints fail to provide the crucial diachronic link between the functional factor and the existing synchronic state.

In my opinion, such theories are rather primitive and they entirely miss the chance to provide subtle and sensitive explanations for the way the cross-linguistic regularities cited above arise. A much more elegant theory, and one that accounts for the fact that there are so few absolute universals, is that developed in the work of Joseph Greenberg, to which we now turn.

4   Diachronic typology

In Greenberg's approach, language states are the product of change. Cross-linguistic comparison is informed by the idea that synchronic states represent different stages of development of subsystems of grammar. For instance, the fact that all languages have oral vowel phonemes and only some languages have nasal vowel phonemes is due to the fact that nasal vowels develop out of oral vowels in the context of a nasal consonant, which subsequently is lost. In a final stage, vowel nasality can also be lost, taking us back to the original situation – a language with only oral vowels. The most basic path of change is (Greenberg, 1978a):

(11)   VN   >   ṼN   >   ṽ   >   v
         I   II   III   IV

A language in stages I, II, or IV has only oral vowel phonemes. Only in stage III are there nasal vowel phonemes. Since at all stages oral vowels exist, the statements in (7) and (8) are true: all languages have oral vowel phonemes and languages with nasal vowels also have oral vowels. In general then, nasal vowels are less common in the languages of the world because there is only one way for them to develop: from oral vowels in a restricted context. For the same reason, statement (9), which other theories cannot explain, is true: nasal vowels will be less frequent in running discourse than oral vowels. A theory that simply states that nasal vowels are marked misses the subtlety of this situation and the diachronic explanation for it.

In "How does a language acquire gender markers?" Greenberg (1978b) postulates a universal diachronic sequence, based on numerous examples from related and unrelated languages, that leads from demonstrative to definite article to non-generic article to Noun marker (a classificatory marker or gender).

(12)   DEMONSTRATIVE > DEFINITE ARTICLE > NON-GENERIC
         ARTICLE > NOUN MARKER

Without the discovery of this diachronic trajectory or path, languages with each of these Noun treatments might be considered as constituting independent types with no basis for comparison. Greenberg's brilliant discovery was that, in unrelated families and languages, parts or all of this path of change are attested, and, furthermore, that the progression along the path is unidirectional. The changes always move in the direction of the arrows, and never in reverse.

The relation among these structures, when only viewed synchronically, is comparable to a purely synchronic view of an acorn, an oak seedling, a full grown oak tree, and wood products, such as lumber. As individual entities they appear to have little in common, but on a developmental account, one becomes the other in a unidirectional fashion. Linguistic theories that just compare synchronic states are like a hypothetical biological theory that compared the seeds of various plants with no regard to what type of developmental trajectory a seed is meant to embark upon. Such a theory would also study a seedling without considering its past and future development. Such a theory of biology would have little chance of explaining the properties of seeds or seedlings or full-grown trees and the wood products that result from them. Similarly, a linguistic theory that compares only the synchronic states of languages is unlikely to hit upon valid explanations for the diversity of states attested in the languages of the world.

5   Grammaticization

The stages on the path in (12) are related to one another by the process of grammaticization. Grammaticization is the process by which constructions arise in languages and the lexical items in them become grammatical morphemes (Bybee *et al.*, 1994; Heine *et al.*, 1991; Hopper and Traugott, 1993; Meillet, 1958 [1912]). The diachronic path in (12) starts with grammatical morphemes (demonstratives) that then become more grammatical. But there are many cases in which the lexical source of a grammatical morpheme can be identified. Recent research has identified numerous paths of grammaticization that are known to have occurred in many unrelated languages. Bybee *et al.* (1994), and Heine and Kuteva (2002) document the cross-linguistic validity of numerous paths of grammaticization.

For instance, in Bybee *et al.* (1994), we used a cross-linguistic sample of seventy-six languages, selected to be maximally unrelated genetically, to study the diachronic origins of tense, aspect, and mood markers. The three paths of change, I–III, for tense and aspect, first proposed in Bybee and Dahl (1989), were robustly evidenced in these unrelated languages, although other, less common paths, are also found. The categories named on these paths, such as anterior, perfective, etc., have also been verified as cross-linguistically applicable in Bybee (1985) and Dahl (1985).

I. The perfective path

(i) "be," "have" + PP > RESULTATIVE
(ii) "come (from)" } >ANTERIOR > PERFECTIVE/PAST
(iii) "finish" > COMPLETIVE

Examples

(i) A stative auxiliary plus a past participle for anterior and past/perfective is documented in Romance and Germanic.

> (13) French
> *il   a   chanté.*
> he has sing–PP
> "He sang."

(ii) "Come from" develops into anterior and past in dialects of Atchin (Oceanic) (Bybee *et al.*, 1994), Teso, and Jiddu (Heine and Reh, 1984).

> (14) Jiddu (Heine and Kuteva, 2002, 72)
> *y-   aam-ooku*
> 3:M eat-come
> "He has just eaten."

(iii) Many languages have anteriors from "finish" (e.g. Bongu, Temne, and Lao, see Bybee *et al.*, 1994), but the entire path can be reconstructed in Bantu languages (Voeltz, 1980).

II. The present/imperfective path

(i) "be located at"
(ii) "movement while" } > PROGRESSIVE > PRESENT/IMPERFECTIVE
(iii) reduplication

Examples

(i) Heine *et al.* (1991) report over 100 African languages with a locative source for progressive.

> (15) Godié (Marchese, 1986, 63)
> *ɔ   kʊ̀   ɓlɪ-dʌ.*
> he be. at sing-place
> "He is singing."

(ii) Movement sources for progressives are found in Spanish, Tojolabal, Tok Pisin, and others (see Bybee *et al.*, 1994).

(16) Spanish
Andaba   escribiendo   para los periódicos.
go:IMPF:3S   write:GER   for the newspapers
"He was writing for the newspapers."

(iii) Reduplication starts out as iterative, then can become progressive and eventually imperfective, e.g. in Nakanai, Rukai, Gugu-Yalanji, and Trukese (Bybee *et al.*, 1994).
Nakanai (Johnston, 1980)

(17) *Eia o-io   sa-sapa.*
3S   at-there REDUP-sweep
"She is there sweeping."

(18) *Eia sa-sapa   te   la   kavikoki.*
3S   REDUP-sweep PREP   NM   morning
"She sweeps in the mornings."

(iv) Progressives have become imperfectives in Yoruba, Scots Gaelic, and Turkish (Comrie, 1976); the progressive has become a present in the Chamus dialect of Maa.

III. Future

(i) "want"
(ii) "movement towards" } > INTENTION > FUTURE
(iii) "soon," "after"

Examples
(i) Desire futures occur in English, Danish, Dakota, Serbo-Croatian, Swahili, etc. (see Bybee and Pagliuca, 1987).

(19) I'll try to find it.   *'ll < will < willan* "to want"

(ii) Movement futures occur in English, Spanish, Zulu, and many other African languages (Heine and Kuteva, 2002).

(20) *Va a llover.*
"It's going to rain."

(iii) Temporal Adverbs give rise to futures in Trukese, Bari, Chepang, and Tok Pisin (Bybee *et al.*, 1994).

(21) Tok Pisin: *by and by* > *baimbai* > *bai* (Romaine 1995)
      em bai tupela sindaun.
      "The two of them will sit down."

(iv) An intermediate stage of *intention*, especially of first person subjects, is
      well documented for all future sources (Bybee *et al.*, 1994).

This remarkable similarity in grammaticization paths across unrelated languages strongly suggests that universals of diachronic development be included in a theory of language universals. I would further argue that the diachronic universals are much stronger than any synchronic universals we can formulate concerning the presence and meaning of tense and aspect markers in the languages of the world. Given the seven common category types involved in the paths above – anterior, perfective, past, progressive, present, imperfective, and future – a very large number of possible synchronic tense/aspect systems can be derived. The existence of anterior, progressive, and future are independent of any other categories. All or any one of them can occur in a language with or without perfective/imperfective or present/past. Thus it appears that the paths are independent in the sense that a development along one path does not affect a development along other paths. Nor does a development along one path preclude other developments along the same path during the same time period. In fact, there are only two generalizations that we have observed that affect multiple paths in a language.

First, since present, past, perfective, and imperfective tend to be inflectional – meaning that they belong to obligatory categories – if a language has a past tense, then it also has a present tense (sometimes expressed by zero). Similarly, if a language has an imperfective, that implies the existence of a perfective (again, possibly expressed by zero). Languages may also have both types of opposition. In that case, the imperfective has a tense distinction and typically the perfective has past as a default interpretation (Dahl, 1985). However, there do not appear to be any restrictions on which other tense or aspect categories can appear in a language with present/past or perfective/imperfective.

The second restriction has to do with how far grammaticization progresses in languages of different types. As Dahl (1985) discovered, past and perfective tend to have inflectional expression, so an analytic language which lacks inflection is also extremely likely to lack a past or perfective. In Bybee *et al.* (1994) this finding was replicated on a different sample. Bybee (1997) interprets this constraint as owing to the nature of grammaticization in analytic languages. It appears that such languages do not carry grammaticization to the end points in the paths but rather go no farther than, e.g., progressive and anterior, which are common categories in analytic languages. Of course, if all languages carried grammaticization to the fullest extremes, there would be no analytic languages, i.e. no language lacking inflection. As Sapir (1921) pointed out, morphological typology corresponds to semantic typology. Some languages do not express the very abstract relational meanings (Sapir's "pure relational concepts") with grammatical markers. Bybee (1997) has argued that such meanings, to the extent that they occur at all, arise only by inference in analytic languages.

If these are the only restrictions on grammaticization, then the possible combinations of aspect and tense categories is rather free – a language could have a construction at any point along any of these paths, or it could have multiple constructions traversing the same path, as many languages do. As a result, the possible synchronic combinations of tense/aspect constructions are relatively unconstrained (see Dahl, 1985). Thus the very robust and very specific paths of development shown above constitute much stronger cross-linguistic statements than any statements we could devise about synchronic states.

6   Similarities among the paths of change

Even the earliest work on grammaticization recognizes that the same set of processes is at work in creating these different paths of change. In recent years, researchers have commented on the semantic and pragmatic changes that occur in constructions as they grammaticize. Grammatical meaning is more abstract, more generalized, more subjective and discourse-oriented than lexical meaning. What mechanisms are responsible for the creation of grammatical meaning?

Although there is still much to learn, substantial progress has been made already in the identification and study of some important mechanisms of change. Here I will emphasize the role of repetition in creating the semantic and phonological changes in grammaticization, and the role of pragmatic inference. Other mechanisms of course exist, but my point is to illustrate the universality and basicness of the mechanisms underlying the paths laid out above and not to provide a full account of grammaticization.

6.1   The role of repetition

Grammaticization is always accompanied by a sharp increase in frequency of use of the construction undergoing change. The frequency increase is both a result of the process and a contributor to it, as repetition has certain effects on neuromotor and cognitive representations.

Some recent studies of grammaticization have emphasized the point that grammaticization is the process of automatization of frequently occurring sequences of linguistic elements (Boyland, 1996; Haiman, 1994; Bybee, 2002a). Boyland (1996) points out that the changes in form that occur in the grammaticization process closely resemble changes that occur as non-linguistic skills are practiced and become automatized. With repetition, sequences of units that were previously independent come to be processed as a single unit or chunk. This repackaging has two consequences: the identity of the component units is gradually lost, and the whole chunk begins to reduce in form. These basic principles of automatization apply to all kinds of motor activities: playing a musical instrument, tying your shoe laces, driving a car. They also apply to grammaticization. A phrase such as *(I'm) going to (VERB)*, which has been frequently used over the last couple of centuries, has been repackaged as a single processing unit. When a sequence of actions is automated, it gains in fluency. The component gestures (in this case, articulatory) reduce and overlap. Thus *going to* undergoes both vowel and consonant reduction, yielding variants such as [gə̃nə].

Repetition of grammaticizing constructions leads to habituation. The earliest discussion of grammaticization recognized that grammatical morphemes lose components of their original lexical meaning and become much more general and abstract. For instance, *will* loses the volitional aspect of its meaning and *be going to* loses the spatial movement components. This process has been called "bleaching" or "generalization of meaning." The latter term is especially appropriate, because the loss of specificities of meaning makes a morpheme applicable in a wider range of contexts. For example, if *will* does not signal volition, it can be used with a wider range of subjects, including inanimate objects.

Repetition itself diminishes the force of a word, phrase, or construction. Examples are well known: *iterate* doesn't seem to mean "repeat" quite strongly enough, so English-speakers tend to add *re-*; with repetition the strength of that fades and we have to say *reiterate again*. In grammaticization, the generalization or bleaching of the meaning of a construction is caused by frequency, but it also contributes to additional frequency, since a generalized construction can be used in more contexts, and thus the change is propelled along the path, gaining momentum as it goes.

Automatization and habituation through repetition are ongoing in all languages at all times, i.e. they are universally present when people use language. These two processes explain a number of properties of the grammar of human languages: (i) grammatical morphemes are reduced phonologically, and dependent, via affixation and cliticization, on lexical material; (ii) grammatical meaning is highly general and abstract in nature.

6.2   Pragmatic inferences

Pragmatic inference is an important mechanism of change in grammaticization. It has been studied intensely by Elizabeth Traugott in various works (e.g. Traugott, 1989; Traugott and Dasher, 2002). It is widely accepted that an important feature of the communication process is the ability to make inferences: the

Social motivation causes repetition.

speaker must be able to judge which details the hearer can supply and formulate his/her utterances accordingly, and the hearer must fill in details not supplied by the speaker. Thus, the hearer is constantly asking "why is s/he asking me or telling me this?" The workings of pragmatic inference in producing semantic change are nicely demonstrated by an example presented in Hopper and Traugott's (1993) book on grammaticization. In Shakespeare's English, *be going to* had its literal meaning of movement in space towards some goal. However, given the apparent interest of human beings in goals and purposes, even in Shakespeare's English, the information value of *be going to* was less about movement in space and more about purpose. Consider example (22):

(22)   *Duke* Sir Valentine, whither away so fast?
        Val.   Please it your grace, there is a messenger
                That stays in to bear my letters to my friends,
                And I am going to deliver them.
                            (1595, Shakespeare, *Two Gentlemen of Verona*, III.i.51, in
                                            Hopper and Traugott, 1993)

Note that even though the Duke asks about movement ("Where are you going so fast?"), what he really wants to know is Valentine's intention or purpose. Note also that, although Valentine answers in terms of movement, he does not say exactly where he is going; rather he states his intention.

When the same pattern of inference occurs frequently with a particular grammatical construction, those inferences can become part of the meaning of the construction. If *be going to* is frequently used to talk about intentions, it begins to have intention as part of its meaning. The literature on grammaticization is full of such instances (Traugott, 1989; Bybee *et al.*, 1994).

Note that common paths of change, such as the development from movement towards a goal to Future would not be attested across languages unless users of these languages made very similar inferences under similar conditions. That is, the repetition across languages of the change in meaning from "movement towards a goal" to "intention" is evidence that speakers in different cultures tend to infer intentions in the same context; similarly, changes from temporal sequence (as English *since*, originally meaning "after the time that") to causation indicate that language users are prone to infer causation.

7   Synchronic patterns as emergent

Lindblom *et al.* (1984) explain how a complex system can emerge from the repetition of many local actions by using the example of how termites build a nest. The nest has a complex architecture, with pillars and arches and yet it is built without a master plan. Each termite repeats a simple sequence of actions that result in the elaborate nest. The termites each carry a small amount of gluti-nous sand seasoned with pheromones; the termite drops its load of sand when it detects a concentration of pheromones. If they begin on a flat surface, at first the deposits are randomly placed. However, very soon local peaks of pheromones and sand begin to appear and these attract even more deposits. The arches are formed when two peaks are very close to one another, and the great quantity of pheromones makes it very likely that more deposits will unite the pillars in an arch.

The mechanisms discussed here produce change over a long period of time by operating in real time in individual usage-events. Change by automatization and inferencing build up over multiple repetitions as language is being used by individual speakers. These mechanisms operate on language-specific material in a predictable way, producing the paths of change discussed above. The paths of change then produce the synchronic linguistic structures. Because they were produced by the same mechanisms across languages, they resemble one another. Because they were produced in different languages with different linguistic material as input to the process, with some differences in the contexts of use, the outcomes are similar but not identical. As a result, absolute universals of language are rare. Moreover, certain minor paths of change are also possible: since only the mechanisms of change are universal, the way they interact with one another, with language-particular material, and with the social context may produce variations on these paths of change.

As an example of a minor path of change, consider a development that can occur in the perfective path, given above in Section 5. Bybee *et al.* (1994) find that a possible development of a resultative coming from "have" or "be" plus a participial verb form is an evidential of inference from results or indirect evidence. This development is found in the GRAMCATS sample in Udmurt (Uralic), Inuit, and Tucano (Tucanoan), and it is also known to have occurred in Turkish, Bulgarian, Macedonian, and Georgian. Thus, while it appears that the most common path for a resultative is to take on anterior functions and eventually develop into a past or perfective, in these languages the resultative develops into a past evidential. While such a development might constitute an exception to the general path of change, the mechanism that produced the change is one of the well-attested mechanisms: change by pragmatic inference. If a speaker makes an assertion citing the results of a past action (*Tom is gone*), the hearer is entitled to infer that the speaker knows the past action largely through its results (that Tom is no longer here, rather than that the speaker witnessed Tom's leaving). If such an inference is commonly made, it becomes part of the meaning and the construction would come to mean "Tom must have gone" rather than "Tom is gone." From the resultative evidential function, the construction could generalize to other evidential functions (Bybee *et al.*, 1994, 95–97). Thus, while this development is somewhat restricted in terms of the

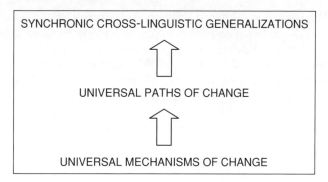

Figure 8.1   The relations among three tiers of cross-linguistic phenomena.

number of languages that undergo it, it is produced by the same mechanisms as the more widespread changes.

Figure 8.1 presents this view of language universals. At the most basic level are the mechanisms of change. These mechanisms are operative as language users produce many local and specific actions in the process of communicating. The repetition of communicative acts leads to automatization and reduction of form, habituation and generalization of meaning, as well as the conventional-ization of pragmatic inference.

These mechanisms create paths of change which are often similar cross-linguistically. As a by-product of these paths, synchronic states may also bear some resemblance to one another.

8   Application to phonology: the status of /h/ in the languages of the world

Another area where diachronic universals are stronger than synchronic state-ments is in phonology. There are general paths of phonological change that principally lead to weakening and reduction (Browman and Goldstein, 1992; Mowrey and Pagliuca, 1995). In the case of consonants, it is common for stops to become fricatives and, further, for fricatives to lose their supraglottal articulation and end up, in the case of voiceless fricatives, reduced to simple glottal frication, or [h]. The glottal fricative itself, being weakly articulated and acoustically less salient, is subject to loss. Such changes are more common in certain positions in the word and syllable than in others. In general, reduction is favored in word-final and syllable-final position, which are characterized by less articulatory force.

It is important to note that the implementation of any sound change is a com-plex phenomenon, involving differential progress of the change in phonetic and

lexical environments and different effects of the change in terms of contrasting segments. These factors are extremely important for an eventual understanding of how and why sound change takes place, as well as for the eventual outcome of the change. However, if we abstract the general patterns from these factors which will differ for each sound change, universal paths of change are evident since the underlying forces that cause change are the same across languages. The particular changes discussed here are due to the reduction of gestures that occurs when speech becomes more and more automated with use.[3]

Commonly reported changes creating and subsequently eliminating [h] are seen in (23–25).[4]

(23) $p > f > h > \emptyset$

Parts of this path (23) are documented in different languages: Japanese has undergone a change that reduced all prevocalic instances of /p/ to a fricative that assimilates to the place of articulation of the following vowel – [ha], [çi], [ɸɯ], [he], [ho]. The frequently reported absence of /p/ in the languages of the world is very likely due to the propensity of /p/ to undergo weakening (Maddieson, 1984, 36–37), which in turn has a phonetic explanation. Spanish and other Romance languages have undergone a change that reduced word-initial [f] to [h] and further to $\emptyset$.

The path in (24) is also common and it converges with (23) (just as grammaticization paths converge) to create [h] which eventually deletes.

(24) $s > h > \emptyset$

Such changes are amply documented in syllable-final position in dialects of Spanish in Andalusia, the Caribbean, and other Latin American dialects. Word-initial [s] also weakens to [h] in Ancient Greek (Méndez Dosuna, 1996) and in Mexican dialects of Spanish.

Finally, the path in (25) is documented, though less commonly as velar fricatives in general are less common in the languages of the world (Maddieson, 1984). This path creates a [h] as do the others, and it is also subject to deletion.

(25) $x > h > \emptyset$

Instances of /h/ in Germanic languages correspond to Proto-Indo-European *k (Latin *cord*-; English *heart*) and are postulated to have evolved through a velar fricative stage. Indeed the velar fricative occurs in Old and Middle English,

---

[3] The evidence that phonetically conditioned sound change is a part of the continuing automation process is the fact that many sound changes show evidence of lexical diffusion from the most frequent words to the least frequent (Phillips, 1984; Bybee, 2002b). On some of the complexity of the changes discussed below, see Pensado (1993), Méndez Dosuna (1996).

[4] These examples, the cross-linguistic survey, and the general theoretical framework are taken from Bybee (2001).

as it does in German *Nacht* "night" (cf. Latin *noct-*). In some dialects of British English, initial /h/ is now deleting. In southern Spain and American dialects of Spanish, an earlier /x/ is produced as [h] (Penny, 1991).

Thus, all three converging paths are attested in independent cases, and I suspect that a concentrated study would turn up many more cases in more widely dispersed languages.[5] The cross-linguistic validity of these paths of change, then, is secure. However, any synchronic statements that we might attempt for the status of /h/ in phoneme inventories do not succeed. Synchronically, we find languages in which /h/ is restricted to syllable-initial or word-initial position, and we find languages in which /h/ is favored in syllable-final position. American English is an example of the first type, where /h/ does not occur finally, but does occur word-initially (*house* [haus]), and syllable-initially before a stress (*vehicle* ['viːkl] vs. *vehicular* [vɪ'hɪkjulr]). Certain dialects of Spanish provide examples of the second type, where /h/ only occurs syllable-finally or word-finally.

The prediction of diachronic typology, then, is that in the languages of the world, there will be languages in which /h/ occurs as a phoneme and is favored in syllable-final position because it is the reduced form of earlier fricatives such as /f/, /s/, and /x/; in addition, there will be languages in which /h/ is a phoneme, but it does not occur in final position (having been deleted there). To test this hypothesis, I used a sample of seventy-six languages selected to be maximally unrelated, the GRAMCATS sample (Bybee *et al.*, 1994). Forty-five of these languages have /h/ as a phoneme. The hypotheses suggested by the diachronic patterns are borne out in this sample, as shown in (26):

(26)   i. seven languages allow all consonants in coda position, including /h/;

        ii. twelve languages allow /h/ but with restrictions on other consonants: four of these allow /h/ but have heavy restrictions on other consonants (Chacobo allows only fricatives, Koho allows no obstruents at all, Palantla Chinantec allows only velars, Slave allows only /ʔ/ and /h/);

       iii. one language allows /h/ in syllable-final position but not in syllable-initial (Palaung);

      iv. twenty-five languages do not have syllable-final /h/ – ten of these have heavy restrictions on coda position but fifteen allow many other consonants in this position.

More languages preclude /h/ from codas than allow it (see [iv]), but a significant minority not only allows /h/ there, but seems to favor it in the sense that it is one of a small set of allowed coda consonants, as shown in (ii).

---

[5] For multiple examples of (24), see Méndez Dosuna (1996).

No implicational universals can be formulated to cover the situation. It cannot be said that /h/ in codas implies the existence of obstruents in codas (as, e.g., nasals do), nor is the reverse true. Similarly, the evidence would not support an OT constraint forbidding /h/ from codas. There are simply no synchronic universals concerning /h/ in the codas of syllables.

The diachronic paths explain the ambiguous distribution of /h/ in the languages of the world. Since /h/ is both the outcome of weakening and often subject to further weakening itself, a cross-linguistic situation is created in which the frequent occurrence of /h/ in syllable-final position is in itself an unstable situation. Thus, the simple synchronic distribution of phonemes does not always serve to indicate the naturalness or unmarkedness of a phoneme in a certain position; rather the diachronic trajectory for each phoneme needs to be taken into account. As in other cases, considering the diachronic paths of change takes us one more step towards an understanding of language universals.

9   Conclusion

In this chapter, I have argued for the necessity of taking diachrony into account in the formulation of language universals. In my view, linguistic theory must look beyond synchronic generalizations about particular language states to the formational mechanisms that bring linguistic structure into being. Language states come about through the complex interplay of processes at work as language is used. To assess the place of language in the context of human cognitive abilities, it is important to note that most of the processes at work as language is used apply to non-linguistic activities as well. Thus automation, habituation, and categorization can be seen to operate in non-linguistic abilities. Language is highly evolved but not totally distinct from other neuromotor and cognitive abilities (Bybee, 1998).

Discovering cross-linguistic similarities and then positing them as inherent to the language acquisition device oversimplifies the way similarities among languages arise. In addition, it obscures the relation between linguistic abilities and more general cognitive abilities. Only by a detailed study of the mechanisms behind the linguistic changes that create grammatical and phonological systems will we be able to discover what is truly universal in human language.

References

Aarsleff, H. 1982. *From Locke to Saussure. Essays on the Study of Language and Intellectual History*. Minneapolis: University of Minnesota Press.

Abbot, M. 1991. Macushi. In C. D. Derbyshire and G. K. Pullum (eds.), *Handbook of Amazonian Languages,* Volume III. Berlin: Mouton de Gruyter. 23–160.

Abdoulaye, M. L. 1992. Aspects of Hausa morphosyntax in Role and Reference grammar. Ph.D. dissertation, University at Buffalo. (Available on RRG website.)

Acero, J. J. 1993. *Lenguaje y filosofía*. Barcelona: Octaedro.

Ackema, P., and M. Schoorlemmer. 1994. The middle construction and the syntax–semantics interface, *Lingua* 93: 59–90.

Ackerman, F., and P. LeSourd. 1997. Toward a lexical representation of phrasal predicates. In A. Alsina, J. Bresan, and P. Sells (eds.), *Complex Predicates*. Stanford: CSLI Publications. 67–106.

Ackerman, F., and G. Webelhuth. 1998. *A Theory of Predicates*. Stanford University: CSLI.

Aikhenvald, A. Y. 2002. Typological parameters for the study of clitics, with special reference to Tariana. In Dixon and Aikhenvald (2002b), 42–78.

Aksu-Koç, A. A., and D. I. Slobin. 1985. Acquisition of Turkish. In Dan Slobin (ed.), *The Crosslinguistic Study of Language Acquisition*. Volume I: *The Data*. Hillsdale, N.J.: Laurence Erlbaum Associates. 3–24.

Alexandrova, G., and O. Arnaudova (eds.). 2001. *The Minimalist Parameter*. Amsterdam: John Benjamins.

Anonymous. 1980. *Ute Reference Grammar*. Ignacio, Colo.: Ute Press.

Arens, H. 1969. *Sprachwissenschaft. Der Gang ihrer Entwicklung von der Antike bis zur Gegenwart*. Munich: Verlag Karl Alber.

Aronoff, M., and S. Sridhar. 1983. Morphological levels in English and Kannada; or atarizing Reagan, *Papers from the Parasession on the Interplay of Phonology, Morphology, and Syntax. Chicago Linguistic Society* 19: 3–16.

Ashton, E. 1944. *Swahili Grammar*. London: Longman.

Bach, E., and R. T. Harris (eds.). 1968. *Universals in Linguistic Theory*. New York: Holt, Rinehart and Winston.

Baker, M. C. 1985. The Mirror Principle and morphosyntactic explanation, *Linguistic Inquiry* 16: 373–416.

1988. *Incorporation. A Theory of Grammatical Function Changing*. Chicago: University of Chicago Press.

1996. *The Polysynthesis Parameter*. Oxford: Oxford University Press.

2001. *The Atoms of Language: The Mind's Hidden Rules of Grammar*. New York: Basic Books.

Bakker, D., and K. Hengeveld. 1999. Relatieve zinnen in typologisch perspectief, *Gramma/TTT* 7. 3: 191–214.

Barlow, M., and C. A. Ferguson (eds.). 1988. *Agreement in Natural Language. Approaches, Theories, Descriptions*. Stanford: CSLI.

Barnes, J. 1984. Evidentials in the Tuyuca verb, *International Journal of American Linguistics* 50: 255–271.

Bartlett, B. E. 1987. The grammarian's contribution to the study of semantics. Renaissance to Enlightenment. In D. Buzzetti and M. Ferriani (eds.), *Speculative Grammar, Universal Grammar, and Philosophical Analysis of Language*. Amsterdam: John Benjamins. 23–41.

Bates, E., and B. MacWhinney. 1982. Functionalist approaches to grammar. In E. Wanner and L. Gleitman (eds.), *Language Acquisition: The State of the Art*. Cambridge: Cambridge University Press. 173–218.

Beard, R. 1995. *Lexeme Morpheme Base Morphology*. Stony Brook, N.Y.: SUNY Press.

Berlin, B., and P. Kay. 1969. *Basic Color Terms*. Berkeley: University of California Press.

Berrah, A. R., and R. Laboissiere. 1997. Phonetic code emergence in a society of speech robots: explaining vowel systems and the MUAF Principle, *Proceedings Eurospeech 97* (Rhodes, Greece): 2395–2398.

Bickel, B. 1995. *Aspect, Mood and Time in Belhare: Studies in the Semantics–Pragmatics Interface of a Himalayan Language*. Zurich: Zurich University Press.

Bloomfield, L. 1933. *Language*. New York: Holt.

Boeckx, C., and M. Piattelli-Palmarini. 2005. Language as a natural object, linguistics as a natural science, *Linguistic Review* 22: 351–370.

Boeckx, C., and J. Uriagereka. In press. Minimalism. In G. Ramchand and C. Reiss (eds.), *Handbook of Interfaces*. Oxford: Oxford University Press.

Boer, B de. 2000. The emergence of sound systems through self-organization. In J. R. Hurford, C. Knight, and M. Studdert-Kennedy (eds.), *The Evolutionary Emergence of Language*. Cambridge: Cambridge University Press. 177–198.

Boersma, P. 1997. *The Elements of Functional Phonology*, ROA-173, Rutgers Optimality Archive, http://ruccs.rutgers.edu/roa.html.

Booij, G. 1987. Lexical Phonology and the organisation of the morphological component. In E. Gussmann (ed.), *Rules and the Lexicon*. Lublin: Redakcja Wydawnictw Katolickiego Uniwersytetu Lubelskiego. 43–66.

1994. Against split morphology. In G. Booij and J. van Marle (eds.), *Yearbook of Morphology 1993*. Dordrecht: Kluwer Academic Publishers. 27–49.

1996. Inherent versus contextual inflection and the split morphology hypothesis. In G. Booij and J. van Marle (eds.), *Yearbook of Morphology 1995*. Dordrecht: Kluwer Academic Publishers. 1–16.

Booij, G., C. Lehmann, J. Mugdan, and S. Skopetas (eds.). 2004. *Morphologie. Ein internationales Handbuch zur Flexion und Wortbildung. Halbband. / Morphology. An International Handbook on Inflection and Word-Formation*, Volume II. Berlin: Walter de Gruyter.

Borgman, D. M. 1989. Sanuma. In Derbyshire and Pullum (1989), 15–248.

Börjars, K. 1998. *Feature Distribution in Swedish Noun Phrases*. Publications of the Philological Society, 32. Oxford: Blackwell.

Botha, R. 1992. *Twentieth-Century Conceptions of Language.* Oxford: Blackwell.

Botne, R. 2003. *To die* across languages: toward a typology of achievement verbs, *Linguistic Typology* 7: 233–278.

Boutin, M. 1994. Aspect in Bonggi. Ph.D. thesis, University of Florida.

Boyland, J. T. 1996. Morphosyntactic change in progress: a psycholinguistic approach. Ph.D. thesis, University of California at Berkeley.

Bracken, H. M. 1983. *Mind and Language. Essays on Descartes and Chomsky.* Dordrecht: Foris.

Bright, W. 1957. *The Karok Language.* Berkeley: University of California Press.

Browman, C. P., and L. M. Goldstein. 1992. Articulatory phonology: an overview, *Phonetica* 49: 155–180.

Brown, P. L. 2001. A grammar of Nias Selatan. Ph.D. thesis, University of Sydney.

Brucart, J. M. 2002. Los estudios de sintaxis en el generativismo: balance y perspectivas. In *Presente y futuro de la lingüística en España. La Sociedad de Lingüística 30 años después*, *Actas del II Congreso de la Sociedad Española de Lingüística* (Madrid, 2000). Madrid: Gredos. 21–51.

Butler, C. 2003. *Structure and Function – A Guide to Three Major Structural–Functional Theories.* Amsterdam: John Benjamins.

Bybee, J. L. 1985. *Morphology. A Study of the Relation between Meaning and Form.* Amsterdam: John Benjamins.

   1988. The diachronic dimension in explanation. In J. Hawkins (ed.), *Explaining Language Universals.* Oxford: Blackwell. 350–379.

   1997. Semantic aspects of morphological typology. In J. Bybee, J. Haiman, and S. Thompson (eds.), *Essays on Language Function and Language Type.* Amsterdam: John Benjamins. 25–37.

   1998. A functionalist approach to grammar and its evolution, *Evolution of Communication* 2. 2: 249–278.

   2001. *Phonology and Language Use.* Cambridge: Cambridge University Press.

   2002a. Mechanisms of change in grammaticization: the role of repetition. In R. Janda and B. Joseph (eds.), *Handbook of Historical Linguistics.* Oxford: Blackwell. 602–623.

   2002b. Word frequency and context of use in the lexical diffusion of phonetically-conditioned sound change, *Language Variation and Change* 14: 261–290.

Bybee, J. L., and Ö. Dahl. 1989. The creation of tense and aspect systems in the languages of the world, *Studies in Language* 13. 1: 51–103.

Bybee, J. L., and W. Pagliuca. 1987. The evolution of future meaning. In A. G. Ramat, O. Carruba, and G. Bernini (eds.), *Papers from the VIIth International Conference on Historical Linguistics.* Amsterdam: John Benjamins. 109–122.

Bybee, J. L., W. Pagliuca, and R. D. Perkins. 1991. Back to the future. In Traugott and Heine (1991), Vol. II, 17–58.

Bybee, J. L., R. Perkins, and W. Pagliuca. 1994. *The Evolution of Grammar: Tense, Aspect and Modality in the Languages of the World.* Chicago: University of Chicago Press.

Cameron-Faulkner, T., and A. Carstairs-McCarthy. 2000. Stem alternants as morphological signata: evidence from blur avoidance in Polish nouns, *Natural Language and Linguistic Theory* 18: 813–835.

Campbell, L. 1985. *The Pipil Language of El Salvador*. Mouton Grammar Library, 1. Berlin: Mouton de Gruyter.

Cantarino, V. 1975. *Syntax of Modern Arabic Prose: The Compound Sentence*. Bloomington: Indiana University Press.

Carlson, G. 1977. Reference to kinds in English. Ph.D. thesis, University of Massachusetts.

Carnie, A., and E. Guilfoyle (eds.). 2000. *The Syntax of Verb-Initial Languages*. Oxford: Oxford University Press.

Carstairs, A. 1987. *Allomorphy in Inflexion*. Beckenham: Croom Helm.

Carstairs-McCarthy, A. 1994. Inflection classes, gender and the Principle of Contrast, *Language* 70: 737–788.

Centineo, G. 1996. A lexical theory of auxiliary selection in Italian, *Probus* 8: 223–271.

Chomsky, N. 1965. *Aspects of the Theory of Syntax*. Cambridge, Mass.: MIT Press.

    1966. *Cartesian Linguistics: A Chapter in the History of Rationalist Thought*. New York: Harper & Row.

    1972. *Studies on Semantics in Generative Grammar*. The Hague: Mouton.

    1973. *Reflections on Language*. New York: Pantheon.

    1981. *Lectures on Government and Binding*. Dordrecht: Foris.

    1986. *Barriers*. Cambridge, Mass.: MIT Press.

    1993. A Minimalist Program for syntax. In Hale and Keyser (1993), 1–37.

    1995. *The Minimalist Program*. Cambridge, Mass.: MIT Press.

    1998. Noam Chomsky's minimalist program and the philosophy of mind. An interview [with] C. J. Cela-Conde and G. Marty, *Syntax* 1: 19–36.

    2000a. *New Horizons in the Study of Language and Mind*. Cambridge: Cambridge University Press.

    2000b. *The Architecture of Language*. Ed. N. Mukherji, B. Narayan Patnaik, and R. Kant Agnihotri. Oxford: Oxford University Press.

    2001. Derivation by phase. In M. Kenstowicz (ed.), *Ken Hale: A Life in Language*. Cambridge, Mass.: MIT Press. 1–52.

    2003. *La arquitectura del lenguaje*. Barcelona: Ed. Kairós.

    2004. Beyond explanatory adequacy. In A. Belletti (ed.), *Structures and Beyond*. Oxford: Oxford University Press. 104–131.

    2005. Three factors in language design, *Linguistic Inquiry* 36. 1: 1–22.

Chomsky, N., and M. Halle. 1968. *The Sound Pattern of English*. New York: Harper & Row.

Chomsky, N., and H. Lasnik. 1993. Principles and parameters theory. In J. Jacobs, A. von Stechow, W. Sternefeld, and T. Vennemann (eds.), *Syntax: An International Handbook of Contemporary Research*. Berlin: de Gruyter. 506–569. (Reprinted in Chomsky, 1995, 13–127.)

Cinque, G. 1999. *Adverbs and Functional Heads. A Cross-Linguistic Perspective*. Oxford: Oxford University Press.

    2000. On Greenberg's Universal 20 and the Semitic DP, *University of Venice Working Papers in Linguistics* 10. 2: 45–61.

Clements, G. N. 1990. The role of sonority in core syllabification. In J. Kingston and M. Beckman (eds.), *Papers in Laboratory Phonology I. Between the Grammar and the Physics of Speech*. New York: Cambridge University Press. 283–333.

Clements, G. N., and E. V. Hume. 1995. The internal organization of speech sounds. In J. A. Goldsmith (ed.), *Handbook of Phonological Theory*. Oxford: Blackwell. 245–306.

Comrie, B. 1976. *Aspect*. Cambridge: Cambridge University Press.

1989. *Language Universals and Linguistic Typology*. Oxford: Blackwell.

1997. Turkic languages and linguistic typology, *Turkic Languages* 1: 14–24.

1998. Rethinking the typology of relative clauses, *Language Design* 1: 59–86.

2001. Languages of the world. In M. Aronoff and J. Rees-Miller (eds.), *The Handbook of Linguistics*. Oxford: Blackwell. 19–42.

2003. On explaining language universals. In M. Tomasello (ed.), *The New Psychology of Language (Cognitive and Functional Approaches to Language)*, Volume II. London: Lawrence Erlbaum Associates. 195–209.

Comrie, B., and M. Haspelmath. 2001. *The Library of Babel*. Berlin and New York: Walter de Gruyter.

Comrie, B., and T. Kuteva. 2005. Relative clause formation. In M. Dryer, M. Haspelmath, D. Gil, and B. Comrie (eds.), *World Atlas of Language Structures*. Oxford: Oxford University Press.

Copleston, F. 1971. *Historia de la filosofía. Volumen IV: De Descartes a Leibniz*. Barcelona: Ariel.

Corbett, G. G. 1983. *Hierarchies, Targets and Controllers: Agreement Patterns in Slavonic*. London: Croom Helm.

1991. *Gender*. Cambridge: Cambridge University Press.

2000. *Number*. Cambridge: Cambridge University Press.

Coseriu, E. 1978. Los universales del lenguaje (y los otros). In E. Coseriu, *Gramática, semántica y universales*. Madrid: Gredos. 148–205.

Cowie, F. 1998. *What's Within?: Nativism Reconsidered*. Oxford: Oxford University Press.

Crain, S., and M. Nakayama. 1987. Structure dependence in grammar formation, *Language* 63: 522–543.

Cram, D., and J. Maat (eds.). 2001. *George Dalgarno on Universal Language*. Oxford: Oxford University Press.

Croft, W. 1990. *Typology and Universals*. Cambridge: Cambridge University Press.

2001. *Radical Construction Grammar: Syntactic Theory in Typological Perspective*. Oxford: Oxford University Press.

2002. *Typology and Universals*. Second edition. Cambridge Textbooks in Linguistics. Cambridge: Cambridge University Press.

2004. Logical and typological arguments for Radical Construction Grammar. In M. Fried and J. Östman (eds.), *Construction Grammar(s): Cognitive and Cross-Language Dimensions*. Constructional Approaches to Language, 1. Amsterdam: John Benjamins. 273–314.

Croft, W., K. Denning, and S. Kemmers (eds.). 1990. *Studies in Typology and Diachrony. Papers Presented to Joseph H. Greenberg on his 75th Birthday*. Typological Studies in Language, 20. Amsterdam: John Benjamins.

Cuenca, M. J., and J. Hilferty. 1999. *Introducción a la lingüística cognitiva*. Barcelona: Ariel.

Dahl, Ö. 1985. *Tense and Aspect Systems*. Oxford: Blackwell.

Dahm-Draksic, T. 1998. A Role and Reference Grammar analysis of case marking in Croatian. MA project, University at Buffalo.

Darnell, M., M. Noonan, and K. Wheatley (eds.). 1999. *Functionalism and Formalism in Linguistics*. Volume I: *General Papers*. Amsterdam: John Benjamins.

Deacon, T. W. 1997. *The Symbolic Species: The Co-evolution of Language and the Brain*. New York: W. W. Norton and Co.

De Mauro, T., and L. Formigari (eds.). 1990. *Leibniz, Humboldt and the Origins of Comparativism*. Amsterdam: John Benjamins.

Derbyshire, D., and G. Pullum (eds.). 1989. *Handbook of Amazonian Languages*, Volume II. Berlin: Mouton de Gruyter.

Di Cesare, D. 1990. The philosophical and anthropological place of Wilhelm von Humboldt's linguistic typology. Linguistic comparison as a means to compare the different processes of human thought. In De Mauro and Formigari (1990), 156–181.

Dik, S. C. 1978. *Stepwise Lexical Decomposition*. Lisse: The Peter de Ridder Press.
    1997. *The Theory of Functional Grammar. Part I: The Hierarchical Structure of the Clause*. Ed. Kees Hengeveld. Amsterdam: John Benjamins.

Dixon, R. M. W. 1972. *The Dyirbal Language of North Queensland.* Cambridge: Cambridge University Press.

Dixon, R. M. W., and A. Y. Aikhenvald. 2002a. Word: a typological framework. In Dixon and Aikhenvald (2002b), 1–41.
    (eds.). 2002b. *Word. A Cross-Linguistic Typology*. Cambridge: Cambridge University Press.

Doke, C. M. 1973 [1927]. *Textbook of Zulu Grammar*. Cape Town: Longman Southern Africa (PTY) Limited.

Donohue, M. 1999. *A Grammar of Tukang Besi*. Berlin: Mouton.

Dowty, D. 1979. *Word Meaning and Montague Grammar.* Dordrecht: Reidel.

Dryer, M. S. 1989. Large linguistic areas and language sampling, *Studies in Language* 13: 257–292.
    1997. Are grammatical relations universal? In J. Bybee, J. Haiman, and S. Thompson (eds.), *Essays on Language Function and Language Type*. Amsterdam: John Benjamins. 115–144.

Eco, U. 1994. *La búsqueda de la lengua perfecta.* Barcelona: Crítica.

Ekmekci, O. F. 1979. Acquisition of Turkish: a longitudinal study on the early language development of a Turkish child. Ph.D. thesis, University of Texas.

Enç, M. 1987. Anchoring conditions for tense, *Linguistic Inquiry* 18: 633–657.

Everett, D. 1986. Pirahã. In D. Derbyshire and G. Pullum (eds.), *Handbook of Amazonian Languages.* Berlin: Mouton de Gruyter. Vol. I, 200–325.

Fabb, N. 1988. English suffixation is constrained only by selectional restrictions, *Natural Language and Linguistic Theory* 6: 527–539.

Facundes, S. da Silva. 2000. The language of the Apurinã people of Brazil (Maipure/Arawak). Ph.D. thesis, State University of New York at Buffalo.

Ferguson, C. A. 1966. Assumptions about nasals: a sample study in phonological universals. In J. H. Greenberg (ed.), *Universals of Language.* Cambridge, Mass.: MIT Press. 53–60.
    1978. Historical background of universals research. In Greenberg (1978a), 7–31.

Feynman, R. 1963. *The Feynman Lectures in Physics*, Volume I. Reading, Mass.: Addison-Wesley.

Fillmore, C. 1987. *Lectures Held at the Stanford Summer Linguistics Institute*. Stanford: Stanford University Press.

Fillmore, C., P. Kay, L. Michaelis, and I. Sag. To appear. *Construction Grammar.* Stanford: CSLI Publications.

Fodor, J. D. 1977. *Semantics. Theories of Meaning in Generative Grammar*. Sussex: The Harvester Press.

Foley, W., and R. Van Valin. 1984. *Functional Syntax and Universal Grammar*. Cambridge: Cambridge University Press.

Forsyth, J. 1970. *A Grammar of Aspect. Usage and Meaning in the Russian Verb*. Cambridge: Cambridge University Press.

Frank, T. 1979. *Segno e significato. John Wilkins e la lingua filosofica*. Naples: Guida.

Freidin, R., and J. R. Vergnaud. 2001. Exquisite connections: some remarks on the evolution of linguistic theory, *Lingua* 111: 639–666.

Genetti, C. 1992. Semantic and grammatical categories of relative clause morphology in the languages of Nepal, *Studies in Language* 16: 405–427.

Givón, T. 1979. *On Understanding Grammar*. New York: Academic Press.

   1984. *Syntax: A Functional–Typological Introduction*. Volume I. Amsterdam: John Benjamins.

   1990. *Syntax: A Functional–Typological Introduction*. Volume II. Amsterdam: John Benjamins.

   1995. *Functionalism and Grammar*. Amsterdam: John Benjamins.

Glinert, L. 1989. *The Grammar of Modern Hebrew*. Cambridge: Cambridge University Press.

Goddard, C. 1998. *Semantic Analysis. A Practical Introduction*. Oxford: Oxford University Press.

   2002. The search for the shared semantic core of all languages. In Goddard and Wierzbicka (2002), 5–40.

Goddard, C., and A. Wierzbicka (eds.). 1994. *Semantic and Lexical Universals. Theory and Empirical Findings*. Amsterdam: John Benjamins.

   2002. *Meaning and Universal Grammar*. Amsterdam: John Benjamins.

Goldberg, A. 1995. *A Construction Grammar Approach to Argument Structure*. Chicago: University of Chicago Press.

   1998. Semantic principles of predication. In J. P. Koenig (ed.), *Discourse and Cognition. Bridging the Gap*. Stanford: CSLI Publications.

   2003. Constructions: a new theoretical approach to language, *Trends in Cognitive Science* 7. 5: 219–224.

González Orta, M. M. 2002. Lexical templates and syntactic variation: the syntax–semantics interface of the Old English speech verb *secgan*. In Mairal and Pérez Quintero (2002), 281–302.

Gonzálvez-García, F. 2003. Reconstructing object complements in English and Spanish. In M. Martínez Vázquez (ed.), *Gramática de Construcciones. Contrastes entre el inglés y el español*. Huelva: Universidad de Huelva. 17–58.

Gorbet, L. P. 1976. *A Grammar of Diegueño Nominals*. New York: Garland.

Gould, S. J. 2002. *The Structure of Evolutionary Theory*. Cambridge, Mass.: Harvard University Press.

Grady, J. 1998. The 'Conduit Metaphor' revisited: a reassessment of metaphors for communication. In J. P. Koenig (ed.), *Conceptual Structure, Discourse, and Language II*. Buffalo: CSLI Publications. 205–218.

Grady, J., T. Oakley, and S. Coulson. 1999. Blending and metaphor. In R. Gibbs and G. Steen (eds.), *Metaphor in Cognitive Linguistics*. Philadelphia: John Benjamins. 101–124.

Greenberg, J. H. 1957. Order of affixing: a study in general linguistics. In J. Greenberg (ed.), *Essays in Linguistics*. Chicago: University of Chicago Press. 86–94.

1963a. Some universals of grammar with particular reference to the order of meaningful elements. In Greenberg (1963b). 73–113.

(ed.). 1963b. *Universals of Language*. 2nd edition. Cambridge, Mass.: MIT Press.

1966. *Language Universals with Special Reference to Feature Hierarchies*. The Hague: Mouton.

1969. Some methods of dynamic comparison in linguistics. In J. Puhvel (ed.), *Substance and Structure of Language*. Berkeley: University of California Press. 147–203.

(ed.). 1978a. *Universals of Human Language*. Volume I: *Method and Theory*. Stanford: Stanford University Press.

1978b. How does a language acquire gender markers? In J. Greenberg, C. Ferguson, and E. Moravcsik (eds.), *Universals of Human Language*. Stanford: Stanford University Press. Vol. III, 47–82.

Grimes, B. 1992. *Ethnologue: Languages of the World*. 12th edition. Dallas: Summer Institute of Linguistics.

Grimshaw, J. 1986. A morphosyntactic explanation for the Mirror Principle, *Linguistic Inquiry* 17: 745–750.

Haegeman, L. 1995. *Introduction to Government and Binding Theory*. Oxford: Blackwell.

Haiman, J. 1985. *Natural Syntax*. Cambridge: Cambridge University Press.

1994. Ritualization and the development of language. In W. Pagliuca (ed.), *Perspectives on Grammaticalization*. Amsterdam: John Benjamins. 3–28.

Hale, K., and S. J. Keyser (eds.). 1993. *The View from Building 20. Essays Presented to Silvain Bromberger on his 50th Birthday*. Cambridge, Mass.: MIT Press.

Hall, C. J. 1992. *Morphology and Mind. A Unified Approach to Explanation in Linguistics*. London: Routledge.

Halle, M., and A. Marantz. 1993. Distributed morphology and the pieces of inflection. In Hale and Keyser (1993), 111–176.

Harris, J. W. 1983. *Syllable Structure and Stress in Spanish: A Nonlinear Analysis*. Cambridge, Mass.: MIT Press.

Harvey, D. 1989. *The Condition of Postmodernity*. London: Blackwell.

Hasegawa, Y. 1996. *A Study of Japanese Clause Linkage: The Connective TE in Japanese*. Stanford: CSLI Publications.

Haspelmath, M. 1996. Word-class-changing inflection and morphological theory. In G. Booij and J. van Marle (eds.), *Yearbook of Morphology 1995*. Dordrecht: Kluwer Academic Publishers. 43–66.

1997. *Indefinite Pronouns*. Oxford Studies in Typology and Linguistic Theory. Oxford: Oxford University Press.

Haspelmath, M., E. König, W. Oesterreicher, and W. Raible (eds.). 2001. *Language Typology and Language Universals. An International Handbook*. Volume 1. Berlin: Walter de Gruyter.

Hawkins, J. A. 1988. Explaining language universals. In J. A. Hawkins (ed.), *Explaining Language Universals*. Oxford: Blackwell. 3–28.

    1994. *A Performance Theory of Order and Constituency*. Cambridge: Cambridge University Press.

Hawkins, J. A., and A. Cutler. 1988. Psycholinguistic factors in morphological asymmetry. In J. A. Hawkins (ed.), *Explaining Language Universals*. Oxford: Blackwell. 280–317.

Hayes, B. P. 1999. Phonetically driven phonology: the role of Optimality Theory and Inductive Grounding. In M. Darnell *et al.* (eds.), *Functionalism and Formalism in Linguistics*. Volume I: *General Papers*. Amsterdam: John Benjamins. 243–285.

Heath, J. 1999. *A Grammar of Koyra Chiini*. Berlin: Mouton de Gruyter.

Heine, B., and M. Reh. 1984. *Grammaticalization and Reanalysis in African Languages*. Hamburg: Helmut Buske.

Heine, B., U. Claudi, and F. Hünnemeyer. 1991. From cognition to grammar: evidence from African languages. In Traugott and Heine (1991), Vol. I, 149–187.

Heine, B., and T. Kuteva. 2002. *World Lexicon of Grammaticalization*. Cambridge: Cambridge University Press.

Heinz Holz, H. 1970. *Leibniz*. Madrid: Tecnos.

Hekking, E., and P. Muysken. 1995. Otomí y Quechua: una comparación de los elementos gramaticales prestados del español. In K. Zimmermann (ed.), *Lenguas en contacto en Hispanoamérica: nuevos enfoques*. Frankfurt am Main: Vervuert. 101–118.

Hengeveld, K. 1989. Layers and operators in Functional Grammar, *Journal of Linguistics* 25. 1: 127–157.

    1992. *Non-verbal Predication: Theory, Typology, Diachrony*. Functional Grammar Series, 15. Berlin: Mouton de Gruyter.

    1998. Adverbial clauses in the languages of Europe. In J. van der Auwera (ed.), *Adverbial Constructions in the Languages of Europe*. Empirical Approaches to Language Typology / Eurotyp 20–3. Berlin: Mouton de Gruyter. 335–419.

Hengeveld, K., J. Rijkhoff, and A. Siewierska. 2004. Parts-of-speech systems and word order, *Journal of Linguistics* 40. 3: 527–570.

Hjelmslev, L. 1971. *Prolegómenos a una teoría del lenguaje*. Madrid: Gredos.

Hockett, C. F. 1963. The problem of universals in language. In J. H. Greenberg (1963b), 1–29.

Holisky, D. 1981a. *Aspect and Georgian Medial Verbs*. New York: Caravan.

    1981b. Speech theory and Georgian aspect. In P. Tedeschi and A. Zaenen (eds.), *Tense and Aspect*. Syntax and Semantics, 14. New York: Academic Press. 127–144.

Holton, D., P. Mackridge, and I. Philippaki-Warburton. 1997. *Greek. A Comprehensive Grammar of the Modern Language*. London: Routledge.

Hopper, P., and E. Traugott. 1993. *Grammaticalization*. Cambridge: Cambridge University Press.

Hurford, J. R., M. Studdert-Kennedy, and C. Knight. 1998. *Approaches to the Evolution of Language: Social and Cognitive Bases*. Cambridge: Cambridge University Press.

Huybregts, R., and H. van Riemsdijk. 1982. *Noam Chomsky on the Generative Enterprise*. Dordrecht: Foris.

Hyman, L. M. 1984. Form and substance in language universals. In B. Butterworth, B. Comrie, and Ö. Dahl (eds.), *Explanations for Language Universals*. The Hague: Mouton. 67–86.

2003. Suffix ordering in Bantu. In G. Booij and J. van Marle (eds.), *Yearbook of Morphology 2002*. Dordrecht: Kluwer Academic Publishers. 245–281.

Hymes, D. H. 1983. *Essays in the History of Linguistic Anthropology*. Amsterdam: John Benjamins.

Jackendoff, R. 1977. *X′ Syntax: A Study of Phrase Structure*. Cambridge, Mass.: MIT Press.

1990. *Semantic Structures*. Cambridge, Mass.: MIT Press.

1994. *Patterns in the Mind*. New York: Basic Books.

2002. *Foundations of Language*. Oxford: Oxford University Press.

2003. Foundations of language: brain, meaning, grammar, evolution. Unpublished manuscript.

Jenkins, L. 2000. *Biolinguistics*. Cambridge: Cambridge University Press.

Johnson, M. 1987. *The Body in the Mind: The Bodily Basis of Meaning, Reason and Imagination*. Chicago: University of Chicago Press.

Johnston, R. L. 1980. *Nakanai of New Britain*. Pacific Linguistics Series B, no. 70. Canberra: Australian National University.

Joseph, B. D., and J. C. Smirniotopoulos. 1993. The morphosyntax of the Modern Greek verb as morphology and not syntax, *Linguistic Inquiry* 24: 388–398.

Kauffman, S. 1993. *The Origins of Order*. Oxford: Oxford University Press.

Kay, P., and C. Fillmore. 1999. Grammatical constructions and linguistic generalizations: the What's X doing Y? construction, *Language* 75. 1: 1–34.

Kayne, R. 1975. *French Syntax: The Transformational Cycle*. Cambridge, Mass.: MIT Press.

1994. *The Antisymmetry of Syntax*. Cambridge, Mass.: MIT Press.

2003. Some notes on comparative syntax, with special reference to English and French. Ms., New York University.

Keenan, E. L. 1972. The logical status of deep structures. In L. Heilmann (ed.), *Proceedings of the Eleventh International Congress of Linguists*, Bologna: le Mulino. (Re-edited in E. L. Keenan. 1987. *Universal Grammar: 15 Essays*. London: Croom Helm.)

Keenan, E., and B. Comrie. 1977. Noun phrase accessibility and universal grammar, *Linguistic Inquiry* 8: 63–99.

Keyser, S. J. 1978. *Recent Transformational Studies in European Languages*. Cambridge, Mass.: MIT Press.

Kiparsky, P. 1982. From Cyclic Phonology to Lexical Phonology. In H. van der Hulst and N. H. S. Smith (eds.), *The Structure of Phonological Representations*. Dordrecht: Foris. Part 1, 131–175.

Kirsch, B., S. Skorge, and S. Magona. 1999. *Teach Yourself Xhosa*. London: Hodder and Stoughton Educational.

Kita, S. 1999. Japanese enter/exit verbs without motion semantics. *Studies in Language*, 23: 317–340.

Klamer, M. 1998. *A Grammar of Kambera*. Berlin: Mouton de Gruyter.

Koerner, E. F. K., and R. E. Asher (eds.). 1995. *Concise History of the Language Sciences. From the Sumerians to the Cognitivists*. New York: Elsevier.

Kohler, K. J. 1998. The development of sound systems in human language. In J. R. Hurford, M. Studdert-Kennedy, and C. Knight (eds.). 1998. *Approaches to the Evolution of Language: Social and Cognitive Bases*. Cambridge: Cambridge University Press. 265–278.

Kolesnikova, V. D. 1966. *Sintaksis èvenkijskogo jazyka*. Moscow/Leningrad: Nauka.

Koptjevskaja-Tamm, M. 1993. *Nominalizations*. London: Routledge.

Kornfilt, J. 1997. *Turkish*. London: Routledge.

Kossmann, M. 1997. *Grammaire du parler berbère de Figuig (Maroc oriental)*. Louvain, Paris: Peeters.

Kövecses, Z., and G. Radden. 1998. Metonymy: developing a cognitive linguistic view, *Cognitive Linguistics* 9. 1: 37–77.

Ladefoged, P. 1971. *Preliminaries to Linguistic Phonetics*. Chicago: University of Chicago Press.

Ladefoged, P., and I. Maddieson. 1996. *The Sounds of the World's Languages*. London: Blackwell.

Lafont, C. 1993. *La razón como lenguaje*. Madrid: Visor.

Lakoff, G. 1987. *Women, Fire, and Dangerous Things: What Categories Reveal About the Mind*. Chicago: University of Chicago Press.

Lakoff, G., and M. Johnson. 1980. *Metaphors We Live By*. Chicago and London: The University of Chicago Press.

    1999. *Philosophy in the Flesh*. New York: Basic Books.

Lakoff, R. 1969. Review of *Grammaire générale et raisonnée*, *Language* 45: 343–364.

Langacker, R. 1987. *Foundations of Cognitive Grammar*. Volume I: *Theoretical Prerequisites*. Stanford: Stanford University Press.

Lecarme, J. 1996. Tense in the nominal system: the Somali DP. In J. Lecarme, J. Lowenstamm, and U. Shlonsky (eds.), *Studies in Afroasiatic Grammar*. The Hague: Holland Academic Graphics. 159–178.

Lefebvre, C., and P. Muysken. 1988. *Mixed Categories: Nominalizations in Quechua*. Dordrecht: Kluwer.

Legate, J., and C. Yang. 2002. Empirical re-assessment of stimulus poverty arguments, *Linguistic Review*, 19: 151–162.

Lehmann, C. 1984. *Der Relativsatz: Typologie seiner Strukturen, Theorie seiner Funktionen, Kompendium seiner Grammatik*. Tübingen: Gunter Narr.

Lehmann, W. P. 1974. *Proto-Indo-European Syntax*. Austin: University of Texas Press.

Levin, B. 1989. The Basque verbal inventory and configurationality. In L. Marácz and P. Muysken (eds.), *Configurationality: The Typology of Asymmetries*. Dordrecht: Foris. 39–62.

Lewontin, R. 2000. *The Triple Helix*. Cambridge, Mass.: Harvard University Press.

Lier, E. van. 2005. The explanatory power of typological hierarchies: developmental perspectives on non-verbal predication. In C. de Groot and K. Hengeveld (eds.), *Morphosyntactic Expression in Functional Grammar*. Berlin, New York: Mouton de Gruyter.

Lightfoot, D. 1999. *The Development of Language. Acquisition, Change, and Evolution*. Oxford: Blackwell.

Lindblom, B. 1983. Economy of speech gestures. In P. F. MacNeilage (ed.), *The Production of Speech*. New York: Springer Verlag. 217–245.

1986. Phonetic universals in vowel systems. In J. J. Ohala and J. J. Jaeger (eds.), *Experimental Phonology*. Orlando: Academic Press. 13–44.

1990. Explaining phonetic variation: a sketch of the H & H theory. In W. J. Hardcastle and A. Marchal (eds.), *Speech Production and Speech Modelling*. The Hague: Kluwer. 403–439.

1998. Systemic constraints and adaptive change in the formation of sound structure. In J. R. Hurford, M. Studdert-Kennedy, and C. Knight (eds.), *Approaches to the Evolution of Language: Social and Cognitive Bases*. Cambridge: Cambridge University Press. 242–264.

Lindblom, B., P. F. MacNeilage, and M. Studdert-Kennedy. 1984. Self-organizing processes and the explanation of phonological universals. In B. Butterworth, B. Comrie, and Ö Dahl (eds.), *Explanations for Language Universals*. Berlin: Mouton. 181–203.

Lindblom, B., and I. Maddieson. 1988. Phonetic universals in consonant systems. In L. M. Hyman and C. N. Li (eds.), *Language, Speech and Mind*. London: Routledge. 62–78.

Lindblom, B., S. Brownlee, B. Davis, and S.-J. Moon. 1992. Speech transforms, *Speech Communication* 11: 357–368.

Locke, J. L. 1998. Social sound-making as a precursor to language. In J. R. Hurford, M. Studdert-Kennedy, and C. Knight (eds.), *Approaches to the Evolution of Language: Social and Cognitive Bases*. Cambridge: Cambridge University Press. 190–201.

Louali, N., and I. Maddieson. 1999. Phonological contrast and phonetic realization: the case of Berber steps. *14th ICPhS 1999*, San Francisco: 603–606.

Luís, A. R., and A. Spencer. 2005. A Paradigm Function account of 'mesoclisis' in European Portuguese. In G. Booij and J. van Marle (eds.), *Yearbook of Morphology 2004*. Dordrecht: Springer. 177–228.

MacDonald, J., and H. McGurk. 1978. Visual influences on speech perception process. *Perception and Psychophysics*, 24: 253–257.

MacNeilage, P. 1998. The frame/content theory of evolution of speech production, *Behavioral and Brain Sciences* 21: 499–546.

Maddieson, I. 1984. *Patterns of Sounds*. Cambridge: Cambridge University Press.

1997. Phonetic universals. In W. Hardcastle and J. Laver (eds.), *The Handbook of Phonetic Sciences*. Oxford: Blackwell. 619–639.

Mairal, R., and P. Faber. 2002. Functional Grammar and lexical templates. In Mairal and Pérez Quintero (2002), 39–94.

Mairal, R., and M. J. Pérez Quintero (eds.). 2002. *New Perspectives on Argument Structure in Functional Grammar*. Berlin, New York: Mouton de Gruyter.

Mairal, R., and J. Gil. 2003. *En torno a los universales lingüísticos*. Madrid: Cambridge University Press /AKAL.

Marchese, L. 1986. *Tense/Aspect and the Development of Auxiliaries in Kru Languages*. Arlington, Tex.: Summer Institute of Linguistics.

Massam, D. 2001. Pseudo noun incorporation in Niuean, *Natural Language and Linguistic Theory* 19: 153–197.

Matthews, G. H. 1963. *Hidatsa Syntax*. The Hague: Mouton.

McCarthy, J. J. 2002. *A Thematic Guide to Optimality Theory*. Cambridge: Cambridge University Press.

McCawley, J. D. 1968. The role of semantics in grammar. In E. Bach and R. T. Harms (eds.), *Universals in Linguistic Theory*. New York: Holt Rinehart and Winston. 124–170.

1974. English as a VSO language. In P. A. M. Seuren (ed.), *Semantic Syntax*. London: Oxford University Press. 75–95.

McGhee, G. 1998. *Theoretical Morphology*. New York: Columbia University Press.

Mchombo, S. 1993. Reflexive and Reciprocal in Chichewa. In S. Mchombo (ed.), *Theoretical Aspects of Bantu Grammar I*. Stanford: CSLI. 181–208.

McNeill, D. 1966. Developmental psycholinguistics. In F. Smith and G. Miller (eds.), *The Genesis of Language*. Cambridge, Mass.: MIT Press. 15–84.

1970. *The Acquisition of Language*. New York: Harper & Row.

Meillet, A. 1958 [1912]. L'évolution des formes grammaticales. Reprint in *Linguistique historique et linguistique générale*. Paris: H. Champion.

Méndez Dosuna, J. 1996. Can weakening changes start in initial position? In B. Hurch and R. Rhodes (eds.), *Natural Phonology: The State of the Art*. Berlin: Mouton de Gruyter. 97–106.

Mendívil Giro, J. L. 2003. *Gramática Natural. La Gramática Generativa y la Tercera Cultura*. Madrid: Machado Libros.

Miner, K. L. 1986. Noun stripping and loose incorporation in Zuni, *International Journal of American Linguistics* 52: 242–254.

Mithun, M. 1999. The status of tense within inflection. In G. Booij and J. van Marle (eds.), *Yearbook of Morphology 1998*. Dordrecht: Kluwer Academic Publishers. 23–44.

Moreno Cabrera, J. C. 1990. *Lenguas del mundo*. Madrid: Visor.

1995. *La lingüística teórico-tipológica*. Madrid: Gredos.

Morin, Y. C. 1997. Remarques sur l'organisation de la flexion des verbes français, *Review of Applied Linguistics* 77/78: 13–91.

Moure, T. 2001. *Universales del lenguaje y linguo-diversidad*. Barcelona: Ariel.

Mowrey, R., and W. Pagliuca. 1995. The reductive character of articulatory evolution, *Rivista di Linguistica* 7. 1: 37–124.

Mulder, J. G. 1994. *Ergativity in Coast Tsimshian (Sm'algyax)*. Berkeley, Calif.: University of California Press.

Musan, R. 1995. On the temporal interpretation of Noun Phrases. Ph.D. thesis, MIT, Cambridge, Mass.

Newmeyer, F. J. 1998. *Language Form and Language Function*. Cambridge, Mass.: MIT Press.

2004. Grammar is grammar and usage is usage, *Language* 79. 4: 682–707.

Nichols, J. 1984. Functional theories of grammar, *Annual Review of Anthropology* 13: 97–117.

1986. Head-marking and dependent-marking grammar. *Language*, 62: 56–119.

Noonan, M. 1999. Non-structuralist syntax. In F. Newmeyer, M. Noonan, and K. Wheatley (eds.), *Functionalism and Formalism in Linguistics*. Volume I: *General Papers*. Amsterdam, Philadelphia: John Benjamins. 11–31.

Nordlinger, R., and A. Saulwick. 2002. Infinitives in polysynthesis: the case of Rembarrnga. In N. Evans and H.-J. Sasse (eds.), *Problems of Polysynthesis*. Studia Typologica, vol. 4. Berlin: Akademie Verlag. 185–192.

208   References

1981. The listener as a source of sound change. In C. S. Masek *et al.* (eds.), *Papers from the Parasession on Language and Behavior*. Chicago: Chicago Linguistic Society. 178–203.

1983. The origin of sound patterns in vocal tract constraints. In P. MacNeilage (ed.), *The Production of Speech*. New York: Springer. 189–216.

1990. There is no interface between phonology and phonetics: a personal view, *Journal of Phonetics* 18: 153–171.

1997. The relation between phonetics and phonology. In W. J. Hardcastle and J. Laver (eds.), *The Handbook of Phonetic Sciences*. Oxford: Blackwell. 674–694.

Ohala, J. J., and H. Kawasaki. 1984. Prosodic phonology and phonetics. In C. Ewen and J. Anderson (eds.), *Phonology Yearbook 1*. Cambridge: Cambridge University Press. 113–127.

Olson, M. 1981. Barai clause junctures: toward a functional theory of interclausal relations. Ph.D. thesis, Australian National University, Canberra.

Ouhalla, J. 1991. *Functional Categories and Parametric Variation*. London: Routledge.

Panther, K. U., and G. Radden (eds.). 1999. *Metonymy in Language and Thought*. Amsterdam: John Benjamins.

Payne, D., and T. Payne. 1989. Yagua. In Derbyshire and Pullum (1989), 249–474.

Penny, R. 1991. *A History of the Spanish Language*. Cambridge: Cambridge University Press.

Pensado, C. 1993. Sobre el contexto del cambio *F* > *h* en Castellano, *Romance Philology* 48: 147–176.

Pérez Quintero, M. J. 2002. *Adverbial Subordination in English*. Language and Computers; Studies in Practical Linguistics, 41. Amsterdam: Rodopi.

Phillips, B. S. 1984. Word frequency and the actuation of sound change, *Language* 60: 320–342.

Pinillos, J. L. 1997. *El corazón del laberinto*. Madrid: Espasa-Calpe.

Pinker, S. 1994. *The Language Instinct*. New York: Morrowo.

Plank, F. 1994. Inflection and derivation. In R. E. Asher (ed.), *The Encyclopaedia of Language and Linguistics*. Oxford: Pergamon Press. Vol. III, 1671–1678.

1999. Split morphology: how agglutination and flexion mix, *Linguistic Typology* 3: 279–340.

Plank, F., and E. Filiminova. 2000. The Universals Archive: a brief introduction for prospective users, *Sprachtypologie und Universalienforschung* 53: 97–111.

Pollock, J. Y. 1989. Verb movement, universal grammar, and the structure of IP, *Linguistic Inquiry* 20: 365–424.

1997. *Langage et cognition*. Paris: Presses Universitaires de France.

Posner, R. 1996. *The Romance Languages*. Cambridge: Cambridge University Press.

Price, G. 2000. *Encyclopedia of the Languages of Europe*. Oxford: Blackwell.

Prince, A., and P. Smolensky. 1993. Optimality Theory: constraint interaction in Generative Grammar. Ms., Rutgers University and University of Colorado.

1997. Optimality: from neural networks to universal grammar, *Science* 275: 1604–1610.

Pullum, G. 1996. Learnability, hyperlearning, and the poverty of the stimulus. Paper presented at the parasession on learnability, 22nd Annual Meeting of the Berkeley Linguistic Society.

Pullum, G., and B. Scholz. 2002. Empirical assessment of stimulus poverty arguments, *Linguistic Review* 19: 9–50.

Radden, G. 1992. The cognitive approach to natural language. In M. Pütz (ed.), *Thirty Years of Linguistic Evolution. Studies in Honour of René Dirven on the Occasion of his Sixtieth Birthday*. Philadelphia: John Benjamins. 513–541.

Radford, A. 1988. *Transformational Grammar*. Cambridge: Cambridge University Press.

1997. *Syntax. A Minimalist Introduction*. Cambridge: Cambridge University Press.

Rappaport, H. M., and B. Levin. 1998. Building verb meanings. In M. Butt and W. Geuder (eds.), *The Projection of Arguments: Lexical and Compositional Factors*. Stanford: CSLI Publications. 97–134.

Rice, K. D. 2000. *Morpheme Order and Semantic Scope. Word Formation in the Athabaskan Verb*. Cambridge: Cambridge University Press.

Rijkhoff, J., D. Bakker, K. Hengeveld, and P. Kahrel. 1993. A method of language sampling, *Studies in Language* 17. 1: 169–203.

Rijkhoff, J., and D. Bakker. 1998. Language sampling, *Linguistic Typology* 2–3: 263–314.

Ritter, E. 1991. Two functional categories in noun phrases: evidence from Modern Hebrew. In S. D. Rothstein (ed.), *Perspectives on Phrase Structure: Heads and Licensing*. Syntax and Semantics, 25. San Diego: Academic Press. 37–62.

Rizzi, L. 1990. *Relativized Minimality*. Cambridge, Mass.: MIT Press.

Romaine, S. 1995. The grammaticalization of irrealis in Tok Pisin. In J. Bybee and S. Fleischman (eds.), *Modality in Grammar and Discourse*. Amsterdam: John Benjamins. 385–427.

Romero-Figueroa, A. 1997. *A Reference Grammar of Warao*. Lincom Studies in Native American Linguistics, 6. Munich: Lincom.

Ross, J. R. 1967. Constraints on variables in syntax. Ph.D. thesis, MIT, Cambridge, Mass.

Ruhlen, M. 1987. *A Guide to the World's Languages*, Volume I: *Classification*. Stanford: Stanford University Press.

Ruiz de Mendoza, F. J., and O. Díez Velasco. 2003. On metonymic thinking: some notes on the role of high-level metonymies in English. In C. Inchaurralde and C. Florén (eds.), *Interaction and Cognition in Linguistics*. Frankfurt, New York: Peter Lang. 189–210.

Sadler, L., and A. Spencer. 2001. Syntax as an exponent of morphological features. In G. Booij and J. van Marle (eds.), *Yearbook of Morphology 2000*. Dordrecht: Kluwer Academic Publishers. 71–96.

Salmon, V. 1969. Review of *Cartesian Linguistics* by Noam Chomsky, *Journal of Linguistics* 5: 165–187.

Sampson, G. 1999. *Educating Eve: The Language Instinct Debate*. London: Cassel Academic Publishers.

Sapir, E. 1921. *Language*. New York: Harcourt, Brace and World.

Schwartz, J.-L., L.-J. Boë, N. Vallée, and C. Abry. 1997. The dispersion–focalization theory of vowel systems, *Journal of Phonetics* 25: 255–286.

Siegel, D. 1974. Topics in English morphology. Ph.D. thesis, MIT. (Published by Garland Publishing, Inc., New York, 1979.)

210   References

1977. The Adjacency Condition and the theory of morphology. In *Proceedings of the Eighth Meeting of the North Eastern Linguistics Society*. Amherst: University of Massachusetts. 189–197.

Slaughter, M. M. 1982. *Universal Languages and Scientific Taxonomy in the Seventeenth Century*. Cambridge: Cambridge University Press.

Smith, C. 1997. *The Parameter of Aspect*. 2nd edition. Dordrecht: Reidel.

Spencer, A. 1991. *Morphological Theory*. Oxford: Blackwell.

1992. Nominal inflection and the nature of functional categories, *Journal of Linguistics* 28: 313–341.

1999. Chukchee and polysynthesis. In V. E. Raxilina and J. G. Testelec (eds.), *Tipologija i Teorija Jazyka – ot opisanija k ob"jasneniju. K 60-letiju Aleksandra Evgen'evicha Kibrika*. Moscow: Jazyki russkoj kul'tury. 106–113.

2000. Morphology. In M. Aronoff and J. Rees-Miller (eds.), *Handbook of Linguistics*. Oxford: Blackwell. 213–237.

2001. The paradigm-based model of morphosyntax, *Transactions of the Philological Society* 99: 279–313.

2003a. Periphrastic paradigms in Bulgarian. In U. Junghanns and L. Szucsich (eds.), *Syntactic Structures and Morphological Information*. Berlin: Mouton de Gruyter. 249–282.

2003b. Putting some order into morphology: reflections on Rice (2000) and Stump (2001), *Journal of Linguistics* 39: 1–26.

2005. Towards a typology of 'mixed categories.' In Orhan C. Orgun and Peter Sells (eds.), *Morphology and the Web of Grammar: Essays in Memory of Steven G. Lapointe*. Stanford University: CSLI. 95–138.

Stahlke, H. 1970. Serial verbs, *Studies in African Linguistics* 1: 60–99.

Studdert-Kennedy, M. 1998. The particulate origins of language generativity. In J. R. Hurford, M. Studdert-Kennedy, and C. Knight (eds.), *Approaches to the Evolution of Language: Social and Cognitive Bases*. Cambridge: Cambridge University Press. 202–221.

Stump, G. T. 1998. Inflection. In A. Spencer and A. Zwicky (eds.), *Handbook of Morphology*. Oxford: Blackwell. 13–43.

2001. *Inflectional Morphology. A Theory of Paradigm Structure*. Cambridge: Cambridge University Press.

2005. Some criticisms of Carstairs–McCarthy's conclusions. In G. Booij and J. van der Marle (eds.), *Yearbook of Morphology 2005*. Dordrecht: Springer Verlag, 283–303.

Talmy, L. 2001. *Toward a Cognitive Semantics*. Cambridge, Mass.: MIT Press.

2003. Concept structuring systems in language. In M. Tomasello (ed.), *The New Psychology of Language (Cognitive and Functional Approaches to Language Structure)*. Volume II. Mahwah, N.J.: Lawrence Erlbaum. 15–46.

Tomasello, M. 2003. *Constructing a Language: A Usage-based Theory of Language Acquisition*. Cambridge, Mass.: Harvard University Press.

Tomcsányi, J. 1988. Roles y Referencia en Bribri: aspectos de la determinación funcional en las estructuras sintácticas. Ph.D. thesis, Universidad Nacional de Costa Rica.

Toratani, K. 1998. Lexical aspect and split intransitivity in Japanese, *CLS* 34: 377–391.

Tournadre, N. 1996. *L'ergativité en tibétain: approche morphosyntaxique de la langue parlée*. Louvain, Paris: Peeters.

Traugott, E. C. 1989. On the rise of epistemic meanings in English: an example of subjectification in semantic change, *Language* 65: 31–55.

Traugott, E. C., and B. Heine (eds.). 1991. *Approaches to Grammaticalization*. Amsterdam: John Benjamins.

Traugott, E. C., and R. B. Dasher. 2002. *Regularity in Semantic Change*. Cambridge: Cambridge University Press.

Travis, L. 1989. Parameters of phrase structure. In M. Baltin and A. S. Kroch (eds.), *Alternative Conceptions of Phrase Structure*. Chicago: University of Chicago Press. 263–279.

Trubetzkoy, N. S. 1939. *Grundzüge der Phonologie*. Travaux du Cercle Linguistique de Prague, 7. Prague: Cerde Linguistique de Prague.

Ulbaek, I. 1998. The origin of language and cognition. In J. R. Hurford, M. Studdert-Kennedy, and C. Knight (eds.), *Approaches to the Evolution of Language: Social and Cognitive Bases*. Cambridge: Cambridge University Press. 30–43.

United Nations. 1948. Universal Declaration of Human Rights. General Assembly Resolution 217 A(III), December 10, 1948. Page 2528. ICPhS99. San Francisco.

van der Auwera, J., and V. A. Plungian. 1998. Modality's semantic map, *Linguistic Typology* 2: 79–124.

Van Valin, R. D. 1991. Another look at Icelandic case marking and grammatical relations, *Natural Language and Linguistic Theory* 9: 145–194.

   2001a. *An Introduction to Syntax*. Cambridge: Cambridge University Press.

   2001b. Functional linguistics. In M. Aronoff and J. R. Miller (eds.), *The Handbook of Linguistics*. Oxford: Oxford University Press. 319–336.

   2005. *The Syntax–Semantics–Pragmatics Interface: An Introduction to Role and Reference Grammar*. Cambridge: Cambridge University Press.

Van Valin, R. D., and R. LaPolla. 1997. *Syntax: Structure, Meaning & Function*. Cambridge: Cambridge University Press.

Van Valin, R. D., and D. Wilkins. 1993. Predicting syntactic structure from semantic representations: remember in English and Mparntwe Arrernte. In R. Van Valin (ed.), *Advances in Role and Reference Grammar*. Amsterdam: John Benjamins. 499–534.

Vendler, Z. 1967. *Linguistics in Philosophy*. Ithaca: Cornell University Press.

Verkuyl, H. 1973. *A Theory of Aspectuality*. Cambridge: Cambridge University Press.

Voeltz, F. K. E. 1980. The etymology of the Bantu perfect. In L. Bouquiaux (ed.), *L'expansion bantoue*. Paris: Centre National de la Recherche Scientifique. 487–492.

Walton, C. 1986. *Sama Verbal Semantics: Classification, Derivation and Inflection*. Manila: Linguistic Society of the Philippines.

Watters, J. K. 1988. Topics in Tepehua grammar. Ph.D. thesis, University of California, Berkeley.

Weber, D. J. 1989. *A Grammar of Huallaga (Huanuco) Quechua*. University of California Publications in Linguistics, 112. Berkeley: University of California Press.

Weist, R. M. 2002. The first language acquisition of tense and aspect: a review. In R. Salaberry and Y. Shirai (eds.), *Tense–aspect Morphology in L2 Acquisition*. Amsterdam: John Benjamins. 21–78.

Wierzbicka, A. 1972. *Semantic Primitives*. Frankfurt: Athenäum.
    1980. *Lingua mentalis*. Sydney: Academic Press.
    1988. *The Semantics of Grammar*. Amsterdam: John Benjamins.
    1992. In search of tradition: the semantic ideas of Leibniz. *Lexicografica* 8: 10–25.
    1995. Universal semantic primitives as a basis for lexical semantics, *Folia Lingüística*
        30. 1–2: 149–169.
    1996. *Semantics, Primes and Universals*. Oxford: Oxford University Press.
    2001. Leibnizian linguistics. In I. Kenesei and R. M. Harnish (eds.), *Perspectives on
        Semantics, Pragmatics, and Discourse. A Festschrift for Ferenc Kiefer*. Amsterdam:
        John Benjamins. 229–253.
Wilkins, D. 1989. Mparntwe Arrernte (Aranda): studies in the structure and semantics
    of grammar. Ph.D. thesis, Australian National University.
Williams, E. 1981. Argument structure and morphology, *Linguistic Review* 1: 18–114.
Wurm, S. A., P. Mühlhäusler, and D. T. Bynon (eds.). 2003. *Atlas of Languages of
    Intercultural Communication in the Pacific, Asia and the Americas*. Berlin, New
    York: Mouton de Gruyter.
Yang, B. 1994. *Morphosyntactic phenomena of Korean in Role and Reference Grammar:
    psych-verb constructions, inflectional verb morphemes, complex sentences, and
    relative clauses*. Seoul: Hankuk Publishers.
Yang, C. 2002. *Knowledge and Learning in Natural Language*. Oxford: Oxford Univer-
    sity Press.
Zwicky, A., and G. K. Pullum. 1983. Cliticization vs. inflection: English *n't*, *Language*
    59: 502–513.

Index